T0088212

BONES
OF
MY GRANDFATHER
RECLAIMING A LOST HERO
OF WORLD WAR II

CLAY BONNYMAN EVANS

Skyhorse Publishing

Skyhorse Publishing books may be purchased in bulk at special discounts for sales promotion, corporate gifts, fund-raising, or educational purposes. Special editions can also be created to specifications. For details, contact the Special Sales Department, Skyhorse Publishing, 307 West 36th Street, 11th Floor, New York, NY 10018 or info@skyhorsepublishing.com.

Skyhorse® and Skyhorse Publishing® are registered trademarks of Skyhorse Publishing, Inc.®, a Delaware corporation.

Visit our website at www.skyhorsepublishing.com.

10 9 8 7 6 5 4 3 2

Library of Congress Cataloging-in-Publication Data is available on file.

Cover design by Kai Texel
Cover photos courtesy of Clay Bonnyman Evans

Hardcover ISBN: 978-1-5107-3061-8
Paperback ISBN: 978-1-5107-6011-0
Ebook ISBN: 978-1-5107-3062-5

Printed in the United States of America

I've always wished to be laid when I died
In a little churchyard on the green hillside.
By my father's grave, there let me be,
O bury me not on the lone prairie.
—"THE COWBOY'S LAMENT," TRADITIONAL

Death is only a state in which the others are left.
Its reality explodes only in the living.
—WILLIAM FAULKNER

Show me a hero and I will write you a tragedy.
—F. SCOTT FITZGERALD

To my grandfather's "three blondes," who paid a bitter price:

Frances Bonnyman Evans

Alexandra Bonnyman Prosser

Josephine "Tina" Bonnyman

and

To Mark Noah, the right man at the right time—just like Sandy

CONTENTS

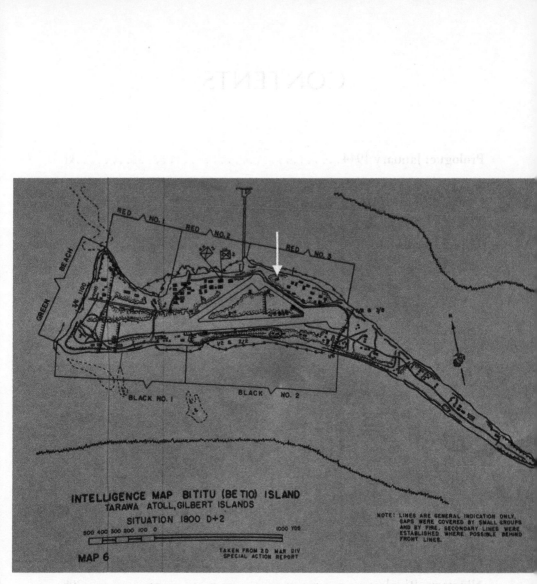

INTELLIGENCE MAP BITITU (BETIO) ISLAND
TARAWA ATOLL, GILBERT ISLANDS

SITUATION 1800 D+2

600 400 300 200 100 0   1000 YDS

MAP 6

TAKEN FROM 2D MAR DIV
SPECIAL ACTION REPORT

NOTE: LINES ARE GENERAL INDICATION ONLY.
GAPS WERE COVERED BY SMALL GROUPS
AND BY FIRE. SECONDARY LINES WERE
ESTABLISHED WHERE POSSIBLE BEHIND
FRONT LINES.

Situation map of Betio island, Tarawa Atoll, Gilbert Islands at 6 p.m. November 22, 1943. The arrow indicates the location of the bunker where Sandy Bonnyman was killed earlier that day. *US Marine Corps Historical Division.*

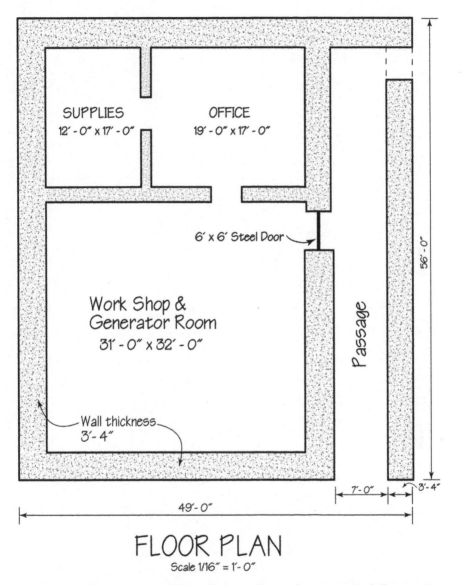

SUPPLIES
12' - 0" x 17' - 0"

OFFICE
19' - 0" x 17' - 0"

6' x 6' Steel Door

Work Shop &
Generator Room
31' - 0" x 32' - 0"

Wall thickness
3'- 4"

Passage

56' - 0"

7'- 0"

3'- 4"

49'- 0"

FLOOR PLAN
Scale 1/16" = 1'- 0"

Schematic of "Bonnyman's Bunker," drawn December 12, 1943, following the battle. *Julie Kunkel rendering; original, Marine Corps Combat Art Collection.*

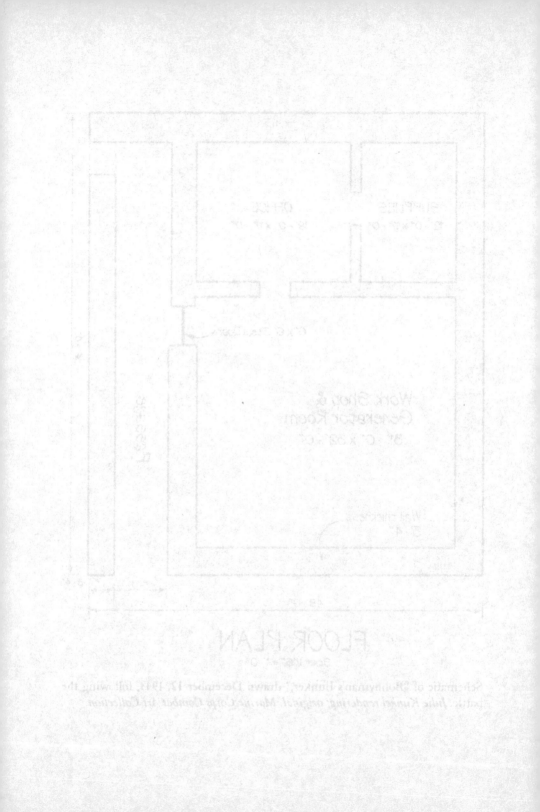

PROLOGUE

JANUARY 1944

She was nine years old when the whispering began in late December 1943.

Golden-haired, athletic, wary, and more than a little impetuous, Frances Bonnyman had attended five schools in the past year. She had liked Mrs. Turley's one-room private academy in Santa Fe, where her family had been living since her father began operating a copper mine in 1938. She loved the exotic mélange of cultures—Spanish, Pueblo, Anglo—in the high-desert town at the foot of the pine-dark, sere Sangre de Cristo Mountains, where she attended Indian dances and picked up Spanish from neighborhood playmates.

She didn't see much of her mother Josephine, or Jo, but that was all right by her. She and her younger sister Tina were well cared for by the cook, Casamira, Sister Michelle, a nun hired by their grand-mother to instruct them in the Catholic faith, and sometimes, the parents of friends and neighbors. Baby Alexandra, called Alix, was born in 1940 and had her own nurse, Miss Rosa Dee.

Fran didn't see a lot of her father, either. Tall, handsome Alexander Bonnyman, Jr.—known to all as Sandy—spent five or six days a week running the mine near Santa Rosa, more than a hundred miles of bad road distant, on the spare plains of eastern New Mexico. But he doted on his oldest daughter when he came home on weekends, holding her hand as they walked in to Sunday Mass at the soaring, ornate Cathedral Basilica of St. Francis of Assisi. Afterwards, they always went to the Capitol Pharmacy soda fountain for a chocolate shake or soda.

Fran would never forget one Sunday in particular, as she watched her father pace the floor with intense agitation, the radio buzzing and crackling in the background with the frightening news that the Japanese Empire had attacked the United States at faraway Pearl Harbor. Seven months later, her father, thirty-two, would board a train to California as a private in the United States Marine Corps Reserve.

Fran missed him and wrote him often on cream-colored stationery with the image of a small, smiling marine in dress blues on top: "When are you coming home? I wish I could see you now!"[1] Sandy wrote to his "big girl" just as often, urging her to keep up her straight A's, go to Communion every Sunday and confession at least every two weeks, be nice to her sisters, and help "Mommie" and Dee. He sent her dollar bills for doing chin-ups and improving her swimming skills.

The summer of 1943, Jo left the girls in Knoxville to stay with their Granny and Grandfather Bonnyman. But at summer's end, instead of taking them back to New Mexico, she enrolled Fran in school in Tennessee, left frail, sickly Tina in Knoxville, and moved with baby Alix and Dee to Mooney's Cottages, a cluster of new, Key West-style bungalows on the beach in Fort Lauderdale. Jo returned in November to take Fran to Florida, leaving Tina with her grandparents.

As Christmas approached, Fran was excited to hear hopeful chatter among the adults that her father might come home to visit. Her cousin Sandy, just six months older, had received a V-Mail in mid-December, postmarked November 16 and featuring a cartoon crocodile in a marine helmet proclaiming, "To you in the States from us in the South Pacific, Merry Christmas and a Happy New

Year," and the hand-written message, "To Sandy with wishes for the Best of Christmases from Uncle Sandy." But Fran hadn't had a letter in many weeks.

What Fran, her mother, and her grandparents didn't know was that Sandy had sailed from Wellington, New Zealand on November 1, arriving a week later at Mele Bay on the island of Efate in the Solomon Islands, where the Second Marine Division rehearsed amphibious landings in preparation for an assault on a remote coral atoll nobody had ever heard of. But by the end of the month the name would be splashed across front pages as the site of the bloodiest battle in Marine Corps history: Tarawa.

The banner headline in the *New York Times* on November 25 read, "RUINED BERLIN AFIRE AFTER 2D BOMBING; U.S. PLANES SMASH AT TOULON AND SOFIA; 4 JAPANESE DESTROYERS SUNK IN BATTLE." Below the fold, a three-paragraph notice reported that marine assault battalions had "conquered the west end of Betio Island, on Tarawa atoll," under the headline, "WE WIN GILBERTS IN 76-HOUR BATTLE."[2]

Correspondent George F. Horne, whom the *Times* had sent to Honolulu after government news blackouts had rendered his previous beat covering shipping news on the New York waterfront obsolete, was unimpressed. The victory, he wrote, was "not of major nor decisive character," and his dispatch dripped with drollery: "Bemused mathematicians were uncertain today as to the time length of the Gilbert Island occupation. First it was 100 hours, but official rewriting now makes it 76 hours, although lesser statisticians wandering hereabouts with pencil and paper figure slightly more."[3]

The remote Gilbert Islands straddled the Pacific equator and had been under British control until the Japanese had arrived two days after Pearl Harbor. The place had hardly been mentioned in US papers until then, though the *Times* did run a small story in September reporting that American forces had conducted heavy bombing operations on Tarawa. And to many Americans, the foe in the Pacific, those funny little "yellow" men with buckteeth and thick, round spectacles, were a joke compared to the mighty mechanized armies of Nazi Germany. The press had convinced much of the public that the Japanese would be a pushover.

"Early in the war our communiqués were giving the impression that we were bowling over the enemy every time our handful of bombers dropped a few pitiful tons from 30,000 feet," wrote *Time-Life* war correspondent Robert Sherrod. The stories "gave the impression that any American could lick twenty Japs." But the men doing the fighting knew the brutal reality, even if censors prevented them from writing home about it. As one sergeant gloomily observed, "The war being written about in the newspapers must be a different war than we see."[4]

But within days, eyewitness accounts from Sherrod and other intrepid journalists who had gone ashore with the marines had replaced the dismissive dispatches of stateside press conference attendees.

"The battle for Betio, the fiercest, bloodiest and most ruthless I have seen in the two years of the Pacific war, showed how long, hard, and costly that war will be. As it was, we won by the narrowest of margins," wrote a correspondent for the *London Daily Express*.[5]

"Guadalcanal," one "black-faced, red-eyed" private told a correspondent, "was a picnic compared with this."[6]

News of the battle inspired the *Times* to editorialize, "This makes the war against the Japanese a war of extermination in which there is virtually no quarter."[7]

Then, in early December, President Franklin Roosevelt authorized the distribution of film footage from the battle, including dead marines sprawled on the beach and bobbing in the lagoon (some images deemed "too grim" were voluntarily censored by newsreel companies[8]). "Bloody Tarawa," as it was dubbed by the press, shocked millions of Americans out of their racially tinged fantasies that victory over the Japanese would be a cakewalk. And where Horne had seen insignificance, Sherrod sensed history: "Last week some 2,000 or 3,000 United States Marines, most of them now dead or wounded, gave the nation a name to stand beside those of Concord Bridge, the *Bonhomme Richard*, the Alamo, and Little Bighorn, and Belleau Wood. The name was Tarawa."[9]

At Bonniefield, the elegant, Italianate mansion on Kingston Pike in west Knoxville, Fran's grandparents, Alexander and Frances Bonnyman, anxiously scanned the papers and listened to the radio for information about the brutal Gilberts campaign. Some reports had put the casualty rate as high as ninety percent and their son Sandy had almost certainly been in on the fighting.

Alex Bonnyman, the well-connected founder and president of the booming Blue Diamond Coal Company, began making inquiries and ordered a fleet of secretaries to work their contacts for any news of his firstborn son. On December 20, one young woman received an encouraging letter from a friend working in the Department of the Navy in Washington, D.C.

"I went downstairs and looked up [*sic*] and Sandy is in the clear," the Navy man reported. "I then went to the 'Officers' Records' and found what I surmised: had he been hurt, unless there is some recent change I did not find (and don't think there is), the telegram or letter [announcing his death] would have gone to 570 Garcia Street, Sta. [Santa] Fe."[10]

"We haven't heard directly from Sandy since the Gilbert Islands attack," Alex Bonnyman told a friend, "but we did hear indirectly that he was safely out."[11]

If anyone was capable of surviving such furious fighting, it was Sandy. He was tough, smart, strong, and resourceful. And in his thirty-three years he had reveled in every kind of danger and adventure with almost boyish glee.

But official news from the Pacific was still cloaked in censorship, and disturbing rumors reached the family. On December 21, the *Santa Fe New Mexican* reported that local Marine Pfc. Jimmy Simpson, "who was with Bonneyman's [*sic*] 'outfit' . . . lost a good friend . . . [who] was reported killed in the battle for Tarawa island in the Marshall archipelago [*sic*], but the report lacked official confirmation."[12] Though unsettling, the story was so riddled with error it left plenty of room for doubt.

But the Navy man's sleuthing, so heartening to the family, turned out to be no more reliable: Jo Bonnyman had left Santa Fe permanently but neglected to inform the Marine Corps. And so the telegram sent by Marine Corps Commandant Lt. Gen. Thomas Holcomb on December 23 bounced back from Santa Fe as undeliverable. The marines next addressed it to non-existent "Knoxville, Kentucky." On the third try it reached the Bonnymans in Knoxville, Tennessee, and Jo received it in Fort Lauderdale on December 29.[13]

"DEEPLY REGRET TO INFORM YOU THAT YOUR HUSBAND FIRST LIEUTENANT ALEXANDER BONNYMAN JR USMCR WAS KILLED IN ACTION. IN THE PERFORMANCE OF HIS DUTY AND IN THE SERVICE OF HIS COUNTRY TO PREVENT POSSIBLE AID TO OUR ENEMIES PLEASE DO NOT DIVULGE THE NAME OF HIS SHIP OF STATION PRESENT SITUATION NECESSITATES INTERMENT TEMPORARILY IN THE LOCALITY WHERE THE DEATH OCCURRED AND YOU WILL BE NOTIFIED ACCORDINGLY PLEASE ACCEPT MY HEARTFELT SYMPATHY."[14]

That's when "three days of whispering" began, Fran Bonnyman Evans now recalls. Her mother was on the telephone all the time, speaking with a hushed urgency, behind closed doors. Something bad had happened to her father, Fran was sure, but nobody would tell her anything. To her dismay, her father's best friend and business partner, Jimmie Russell, had arrived from Santa Fe, suitcase in hand. And it was Jimmie who finally called the little girl to stand before him, straight as the little marine on her stationery, while her mother hovered behind him.

"Your father won't be coming back," he said. "He's been killed." It was all he said.

Fran knew better than to cry. Her mother, looking elegant in her usual stark, red lipstick, auburn hair tightly curled and coiffed like a movie star's, began to chatter. Jo and Jimmie excitedly told Fran about the deep-sea fishing trip they'd planned for her, how wonderful it would be, on and on, Jo's hands fluttering like birds' wings. But the little girl didn't want to go fishing. She knew they were just trying to distract her.

Her mother never spoke about Sandy again, as if he'd never existed at all. Everyone in Fran's world would soon draw a curtain of silence around the subject—except for Granny. So nine-year-old Fran was left to ponder the terrible news alone. The tall, kind, handsome father whose hand she had so proudly held as they walked into church was gone. Already her memories were blurring around the edges.

Sandy's "three blondes," as he lovingly described them to fellow marines, would soon be broken apart and grow into adulthood knowing as little about their father, how he lived, how he died, as the rest of the world. Their grandparents would dote on them and provide for them into adulthood and beyond, with money, travel, and blue-chip social standing, but still they could not deflect the terrible consequences of losing their father.

Riven by grief, bound by the stoicism expected of their social milieu, Alex and Frances Bonnyman set about in their own ways to preserve their lost son for posterity.

Driven by guilt over his conflicted relationship with his eldest son, Alex channeled his grief into action. Using the influence he had gained as one of the South's most successful coal magnates, he began pulling strings at the highest levels of the military and government in a quest to learn everything he could about his son's death and, more importantly, bring his body home for burial.

But Alex would die a decade later, heartbroken and lost in a wilderness of conflicting official explanations about the whereabouts of Sandy's remains. His younger son Gordon, who had suffered his own wounds fighting in Burma, would take up the search, pursuing even the thinnest of leads for decades, haunted by the loss of the brother he so deeply loved and admired. Yet by the dawn of the next century it seemed that Sandy Bonnyman would ultimately be "buried at sea"—the epitaph carved on the family tombstone—as rising sea levels threatened to inundate the tiny coral spit where he'd fallen.

Sandy's mother, Frances Berry Bonnyman, had always favored the strapping, handsome, sometimes impetuous son who lovingly called her Mumsie, shielding him from his stern Scottish father, quietly enabling his adventurous spirit, and sometimes covering for his mistakes. In losing him, she lost much of her joy in life; she gave away her jewelry, stopped traveling,[15] and began to suffer from illness. But she took control of her son's legacy, polishing up his many virtues—courage, charisma, deep faith, an unquenchable embrace of life—while sanding away rough edges, presenting him as the kind of hero the world expected. His widow would later rue that in death Sandy had become "an absolutely perfect, and eternal, Sir Galahad."[16]

But there was solace, too: Sandy Bonnyman would be awarded the nation's highest military recognition, the Medal of Honor (sometimes referred to as the Congressional Medal of Honor) and his singular actions in the Battle of Tarawa on November 22, 1943, would earn him an enduring place in Marine Corps lore. Generations of marines, historians, and civilians would continue to speak his name with awe and reverence many decades later, and it would be bestowed upon a ship, a bridge, streets, and even a bowling alley. And long after they had forgotten all but the haziest tales of the great battle that freed them from the Japanese, poverty-stricken people living amid the environmental degradation and decaying relics of twenty-first-century Tarawa would still remember the name of the hero Bonnyman and tell their own versions of his mythic feat.

Yet the battle of Tarawa, so shocking and momentous in 1943, is hardly remembered by most twenty-first-century Americans, most of whom know only a handful of shorthand signifiers of the terrible Pacific war—Pearl Harbor, Iwo Jima, Hiroshima. Meanwhile, memories of Sandy Bonnyman have been replaced by the legend of 1st Lt. Alexander Bonnyman, Jr. and, unbeknownst to my family, my grandfather's body remained hidden in the sepulchral sands of Tarawa. We didn't know him any better than the rest of the world.

But my grandfather had been my hero since I was a small boy gazing at that medal, hanging from its fading, pale-blue ribbon against midnight velvet in a gold-painted frame on the wall in all my childhood homes. As I grew older, my hero grandfather became a perfect exemplar against whom I couldn't help measuring myself and, failing to measure up, I turned away. It wasn't until much later in life that I turned toward him again, inspired by a man who wanted to bring my grandfather home, a man who had no reason to care, other than admiration for what Sandy and his fellow marines accomplished at Tarawa.

This book is the story of the quest to find Sandy Bonnyman, in both body and spirit, and bring him home.

ONE
UNKNOWN HERO
2009

In August 1973, my mother, Fran Bonnyman Evans, moved with my father, Dr. Clayton "Gus" Evans, my sister, brother, and me to a spacious new home on the northern rim of the Boulder Valley, northwest of Denver, Colorado.

With its high ceilings, tall south-facing windows, and flourishes of Santa Fe style, the new house was a big a step up from our first home in Boulder, a boxy, low-ceilinged colonial knockoff that was prone to flooding and lay directly in the path of occasional—and literal—hurricane-force winter winds.

Now we could stretch out. My mother bought a long, dark, polished oak table that dimly recalled the one at my Granny Great's house in Knoxville, Tennessee. And now she had a perfect place to hang the portrait of her father, my grandfather, 1st Lt. Alexander "Sandy" Bonnyman, Jr., recipient of the Medal of Honor in World War II: above the fireplace in our sun-splashed living room.

Eugenia Berry Ruspoli, my grandfather's eldest aunt on his mother's side, had commissioned the painting in 1944. Born to a former slave-holding family in Rome, Georgia, "Aunt Jennie" had married an Italian prince, Enrico Ruspoli, in 1901, and inherited his estate, Castle Nemi, when he died just eight years later. Working her Italian connections, she commissioned celebrated Italian portrait and landscape artist Arturo Noci to create a posthumous image of her heroic nephew Sandy.

Noci succeeded beyond even the high expectations of Princess Ruspoli. The portrait is both beautiful and haunting, portraying handsome, blond, blue-eyed Sandy in marine dress blues against a sky roiling with flame-gilded smoke and a distant, impressionistic island studded with battle-blasted trees. A brilliant rainbow of award ribbons, brassy buttons and buckles, and the white disc of his cap stand out from Noci's somber palette of war. My grandfather, too, is somber, his eyes gazing at a distant horizon, as if faintly troubled by some new realization. Subtle and haunting, the painting is far superior to the portrait by Russian-born American artist Nicholas Basil Haritonoff, which now hangs at Oak Hill Museum at Berry College in Rome, Georgia.

At age eleven, I was mesmerized by the image of the hero whose legend had hung like a morning mist in the deep hollows of family lore ever since I could remember, and whose medal my mother always proudly displayed. Until I had outgrown such things, I would at times stand beneath the portrait, venerating my icon, sometimes even seeking his guidance at moments when I felt misunderstood or misused by the living.

Fascinated, like my father, with World War II, I'd spent countless hours slowly flipping through thousands of pages of photos in the immense *Time-Life* coffee table books and multi-volume subscription series about the war. I didn't just love heroes—Batman, the Green Hornet, Tolkien's brave hobbits—I *needed* them. Dissatisfied when I learned of Hitler's desultory suicide, I regaled friends with the "true" story of the Canadian ace pilot who parachuted behind enemy lines to put the bullet in the Nazi madman's forehead . . . then claimed the avenging airman as a relative.

Yet I was strangely incurious about my grandfather, the real-life hero in my bloodline. I did not pause particularly over images from

Tarawa in all those books or ask questions of my mother or aunts. At some point, I did read the citation displayed in a golden frame next to the medal:

The President of the United States takes pride in presenting the MEDAL of HONOR posthumously to FIRST LIEUTENANT ALEXANDER BONNYMAN, JR., UNITED STATES MARINE CORPS RESERVE, for service as set forth in the following CITATION:

'For conspicuous gallantry and intrepidity at the risk of his life above and beyond the call of duty as Executive Officer of the 2d Battalion Shore Party, 8th Marines, 2d Marine Division, during the assault against enemy Japanese-held Tarawa in the Gilbert Islands, 20–22 November 1943. Acting on his own initiative when assault troops were pinned down at the far end of Betio Pier by the overwhelming fire of Japanese shore batteries, 1st Lt. Bonnyman repeatedly defied the blasting fury of the enemy bombardment to organize and lead the besieged men over the long, open pier to the beach and then, voluntarily obtaining flame throwers and demolitions, organized his pioneer shore party into assault demolitionists and directed the blowing of several hostile installations before the close of D-day. Determined to effect an opening in the enemy's strongly organized defense line the following day, he voluntarily crawled approximately 40 yards forward of our lines and placed demolitions in the entrance of a large Japanese emplacement as the initial move in his planned attack against the heavily garrisoned, bombproof installation which was stubbornly resisting despite the destruction early in the action of a large number of Japanese who had been inflicting heavy casualties on our forces and holding up our advance. Withdrawing only to replenish his ammunition, he led his men in a renewed assault, fearlessly exposing himself to the merciless slash of hostile fire as he stormed the formidable bastion, directed the placement of demolition charges in both entrances and seized the top of the bombproof position, flushing more than 100 of the enemy who were instantly cut down, and effecting the annihilation of approximately 150 troops inside the emplacement. Assailed by additional Japanese after he had gained his objective, he made a heroic stand on the edge of the structure, defending his strategic position with indomitable determination in the face of the desperate charge and killing 3 of the enemy before he fell, mortally wounded. By his dauntless fighting spirit, unrelenting aggressiveness and forceful leadership throughout 3 days of unremitting, violent battle, 1st Lt. Bonnyman had inspired his men to heroic effort, enabling them to beat off the counterattack and break the back of hostile resistance in that sector for an immediate gain of 400 yards with no further casualties to our forces in this zone. He gallantly gave his life for his country.'

(signed) Harry S. Truman.

But what I absorbed and remembered from those 395 words barely qualified as a Cliff's Notes version: *Killed fighting the Japanese on a faraway island called Tarawa. Won the Medal of Honor. My mother received the medal when she was twelve years old.* Just knowing my grandfather was a hero, it seemed, was enough.

Perhaps that was no surprise. His heroism was a background to our lives, something to be proud of, but my mother didn't speak of him often. I was too childishly self-absorbed to consider her deeper feelings when the subject of war arose, as when I announced that the Civil War was my "favorite" war. "The Civil War was terribly sad, brother killing brother, father killing son," she said without judgment. "War is sometimes necessary, but it is always a tragedy."

Visiting my Granny Great in Knoxville was an annual summer ritual, but if the adults there ever talked about my grandfather, I don't recall (I was not yet six years old when she died in September 1968). We had occasional visits from my two fun-loving aunts, Alix and Tina, and the odd drop-in by my mother's cousins over the years, but there was never any Sandy talk, and my siblings and I had no other encounters with the Bonnyman clan for most of my childhood.

Then in 1980, my Uncle Gordon—in fact, great-uncle; he was Sandy's younger brother by nine years and patriarch of the clan since the death of my great-grandfather in 1953—orchestrated a reunion at the High Hampton Inn, his family's annual summer hideaway in the remote Appalachian mountains on the border of Georgia and North Carolina. By then I was a brash eighteen-year-old headed off to college, more interested in drinking with like-minded family members than learning our shared history.

Having come of age in the immediate aftermath of Vietnam, I shared the view of my peers and saw military service as a lowly calling, an option only for kids not smart enough to go to college. I wrote furious anti-war poems, plays, and an incensed column in the school newspaper when President Jimmy Carter re-established Selective Service registration for all eighteen- to twenty-six-year-old males in response to the Soviet invasion of Afghanistan. My father, who had served two years as a Russian-language translator for the US Air Force in 1950s Turkey, found me arrogant, selfish, and enti-tled, too loud, too opinionated, too cocksure, *too much*. He warned that I would soon have no friends, no girlfriend, maybe even no family; but, he advised, joining the military might teach me enough discipline and humility to avoid such a fate.

"But I don't want to kill anyone," I said.

"Oh, bullshit," he said. "You're just afraid to die."

We were both right, though at that stage we had no way to talk about it.

My father never openly compared me to Sandy Bonnyman, but he didn't have to. I knew I didn't measure up. My grandfather had been a football star; I'd quit the team in junior high school so I could spend fall afternoons reading science fiction novels that sent me on flights of thrilling imagination. Sandy was, I was certain, a good son; I was rebellious and independent and felt constrained by my family. My grandfather was a gallant Southern gentleman; I was an entitled, party-hearty, spoiled kid who had little use for authority. My grandfather was that greatest of American icons, a successful businessman; I wanted to be, of all things, a writer. Most important, Sandy Bonnyman had sacrificed his life for his country; I wouldn't even consider joining the military.

I knew I was no Sandy Bonnyman; I would win no medals, and no princess would ever commission a famous artist to paint a heroic portrait of *me*. I was a rebel, a punk who walked into the world fists balled, chin outthrust, tuned to see insults wherever I turned my gaze. Though I would never be tested in battle, I would spend a lifetime seeking out adventure, risk, and challenge in a never-ending campaign to prove to the world—to myself—that I was no coward.

For most of her life, my aunt Alix Prejean had no clear idea of how her father had been killed. Just one and a half years old when Sandy Bonnyman left for Marine Corps service, his youngest daughter had a trunkful of letters, photos, and memorabilia, but no memories. She had read the Medal of Honor citation, but like me, hadn't absorbed it.

"All those years I grew up thinking he'd been blown up by a grenade or something," she said.[1]

As the eldest child, my mother, Fran Bonnyman Evans, had long been the designated family spokesperson about her father. Media sought her out whenever a Tarawa anniversary rolled around, and she dutifully answered inquiries from authors, history buffs, even Tarawa veterans. But she never liked talking about her father, and in the 1980s she surrendered her role to Alix, who embraced it with gusto. She joined the American World War II War Orphans Network, visited Camp Tarawa on the big island of Hawaii, where the Second Marine Division had been garrisoned following the battle in December 1943, and began participating in the annual Memorial Day wreath-laying ceremonies at the National Cemetery of the Pacific on Oahu.

In 1994 Joseph Alexander, a retired Marine Corps colonel and military historian, wrote to my mother seeking details about her father's pre-war life for *Utmost Savagery: The Three Days of Tarawa*, a comprehensive history of the battle published in 1995.

"It occurs to me that I don't know much about Alexander Bonnyman other than: played football at Princeton, owned and operated a (several?) copper mines, obviously had kids, probably didn't have to enlist, did so anyway, and was meritoriously commissioned a lieutenant after valorous combat service in Guadalcanal," Alexander wrote, noting that he had gathered a wealth of biographical material on Tarawa's three other Medal of Honor recipients. "Would you care to fill in some of the gaps as to what he was like, both as a man, and a Marine? . . . I'd love to know more."[2]

My mother forwarded the request to Alix, who struck up a correspondence with the author. Alexander had published a well-received monograph on Tarawa, which recounted the canonical narrative of my grandfather's actions. But now, based on a single fifty-year-old eyewitness account, he informed my aunt that, "events atop the bunker were not quite as melodramatic" as he'd previously written. "Your Dad's conspicuous contributions were more in the realm of organizing and leading a demoralized group of men."[3]

According to Harry Niehoff, then seventy-five, a marine corporal when he had fought beside my grandfather on his final day, Sandy had not single-handedly stood against a counterattack of desperate Japanese. Rather, the two men had lain side-by-side on the leading edge of the bunker and fended off the assault together until Sandy was killed instantly by a shot to the head, according to Niehoff. My grandfather, he told Alexander, had directed the assault with cool efficiency but no great ardor. What's more, Niehoff, one of several marines to recommend Sandy for the Medal of Honor, now claimed to have drawn up assault plans long attributed to my grandfather.

My aunt took immediate umbrage at the author's apparent diminution of her father's heroism. But in truth, she knew little more than Alexander about Sandy's life, and was able to provide him with just a few sparse details and tales passed down by family members, some likely apocryphal. But she very much wanted to talk to Niehoff, who may have been the last person to see her father alive.

As it turned out, Sandy Bonnyman had been on Harry Niehoff's mind for decades. He had even sought out my mother after someone sent him a clipping from the *Denver Post* about the 1985 christening of the marine prepositioning ship *1st Lt. Alex Bonnyman* (so named even though my grandfather was always known as Sandy, and his marine buddies called him Bonny) in Beaumont, Texas. Niehoff wrote the paper seeking information about Fran Evans and the *Post* proudly reported that it had "arranged contact."[4] My mother does recall receiving a letter from Niehoff, but in keeping with her long reluctance to dredge up the painful past, she never responded. Ten years later Alix, in keeping with her long campaign to make friends with everyone—she calls herself Aunty Octopus and hugs everyone she meets, no matter what—struck up a friendship with Niehoff that lasted until his death in 2008.

Alix also asked Alexander if he had happened to come across any clues in his research regarding the final disposition of my grandfather's remains. She had seen the ten-foot-long Italian marble

headstone on the Bonnyman family plot in Knoxville, with its chiseled insistence that Sandy had been "Buried at Sea." But she'd heard
lots of other things, too, including that his bones had been buried
as an unknown in the National Cemetery of the Pacific, aka The
Punchbowl, just outside Honolulu. Alexander replied that Sandy
was buried on Betio, "sure enough, but no one can say precisely
which spot."[5]

Yet when *Utmost Savagery* was published in 1995, Alexander
wrote that Sandy's remains, along with those of fellow Tarawa Medal
of Honor recipients William Deane Hawkins and William Bordelon,
"now lie in Oahu's Punchbowl," citing the fiftieth-anniversary edition of *Tarawa: The Story of a Battle* by Robert Sherrod.[6]

That seemed to square with my mother's beliefs. During a 1976
Christmas trip to Hawaii, she took my sister, brother, and me to see
our grandfather's name carved into the marble walls of the Courts
of the Missing at the Punchbowl, gold-painted and sporting a star,
in recognition of his Medal of Honor. She told us he was buried
there.

Yet she knew, or should have known, that he wasn't. She'd written
a letter just a few months earlier to request that a memorial headstone
be placed in the Santa Fe National Cemetery, noting that he was still
"buried at Tarawa where he was killed."[7]

She also had a 1990 letter from the US Navy that confirmed her
father's remains were still somewhere on Betio.

"Regrettably, we cannot provide information on the whereabouts of your father's remains because they were never recovered
from Tarawa. That's why his name appears on the Tablets of the
Missing," wrote Maj. A.E. Edinger. "The ravages of time, battle
damage, and the circumstances of burial made locating and identifying the Tarawa dead a formidable task."[8]

For whatever reason, two decades later nobody in the family
seemed aware of that fact. "After all these years, I just thought, he's

dead and buried and we'll never know," said Alix.[9] But she remained curious, and once she got connected to the internet at her remote home on the island of Maui, she discovered Tarawa on the Web. Jonathan Stevens, whose father Gordon had fought in the battle, created the site in 1998 as "a tribute to the 2nd Marine Division of WWII and a historical resource to further the knowledge of an epic struggle that was an integral part of the march of the United States towards defeat of Imperial Japan."[10]

My aunt began routinely monitoring the site's lively forum, Tarawa Talk, frequented by history buffs, descendants of those killed in the battle, and a slowly dwindling number of Tarawa veterans.

I had never heard of the site when Alix sent me a brief email in late 2009—"Do you know about this?" I clicked the link and what I saw made my jaw drop. It seemed that Joseph Alexander had been right before he'd been wrong: Not only were Sandy Bonnyman's remains not entombed in the Punchbowl, but two separate, independent civilian researchers were now claiming he was still buried on faraway Betio Island along with *hundreds* of other missing marines. And pressure was building for the US Department of Defense to find them and bring them home.

"Efforts to bring home the remains of more than five hundred U.S. service members killed in the World War II Battle of Tarawa received a boost from Congressman Dan Lipinski (IL-03) this week," read a release posted on the Illinois Democrat's website in June 2009. "Before the defense authorization bill passed the House of Representatives on Thursday, Lipinski succeeded in attaching an amendment that calls for the Defense Department to 'recover, identify, and return remains of members of the Armed Forces from Tarawa.'"[11]

Congress had become involved, Stevens noted on Tarawa Talk, thanks to the "ceaseless efforts to find the missing Marines" of the two civilians, Mark Noah and Bill Niven, working separately.[12]

"As the area gets more populated, the chance to get this work done decreases," declared Noah, whose non-profit organization, History Flight, Inc., had been conducting archival and field research in hopes of locating "the lost graves of Tarawa" since 2007.

More than half a century after the US Army Graves Registration Service had quietly declared the remains of nearly half the marines and sailors killed in the battle to be "unrecoverable," the case was about to be reopened. In December 2009, the defense department's Joint POW/MIA Accounting Agency (JPAC) in Honolulu announced that it would send an eleven-man archaeological team to Betio in August and September 2010 to excavate six locations identified by History Flight as potential gravesites. From the very beginning, the name of Alexander Bonnyman, Jr., the lone missing Medal of Honor recipient, was associated with the mission.

"There is a possibility of recovering over two hundred marines, including that of Congressional Medal of Honor recipient Lt. Alexander Bonnyman, who were buried in shallow graves after one of the most horrific battles of WWII," former Navy gunnery officer and Vietnam veteran Kurt Hiete of California announced in an email.[13]

According to documents unearthed by History Flight, my grandfather was recorded as having been interred with thirty-nine other men in a trench known as Cemetery 27, just one of scores of burial sites scattered across Betio, a spit of sand and coconut trees covering less than three-quarters of a square mile just a shade above the equator in the central Pacific. California-based Niven, a marine veteran and former commercial pilot, declared that he'd pinpointed the location of Cemetery 27, while Noah, also a commercial pilot, had been scouring the north side of the islet using every available technology in his own efforts to find the trench.

From the beginning, Mark Noah wanted just one thing: to locate, through whatever means, Tarawa's missing and see them brought back home to their families for burial. He didn't want glory, or credit; he just wanted to see the job done, and he was willing to do anything to assist. "We need to get the government out there and help them do their job," he said in 2008.[14]

Less than two years later, he would come to the conclusion that the government agencies tasked with recovering battlefield remains weren't really interested in finding the lost graves of Tarawa, with or without his help.

It wasn't until my thirties that I found myself drawn back to my grandfather and the history of Tarawa. I finally read journalist Robert Sherrod's short, gut-wrenching 1944 eyewitness account of the battle and Alexander's meticulous 1995 rendering, and dug out the official marine histories from trunks in my mother's basement. In 2003, my mother offered to help pay my way to visit the atoll with Valor Tours, a military-history excursion company out of Sausalito, California. Inclined toward more luxurious travel, she would never dream of going herself. But as the first Bonnyman to visit the place where the great family hero had sacrificed his life, I could be her proxy; she *wanted* me to go. Still deaf to her feelings about her father, I declined, protesting that such a short trip wasn't worth the price.

But seven years later, inspired by the news that my grandfather was still buried on the island and spurred by Mark Noah's passion, I knew I had to go. As the only living grandson of Sandy Bonnyman (my brother had died in 1999 from cystic fibrosis), I had a persistent sense of guilt because I had not followed him into military service. Going to Tarawa was hardly the same thing, but it was an opportunity to give back to my grandfather in a small, belated way while representing my family.

My mother connected me with Kurt Hiete, who had contacted her the year before seeking information about Sandy Bonnyman.

The rangy, affable California Vietnam veteran had visited her in Boulder, politely prompting her to replace the crumbling, faded ribbon on Sandy's Medal of Honor. Kurt enthusiastically urged me to go and spoke on my behalf to Johnie E. Webb, civilian deputy to the commander at JPAC. He also arranged for his American Legion post to make a donation for my travel expenses.

From the moment I decided to go, I was consumed with taking up the role of paladin of my grandfather's legacy. As a kind of penance for my long neglect, I embarked on a quest to exhume his life, and, if I were lucky, perhaps even his body. After all, if my family hadn't even known he still lay sleeping beneath the sands of Tarawa, what *else* was I missing?

I began my excavation with the insignificant atoll that had so briefly captured America's imagination before sinking back into obscurity, lost and forgotten by almost everyone.

TWO
UNKNOWN ISLAND
1000 BCE–2010 AD

Although the seventy-six-hour struggle for Tarawa in 1943 was almost immediately christened the "bloodiest battle in Marine history," it swiftly faded from the public imagination and was soon overtaken by other momentous events in the Pacific war.

For Tarawa, obscurity was the normal state of affairs. Few newspapers bothered to mention that the remote Gilbert Islands were part of Japan's massive December 1941 offensive, focusing instead on more strategically important attacks at Pearl Harbor, the Philippines, Hong Kong, Singapore, and beyond. Even the marines of the Second Division would not hear of Tarawa until less than a week before they headed into the fiery maw of battle. Once they did, they made jokes, singing, "Tuh-RA-wa BOOM de-ay" in the hulls of transport ships and chuckling at the ridiculous name of the islet, "BEE-tee-oh." Most just used Helen and Longsuit, the respective code names for Betio (pronounced BAY-so) and Tarawa (ta-DHA-wa, with a soft "r" and only the lightest emphasis on the middle syllable).

But the humble Gilberts had a long, if mostly uneventful, history before World War II. The islands, which today span both the equator and the International Date Line, were once volcanic cones created by submarine eruptions millennia ago. The broad fringing

reef surrounding Betio today was built during a prehistoric formation during a period of high seas some twelve thousand years ago.[1]
The chain that would come to be known as the Gilberts comprise
sixteen atolls and 117 separate islands spanning millions of square
kilometers of ocean. Today Tarawa is one of the most remote locations in the Pacific, situated one degree north of the equator, 2,390
miles northeast of Brisbane, Australia, and 2,394 miles southwest of
Hawaii. Travel straight north, you won't strike land until Siberia;
south, it's Antarctica.

Tarawa was probably first settled about three thousand years
ago by Southeast Asian people who canoed from the Caroline
Islands some two thousand miles across open ocean.[2] The inhabitants developed a Micronesian dialect and told the story of how
Nareau the spider named the sky "Karawa," the ocean "Marawa,"
and the land between, "Tarawa."[3]

A Portuguese ship searching for Terra Australis, the fabled
southern continent, brought the first recorded Western explorers
to the area in 1606. British Captain Thomas Gilbert first mapped
the wedge-like Tarawa Atoll in 1788, but the surrounding islands
weren't named in his honor until 1820, curiously, by a Russian
admiral.[4] The first American ship, the USS *Peacock*, visited in 1828,
and in 1856 the Rev. Hiram Bingham sailed from Boston on a mission to convert the islanders to Christianity.[5]

The British hoisted the Union Jack over Tarawa in 1892 and
eventually annexed the islands in 1915 to facilitate the extraction of
phosphates—fossilized bird dung useful in making fertilizer and
detergents—from other islands in the region. Germans arrived to
export dried coconut and the United States and Britain bickered
about air- and sea-lane rights, but to Western eyes, Tarawa was just
a sleepy backwater of the British Empire.[6]

Then, following its defeat in World War I, Germany ceded
control of its Pacific colonies, including Micronesia—the Caroline,

Marianas, and Marshall islands—to the burgeoning Japanese empire. By 1940, Japanese residents outnumbered natives on those islands by seventy thousand to fifty thousand.[7] Partially in reaction to sleights, real and perceived, by the United States, Britain, and Australia, Japan withdrew from the soon-to-be-defunct League of Nations and began flexing its muscles across Asia and the Pacific. Japan invaded China in 1937 and in 1940 occupied northern Indochina with the acquiescence of the French colonial government. On June 27, 1941, Japan announced its plans for a Greater East Asian Co-Prosperity Sphere, which was to include Australia, Burma, India, Malaya, New Guinea, New Zealand, and Thailand, spurring immediate embargoes on Japanese goods by the United States and Britain. On July 16, following a military takeover of the government, General Hideki Tojo became Prime Minister. Sensing imminent war, many Europeans, Australians, and New Zealanders began to leave Tarawa over the coming months and Britain started evacuating residents to Australia.

On December 10, 1941, just two days (accounting for the International Date Line) after shocking the world with its bold attacks on Pearl Harbor and British and Dutch colonies in Asia, two Japanese warships anchored in Tarawa's lagoon. Two hundred *rikusentai*—Japan's marines—went ashore and ordered the Western population off the atoll, allowing only the nuns at the Our Lady of the Sacred Heart convent on Bairiki and twenty-two British and New Zealand coastwatchers to remain.

The "Commander of Japanese Squadron" nailed up a declaration outside the post office on Betio: "The Empire of Japan declared war on America Britain and Dutch Indies to break down these hostilities on Dec. 8th and Japanese Naval Forces have occupied Gilbert Islands to day in the morning. It is our duty to secure the military supremacy in to our hands but we have never enmity for the Gilbert people. According the peoples to do the peaceful conduct will be protected sufficiently, but if you will do hostile acts or do not submit my order, you will be punished with heavy penalties."[8]

But the Gilberts' new rulers paid little heed to Tarawa for many months, instead focusing their efforts on building an airstrip for weather monitoring planes on Butaritari atoll some 150 miles north. The Americans did not view the islands as strategically important, and with the exception of a single carrier-based bombing raid in February 1942, ignored them.[9]

All that would go by the wayside on August 17, 1942, when 220 men from Col. Evans Carlson's 2nd Marine Raider Battalion attacked Butaritari in an attempt to divert Japanese resources away from the invasion of Guadalcanal, launched ten days earlier. The assault was a minor disaster, as the Japanese drove the marines back into the sea, leaving nine behind to be captured and later beheaded. Worse, the attack convinced Japanese Fleet Adm. Isoroku Yamamato that the Gilberts might be more important to Japanese war aims than previously assumed, and he issued orders to reinforce, fortify, and build an airstrip on Betio, the western terminus of Tarawa Atoll.

Under the direction of Rear Admiral Tomanari Saichiro, a skilled engineer, Japanese troops, with the help of several hundred Korean forced laborers and Gilbertese men pressed into service, were soon hard at work. They built dozens of steel-reinforced concrete bunkers and pillboxes—some with three-and-a-half-foot-thick walls, standing fifteen or twenty feet high, and covered with tons of sand, coconut logs, and railroad ties, making them both less visible and more impervious to American bombers. They built twenty gun mounts around the island's perimeter and armed them with ten 75mm mountain guns, six 70mm cannon, and nine 37mm field artillery pieces. They also brought in four hulking 8-inch guns and placed them on Betio's south- and west-facing beaches; three still stand today (though long rumored to be booty from the capture of

Singapore in 1942, the Japanese actually purchased them from the British in 1905).

They brought in nine light tanks and countless anti-aircraft and -boat guns, and studded the island with machine-gun positions, creating interlocking fields of fire that left virtually no inch of the coastline open to assault.

To thwart amphibious attack, Japanese forces strung miles of heavy barbed wire around Betio, placed giant blocks of concrete across the reef, and built a three-foot high coconut-log seawall, to block passage of tanks and transports.[10] When the work was mostly done in May, the Sasebo 7th Special Navy Landing Force joined the Yokosuka 6th Special Landing Force on Betio, swelling the garrison to nearly five thousand men.[11]

Built in response to Carlson's small raid on Makin, this massive fortification of Betio would become one of three main factors contributing to merciless carnage some six months later.

When the First Marine Division stormed the beaches of the mosquito-choked jungle island of Guadalcanal in the Solomon Islands on August 7, 1942, Americans back home desperately needed a glimmer of hope. There hadn't been a lot of good news from the Pacific since Pearl Harbor.

On March 11, despite previous assurances that things were going well, Gen. Douglas MacArthur abandoned the island of Corregidor in the dead of night under orders from President Roosevelt, fleeing before a Japanese onslaught that would soon overrun the Philippines and lead to the horrific Bataan Death March. The supremely confident forces of the Japanese Empire had swept across the southwest Pacific and appeared poised to drive into Australia, exposed when most of its troops had been commandeered for the British fight against the Axis powers in North Africa. The Japanese already had taken Manila, the Dutch East Indies, North Borneo, New Britain, and British-held Singapore, once thought invincible, with relative ease. And while it didn't amount to much, a Japanese submarine had even surfaced off Santa Barbara, California to shell an oil refinery, raising the specter of an invasion of the continental United States.

There were, to be sure, a few heartening glimmers. Though of little strategic value, the daring B-25 raids on Tokyo on April 8, 1942, led by Col. James Doolittle, showed the enemy that America could, and would, fight for its life. And in June, US and British sea forces fended off Japan's attack on Midway Island, thanks in part to the work of American code breakers.

Still, the losses continued to pile up, as the Japanese took Burma in May and claimed the southern end of Alaska's Aleutian Islands in June. By July they had also landed in northern New Guinea and the Solomon Islands, threatening to cut off Australia and New Zealand from the United States.

On the American side, a tug-of-war between Navy Adm. Chester W. Nimitz, commander of the Pacific Fleet, and the Army's MacArthur had resulted in a dual strategy for retaking the Pacific. MacArthur favored going straight to the Philippines after retaking New Guinea. Nimitz advocated using amphibious marine assaults to take objectives in an "island-hopping" campaign that would allow the Navy to construct airfields ever closer to the Japanese home islands and ramp up bombing raids. In the end, advisors to President Roosevelt and British Prime Minister Winston Churchill endorsed a pincers strategy, with MacArthur "leapfrogging" in the western theater and Nimitz island-hopping across the central Pacific.

American military planners had expected war with Japan as far back as 1920 and my grandfather had not been far behind: "Everyone thought I was crazy to say in 1932 that such an insignificant people would dare tackle the mighty United States," he wrote his mother.[12] The US military had devised a plan to defend the Central Pacific by 1930, but, assuming the British would defend the seemingly inconsequential Gilbert Islands, had left them out of the equation.[13]

When the US First Marine Division stormed ashore at Tulagi and Guadalcanal, it was the first crucial step in Nimitz's and MacArthur's campaign to take back the Pacific by picking off enemy strongholds and moving north until American bombers could easily attack the Japanese home islands. Following more than six months of grueling close combat, the Second Marine Division was sent in to mop up on Guadalcanal in February 1943.

But where to next? American military planners insisted that any assault have land-based air support.[14] The Marianas, Carolines, and Marshalls were too far afield, but heavy bombers could reach the Gilberts from US bases in the Ellice Islands, eight hundred miles to the southwest. And now that Betio had become a fortress, it threatened to sever traffic between Hawaii and Australia and might be used to thwart an attack on the Marshalls.

There was one more crucial incentive to take Tarawa: In order to reach Tokyo, the Navy and marines believed they would have to master the art of conducting full-scale amphibious assaults on heavily defended beaches. With its broad, fringing reef and flat, sandy beaches, Betio looked like the ideal laboratory to test battle plans, strategy, and technology.

Amphibious warfare traces its roots to the ancient Egyptians and Greeks; the Persian Empire used ships to land ground troops at the battle of Marathon in 490 BCE. But the first full-scale amphibious assault of the modern era, at Gallipoli on the Turkish coast in 1915, became a bloody rout now synonymous with slaughter, resulting in nearly 188,000 Allied casualties. There was widespread belief among military planners after that battle that amphibious warfare could never succeed against modern defenses.

The outlier was the US Marine Corps. In 1921, convinced that the United States would one day have to fight a naval battle with Japan in the Pacific, Marine Maj. Earl Hancock "Pete" Ellis asked permission to conduct undercover reconnaissance in the Marshall and Caroline islands. Ellis returned and wrote "Advanced Base Operations in Micronesia," which became the foundation for marine amphibious warfare in World War II. He determined that success would depend on fast-moving waves of landing vehicles, both naval and air bombing support, and nimble assault teams armed with machine guns, light artillery, light tanks, and combat engineers to demolish beach defenses with explosives and fire.[15]

In 1943 Maj. Gen. Julian Smith, commander of the Second Marine Division, believed he had all that, and more.

"For its part, the U.S. Marine Corps was itching to test itself against a defended beach, a task for which it had been preparing since 1775, the year the Marine Corps was founded," write Tarawa historians Eric Hammel and John E. Lee. "The solution was simple: Betio would be assaulted."[16]

THREE
PARADISE LOST
1943–2010

As I was pondering my first trip to Tarawa in 2010, I read *The Sex Lives of Cannibals*, J. Maarten Troost's wry 2004 memoir about the two years he and his girlfriend spent living in a tropical paradise, sight unseen.

The couple had figuratively closed their eyes and stabbed a finger into a map of the Pacific Ocean, landing on a remote atoll they'd never heard of: Tarawa. But Betio was hardly Gilligan's Island. Its once gorgeous reef was dead and stinking, the water table teemed with bacteria that caused periodic outbreaks of cholera and typhus, mosquitoes carried dengue (aka "break bone") fever, and the beaches were not only mounded with twelve-foot high heaps of garbage, but also mined with human feces. With more than twenty thousand of the poorest residents in the world crammed onto less than a square mile of flat coral sand, Betio was a depressing, hot, uncomfortable tropical slum.

As Troost wrote, "it was a filthy, noxious hellhole. But it was *our* filthy, noxious hellhole."[1] And, in the spirit of my adventurous grandfather, there was no place on earth I'd rather go.

In June 2010 I wrote to Johnie Webb, an Army veteran who had been with the US Department of Defense Joint POW/MIA Accounting Agency since 1975 and now served as its top civilian administrator. Imagining Webb to be some sort of bureaucrat, I wouldn't learn until later that he was one of the founding fathers of America's modern efforts to recover the remains of tens of thousands of missing military personnel. He was friendly, helpful, and enthusiastic about having a member of the Bonnyman family observe the JPAC team's work on Betio in August and September.

I was soon speaking to the agency's director of public affairs, Lt. Col. Wayne Perry, and Maj. Ramon "Ray" Osorio, press liaison for the eleven-man team headed to Betio. They, too, welcomed my visit and promised that I would be given the courtesy of full access to dig sites. Perry suggested I plan to arrive the second week of August, when the work would have begun in earnest. He also suggested I contact Steven C. Barber, a Los Angeles-based videographer hired by JPAC to document the mission.

Barber had teamed up with US Navy veteran Leon Cooper to make a 2009 documentary, *Return to Tarawa: The Leon Cooper Story*. An energetic filmmaker with a knack for sniffing out a good story, he was constantly chasing down celebrities in hopes of breaking into the Hollywood big leagues. Barber had never heard of Tarawa until 1997, when he scored a brief interview with actor Eddie Albert, then ninety-five. Albert was a stage name, and as Navy Lt. Edward A. Heimberger, he had earned a Bronze Star for rescuing injured marines at Tarawa, and performed the grim duty of pulling the dead from the lagoon.

The salty, irreverent Cooper, a Navy coxswain, recalled ferrying marines across the reef and "closing the eyes of the dead" on the beaches. (Military records show that while Cooper did serve as a coxswain, he did not spend time ashore.[2]) Cooper's disgust and sadness over the deplorable conditions he found on Betio when he visited in 2008, and his outrage at learning that there were still marines buried on the island, formed the emotional core of the film, which he produced. Now, JPAC had hired Barber to create a film based on its Tarawa recovery efforts.

"The boss [Perry] and I spoke with Clay Bonnyman [*sic*] the other day," Osorio wrote to Barber after my first phone meeting with the JPAC officials. "We gave him the green light to come out and play, I figured this would work out nicely for your piece."[3]

Heeding Perry's advice, I called Barber to ask him about what to bring, where to stay, and the easiest way to fly to Tarawa. He immediately warned me to prepare for the worst, because I was going to a "third-world hellhole," but unlike Troost, he didn't seem to see much upside to the place. He sent me his itinerary and offered to put in a good word so that I could stay at Our Lady of the Sacred Heart convent, still going strong on neighboring Bairiki, a far less degraded island than Betio.

Speaking in a non-stop rush, the filmmaker also laid out his vision for a film in which I would be the "star." He would shoot me gazing out the window as the Air Pacific 737 approached Tarawa, exploring the island, and if we got lucky, the expression on my face when JPAC located my grandfather.

A couple of days later, Barber sent a boisterous email with a link to a YouTube video, a fundraising pitch that announced, "Medal of Honor winner Alexander Bonnyman . . . will have his grandson Clay embedded with our production crew as the search [for remains] begins in August."

I immediately called him and asked him to remove my name from the video, explaining that I wasn't going to be "embedded" with anyone. He didn't call back, instead sending a curt email: "You're on your own. . . . I had a house lined up for you but when you bailed on me I gave away your spot."[4]

On the suggestion of Kurt Hiete, I also contacted Mark Noah, founder of History Flight. The non-governmental organization had, to date, conducted thousands of hours of archival research and spent more than four months on Betio using every conceivable technology, from ground-penetrating radar to a cadaver-detection dog, in a single-minded mission to locate "the lost graves of Tarawa." JPAC planned to excavate up to six sites identified by Noah's crews during the mission.

"Feel free to drop me a line any time," Mark responded when I emailed. "I'd be happy to show you any and all of our Tarawa info."[5] He also offered to connect me with his local "fixer" on Betio, Kautebiri Kobuti, who could help me find accommodations, and suggested I rent my own car, with the mysterious aside, "so you are independent of all the PT Barnum grandstanding that is going to be happening there at the time."[6]

It would be a long time before I met Mark in person, and even longer before I talked him into explaining why a civilian with no connection to the Marine Corps or Tarawa would so relentlessly seek the graves of men long dead, lost and mostly forgotten by ever-more distant relatives who never met them. But that conversation a month before leaving for Tarawa in 2010 would be only the first of many.

Mark, a bull-stout guy with a fine brush of reddish-brown hair, wire-rimmed glasses, and a round, ruddy face, had racked up thousands of hours of flying time for government and commercial delivery services by the time he founded History Flight in 2003. Dedicated "to preserving and honoring American WWII, Vietnam, and Gulf-War aviation history and aircrew combat veterans," the nonprofit offered flights to the public on its fleet of World War II-era aircraft: the North American B-25H Mitchell bomber, *Barbie III*; a North American AT-6 Texan, used to train P-51 Mustang pilots during World War II; and a Boeing N2S Stearman biplane.

Mark had no formal connection to the military. Born in 1965, he had spent most of his childhood overseas, living in countries

where his father had been posted with the US State Department—
China, Finland, the Philippines, Russia, South Korea, Thailand. He
returned to the United States to attend the prestigious Westminster
School in Simsbury, Connecticut with the likes of H. John Heinz
IV, son of the late US Senator from Pennsylvania and stepson of
former Secretary of State and Democratic presidential nominee
John Kerry. It was, Mark recalled, "an upper-crust education that
resembled the *Dead Poets Society*."

He took a year off before attending college so he could save money
and achieve his dream of becoming a pilot, which eventually helped
pay for his undergraduate degree at Atlanta's Emory University. After
graduating, he spent several years in the music business—mostly
punk—in Atlanta and Los Angeles before deciding to become a
professional pilot. When I met him, he was making his living flying
cargo runs to South America and Central America for United Parcel
Service.

Mark found his way into the MIA recovery community via The
BentProp Project. Founded by physician, scuba diver, and World
War II aviation enthusiast Pat Scannon of California, the nonprofit organization is dedicated to locating and recovering American MIAs, with a special emphasis on downed aircraft in the tiny
western Pacific nation of Palau. Described as "the Indiana Jones of
military archaeology,"[7] Scannon worked closely with JPAC and had
been conducting annual missions to Palau since 1999.

Mark joined BentProp (now known as Project Recover) as a volunteer reconnaissance pilot and first learned of the lost graves of Tarawa
during a 2007 mission to locate a missing aircrew believed to have gone
down in Tarawa's vast, jewel-hued lagoon. It was a story that had not
been merely forgotten, but virtually erased from history. In the years
after the battle, the US government fed a litany of false explanations
to families of the fallen—their loved ones rested in neat rows beneath
white crosses on Betio, or they'd been buried at sea, or anonymously

interred in Hawaii. In truth, as many as half of the 1,049 marines and navy personnel killed in the battle remained unaccounted for.[8]

So how could more than five hundred gravesites have gone missing on the flat, featureless, 1.2-square-kilometer sandy spit that is Betio? Multiple factors played a role.

As soon as the fighting ended on Betio on November 23, 1943, chaplains from the Second Marine Division oversaw the burial of hundreds of Americans killed in the battle. The burials were hasty—most of the bodies had been rapidly decomposing for two or three days in the blazing equatorial heat—but the marines did their best to keep things orderly. Whether they had been buried in scattered individual graves or trenches dug by Navy Construction Battalion (Seabee) bulldozers, identities of the dead were recorded where possible (though hundreds had to be buried as "unknown"), and the location of graves was marked on a map. Marines erected rough markers cobbled together from the shattered remnants of Japanese structures over each individual grave and buried the dead with one set of dog tags—if available—and hung the other from the markers.

But with the planned assault on the Marshall Islands just over two months away, rebuilding the airstrip on Betio was an urgent priority. Jeeps and bulldozers that began rumbling off the pier as soon as the coast was clear destroyed many grave markers, while others were removed to make way for construction. Noah had interviewed a former Navy bomber crewman, Ralls Clotfelter, who recalled seeing his commanding officer punch a Seabee officer for removing crosses to make way for an aircraft parking area.[9]

Seabees were laying down "twelve to eighteen inches of crushed coral rock on top of burial sites," Mark told me. "That's one reason they never found them after the war—nobody thought to look under a parking lot."[10]

To further complicate matters, virtually all the Second Marine Division had packed up and sailed for Hawaii before the end of

November, leaving no witnesses. In early 1944, the US Navy began what it called "beautification and reconstruction," taking down almost all of the original crude grave markers and building a series of orderly "cemeteries" complete with gleaming white crosses, crushed coral ground cover, and borders made from coconut logs or anchor chains. There was just one problem: Most of the "graves" contained no remains.[11]

By the time US Army Graves Registration returned in 1946 with a Catholic chaplain who supervised the burials to reclaim the dead, the island was a very different place. Armed only with shovels, and with little to guide them but the priest's memory, hand-marked maps, and a few aerial photos, the team can be forgiven for failing to locate hundreds of graves. Less forgivable were the subsequent decades of efforts to hide the truth from families of the missing.

"Tarawa," Mark Noah said, "is a double tragedy where 1,113 young Americans lost their lives and the parents, children, and siblings of 495 of them that became 'missing' after the battle never received the truth about the disposition of their family members because the records pertaining to their disappearance were classified until a generation after the parents of the missing themselves deceased."[12]

When Mark returned from Tarawa in 2007, he was determined to do whatever he could to help the families of the missing. He and a paid researcher spent thirty-five days delving deep into the National Archives, Marine Corps Historical Division, and other dusty archives for clues that might allow a modern team to locate the lost graves. Eventually—and not until they'd done battle with several bureaucracies—History Flight obtained copies of Individual Deceased Personnel Files, casualty cards—index cards with typewritten information about death and disposition of remains—and other documents indicating that a minimum of 216 American dead were still buried somewhere on the island.[13] But nobody knew where.

"The missing graves on Tarawa were like a Rubik's Cube," Mark said, "only ten thousand times more difficult to solve."[14]

But Mark had no intention of restricting his search to the dusty stacks of Washington's public archives. He began raising money from friends and private donors. He and his researchers hunted down and interviewed some hundred Tarawa veterans. And in 2008, Mark sent a team of surveyors, historians, and archaeologists armed with magnetometers, GPS locators, a GSSI 3000 Ground Penetrating Radar unit, and even a good, old-fashioned survey wheel, to Betio for a total of eight weeks in the first intensive effort to locate the lost graves since 1946. In May 2009, he self-published a lengthy report, *The Lost Graves of Tarawa*, which retraced the history of the problem and laid out a case—including copies of hundreds of casualty cards—he hoped would spur the Department of Defense into mounting its own mission to Tarawa. History Flight's 2009 report highlighted the case of Alexander Bonnyman, Jr., the only missing Medal of Honor recipient, whose "casualty card showed him buried in #17, 8th Marines Cemetery #2, where he still lies today."[15]

But JPAC was not exactly impressed, arguing that soil disturbances identified by History Flight as possible grave sites "may be the result of Japanese defensive positions, U.S. construction efforts, burial of war dead, prior searches of U.S. burials, or more recent construction activities."[16]

In one of those inexplicable synchronicities of history, Capt. William L. Niven, USMC (retired), had also stumbled across the mystery of Tarawa's MIAs, and in 2007 he spent some $50,000 of his own money to self-publish the first book on the subject, *Tarawa's Gravediggers*. Alternately described by the author as a "non-fiction novel"[17] and a "comprehensive research study (that) accurately identifies and locates the undiscovered graves of many Marines and Sailors killed in action during the battle for the island of Betio,"[18] the spiral-bound, professionally printed volume covered some of the same ground as History Flight's later report.

With help from historians at JPAC and its sister agency, the Pentagon's Defense Prisoner of War/Missing Personnel Office (DPMO), Bill had painstakingly developed what he believed to be the first accurate roster of 1,104 US service personnel killed in the battle using official reports, chaplain diaries, journalist accounts, and other documents. He hired a Virginia-based cartographic company to help him overlay battle-era maps and photos of Betio with Google Earth images and eventually arrived at a set of precise geographical coordinates where he believed the lost marines would be found.[19]

Bill had been a marine pilot, and in another incidental parallel to Mark Noah, flew cargo jets for Federal Express and Flying Tigers. He had always been interested in Marine Corps history, and among all the campaigns of World War II, Tarawa was the one that most captured his imagination—especially the story of Sandy Bonnyman. Bill visited Tarawa in 1989 in part to "retrace his footsteps to the place where he was killed."[20]

Bill's book deserves to be known as the pebble that started the avalanche of government and public interest in the Tarawa fallen who had never come home from the battle. After seeing him on MSNBC on Memorial Day 2008, James Balcer, Democratic alderman of the 11th Ward of Chicago and a marine veteran who fought in Vietnam, tracked Bill down and invited him speak to the city council. Bill declined, but sent a copy of his book to Balcer, who persuaded the council to send a resolution to JPAC and President George W. Bush, requesting that a recovery mission be dispatched to Tarawa posthaste.

US Rep. Dan Lipinski, Democrat of Illinois, then picked up the ball and introduced House Resolution 2647, which directed JPAC to review research conducted by civilians and "do everything feasible" to recover Tarawa's lost marines.[21] That suggestion became an order with the passage of the 2010 National Defense Authorization Act—thanks to a big push from US Sen. Dick Durbin of Illinois, the ranking Democrat on the Senate Armed Services Committee—which not only directed JPAC to conduct a mission to Tarawa, but also mandated that the agency increase the number of remains identified to 200 per year by 2015. It was an enormous boost in expectations: In 2009, the agency identified eighty MIAs, and in 2012, sixty.[22]

JPAC had by then begun to meet with both Bill Niven and Mark Noah. The two men knew of each other's work and had spoken. The relationship was cordial, but competitive.

"Mark Noah is a patriot," Bill said. "But I think he's wrong."[23]

"Bill's a nice guy," Mark said. "But he hasn't been to Tarawa since 1989 and he hasn't done the fieldwork we have."[24]

When the time came for the DPMO—the Washington-based agency tasked with oversight of recovery efforts—to put together a plan for the 2010 mission on Betio, the agency put its chips on Noah's History Flight.

"In 2009, JPAC and DPMO researchers conducted a review of the History Flight report and in September 2009 a small investigation and coordination team mapped and developed a recovery plan for the possible mass grave locations determined by History Flight. JPAC and DPMO researchers also held meetings with [name redacted, but almost certainly Bill Niven] and Mr. Mark Noah, of History Flight in April 2010 to evaluate the available historical evidence concerning these possible mass grave locations," according to a 2010 JPAC email.[25]

Despite Bill Niven's efforts, outsiders gave credit to History Flight for rolling up its sleeves and getting its hands dirty.

"JPAC's MIA recovery mission is based entirely on the excellent work done by Mark Noah and History Flight," Jim Hildebrand posted on Tarawa on the Web. "First they did all their homework on the MIA problem. Then they took a team to Betio, equipped with ground-penetrating radar, to look for unexhumed graves/bodies. . . . They also provided GPS locations to JPAC. My impression is that the information was so good, it could not be ignored by JPAC."[26]

All this was good news to those who wanted to see the Tarawa marines recovered and brought home to their families. But behind the scenes, JPAC was riven with factionalism, and some scientists at its Central Identification Laboratory in Honolulu were lobbying against the little NGO that could, History Flight, and its methods.

As I prepared for my trip, I discovered that nobody had ever heard of Tarawa. The staff at Boulder's venerable Changes in Latitude travel store, whose map of the world was stuck with hundreds of brightly colored pins designating far corners of the world visited by well-heeled locals, had to consult a guidebook to look up Kiribati (the modern name for the independent nation that includes the Gilbert Islands, it's pronounced KIHD-uh-boss) when I walked in. Even the nurses at the local clinic that did nothing but provide shots and advice to people traveling to weird places overseas hadn't heard of it.

I began to receive advice from Tarawa Talk members who had traveled to Betio, and it didn't sound good. Dennis Covert, a US Navy veteran who visited Tarawa in 2008, warned, "Sanitation is poor or lacking. Betio is overpopulated . . . people, pigs, dogs, kids, trash litter, excrement, etc., all mixed in crowded conditions. The Betio lagoon is regarded as a cauldron of infectious diseases, which are continuously re-cycled back to the people through their consumption of contaminated fish." Seven people on South Tarawa had died from dengue fever just prior to his trip, Covert said, and "hepatitis is widespread and the majority of the population has intestinal parasites and worms."[27] Never mind that the atoll's contaminated water table leaves residents vulnerable to giardiasis, cryptosporidiosis, dysentery, typhoid, salmonellosis, internal parasites, and cholera, all contributors to the highest infant-mortality rate in the Pacific region.[28]

Dennis sent me a detailed list of essentials to bring, everything from a mosquito head-net to a prescription antibiotic and Lifesaver candy to hand out to the children who would happily swarm any *i-Matang*—foreigner—they saw.

"Oh my God, it's not that bad," Kelle Rivers said with a laugh when we met at Dot's Diner in Boulder. "You make it sound like you're going into a war zone."

I had reason to trust Kelle, a longtime friend and, briefly, girlfriend who had been living in Thailand for years and just happened to be visiting her family in Colorado. In 1994, I had hugged her one last time and watched her disappear down the jetway at Denver's Stapleton International Airport, on her way to a Peace Corps assignment in Kiribati. She had been posted to Abemama, seventy-six miles (and twenty-four hours by boat, as she would learn to her dismay) south of Tarawa, teaching at Tetongo Primary School and swimming daily in warm, crystalline waters. It wasn't all paradise—she battled ants, loneliness, and little for a vegetarian to eat—but it was close.

"I'm writing by the light of a little oil lamp—actually it's an old jar with a wick and oil. I have it hanging inside my little thatched-roof sleeping house. It's spreading a faint pinkish light through my mosquito net, enough to read this letter. All I can hear right now is a cricket, the ocean, the wind, and an occasional bird in a nearby tree," she had written in her first letter to me.[29]

But she acknowledged that Kiribati's capital, Tarawa, where she had to attend meetings and conferences at the Peace Corps office, made for quite a different experience. Teeming with more than half of Kiribati's one hundred thousand residents, South Tarawa was constantly abuzz with noise from passing minibuses blaring tinny Christian music and streams of barefoot girls and boys in colorful school uniforms walking along the narrow shoulder of the atoll's lone paved road at all times of day or night, as well as countless pigs and scabby, feral dogs and cats. But Kelle adored the people. There was little crime to speak of, and she encouraged me to swim in the lagoon, that aforementioned "cauldron of infectious diseases." After all, she had, and lived to tell the tale.

I told Kelle my goal was to trace my grandfather's footsteps.

"Well, that should take you about five minutes," she said, understanding the scale of Betio in a way I could not. "And seriously, it's not that bad. You're not going there for a beach vacation, anyway."

She was right. My grandfather had come to Tarawa literally in the dark, uneasy, but eager to defeat the enemy, and hoping his war might end soon so he could go home to his family. My arrival would be very different, but I was on a mission, too: to exhume a tragic episode from my family's past that had been buried for far too long.

FOUR
RESTLESS SPIRIT
1868–1928

This is everything I knew—or thought I knew—about my grandfather a month before my departure to Betio: *Grew up in Knoxville; went to Princeton, where he played football; married my grandmother, Josephine Bell; moved to New Mexico and became a successful mine owner; joined the marines in a patriotic fervor after Pearl Harbor, though he didn't have to go; killed at Tarawa; received the Medal of Honor.*

There's also this anecdote, recounted to me by nearly every Bonnyman family member who had known him, however briefly, and repeated by relatives born decades after his death: Even as an adult, Sandy delighted in alarming observers with daredevil antics at the swimming pool at his childhood home, Bonniefield. He would scramble up the backside of a small bathhouse at the eastern end of the pool, take a few loping strides up the slanted tile roof, then launch his long, muscled body over twelve feet of concrete into the water.

"It was quite a dive," said Robert McKeon, a nephew who witnessed the feat. "I don't know how he didn't kill himself."[1]

And there was this: During the 1980s, I worked for another of my grandfather's nephews, Alexander "Sandy" McKeon (my father used to joke that the Bonnymans lost the baby-name book, as there seem to be only about five names to go around) who owned several ranches in California's central valley. Sandy McKeon remembered his uncle from boyhood, and knew how much I idolized him.

"He wasn't perfect, you know," he casually mentioned one blazing afternoon as we trailed cattle across sun-crisped, rolling hills. "I'll bet you didn't know he was once shot in a bar fight in Santa Fe."

My hackles rose immediately. Angry responses galloped through my head: *Why haven't I heard this before? You're just jealous; you may have done your little hitch in the Army, but you hardly served with the same distinction as your uncle. And if there really was a "bar fight," who's to say he started it?*

But when I pressed him for details, he had none. Fuming, I spurred my horse and headed toward the front of the herd. Only years later would I come to understand that my deeply Catholic cousin wasn't trying to insult my grandfather so much as remind me that all fall short of perfection.

The next time I called home, my mother confirmed that her father had been shot. But she was just six years old at the time and the only thing she remembered was how big his feet were as he lay on the couch recuperating.

The first known reference to Scottish surname Bonnyman in North America was published June 9, 1682, in a history of the Bruton Church in Williamsburg, Virginia. My great-grandfather, Alexander Bonnyman Sr., was two when he arrived with his family from Scotland in 1870. George and Ann Toner Bonnyman and their five children settled in Lexington, Kentucky. It's not clear how (or if) George Bonnyman made a living, but he often "would go on [drinking] sprees."[2] Young Alex was often sent by his mother to retrieve his father from local taverns, an experience that would lead to lifelong abstemiousness.

Just five feet, six inches tall, Alex had short, powerful legs and a long torso that made him appear as tall as many a six-footer when seated. His thick, wavy brown hair, round cheeks, and bright blue eyes gave him a cheery avuncular appearance that belied his formal and sometimes demanding personality.

Accepted at age sixteen to study engineering at the University of Kentucky, Alex Bonnyman was already teaching math to undergraduates at the age of nineteen.[3] He had finished all his mathematical and engineering work but still had a few electives to take when his father, who never fully approved of his son's "cow college," abruptly informed him that he would be shipped off to study at the Edinburgh School of Medicine. In an early demonstration of will and determination—some would say stubbornness—Alex refused. His father immediately withdrew financial support, forcing Alex to drop out of school (the university awarded him an honorary doctorate of law in 1950).

But Alex had learned enough of engineering to find work with several Southern railroad companies. He became chief engineer for the Atlantic, Birmingham, and Atlanta Railroad in 1899, where he supervised construction of more than 600 miles of rail.

While in Georgia, he met Frances Rhea Berry, youngest daughter of Capt. Thomas Berry, a Confederate veteran turned wealthy cotton merchant and plantation owner, and Frances Rhea, daughter of a former slave-holding family with a plantation near Gadsden, Alabama. Born in 1878, my great-grandmother lived a genteel life, cared for by servants and schooled by a governess on an idyllic plantation outside the town of Rome. Like her future son, she grew up loving animals and exploring the outdoors.

Alexander Bonnyman was thirty-eight when he proposed to Frances, ten years his junior. Her Episcopalian family did not approve of her marriage to an immigrant and, worse, a Catholic. But in an early demonstration of the independent streak she would share with her oldest son, Frances not only married Alex in 1906, but also converted to Catholicism. The couple's first three children were born in Atlanta, including Alexander Jr. on May 2, 1910.

Having learned a great deal about mining while working the railroads, Alex moved his family to Knoxville in 1912 to take a job with the Campbell Coal Mining Company, owned by the wealthy husband of his wife's sister Laura. Four years later, with help from my great-grandmother's inherited fortune, he bought a coal mine near Hazard, Kentucky and started Blue Diamond Coal Company. The company's mines in Kentucky, Tennessee, and Virginia made a "major contribution" to the American campaign in World War I and would ship more than a million tons of coal a year during World War II.[4]

Alex built Bonniefield on twenty-six acres west of Knoxville in 1916.[5] Designed by Charles Barber, the South's most famous Beaux-Arts architect, the mansion was lavishly appointed with sculpted tile floors, shiny hardwood stairs, a generously lit sunroom, and a swimming pool. Ivy-twined and surrounded by wide swaths of well-tended lawn, ornate gardens, and carefully sculpted shrubbery, the estate's north side dropped off into a steep ravine, where a railroad track split the tangled Tennessee wilderness. Here the Bonnymans' many servants, cooks, nannies, drivers, and groundskeepers, both black and white, helped raise four children.

As the firstborn son of a cultured conservative Scotsman and a daughter of the plantation South, my grandfather was both privileged and doted upon. Cared for as an infant by an African American nurse named Minerva, by the time he was walking and talking he was his father's greatest pride. Wearing long, curly, blond locks and dressed in white gowns, knee socks, and buckle shoes as a toddler, he was barely distinguishable from a little girl. But he was, from the beginning, all boy, and as soon as he could he was off exploring the woods at the back of Bonniefield, dropping a fishing line into the Tennessee River just down the hill, or riding his little black pony, Tap, at Galbraith Springs, a summer resort seventy miles northeast of Knoxville.

My great-grandmother insisted that the children be well educated, and they were among the first students to attend Mrs. J.A. Thackston's School when it opened in Knoxville in 1920. She read to them often from *The Harvard Classics* and the red-leather-bound series, *The Children's Hour*, which contained young Sandy's favorite poem, Whitman's "O Captain! My Captain!"

> The ship is anchored safe and sound, its voyage closed and done;
> From fearful trip, the victor ship, comes in with object won;
> Exult, O shores, and ring, O bells!
> But I, with mournful tread,
> Walk the deck my Captain lies,
> Fallen cold and dead.[6]

The Bonnymans brought the children up to be devout Catholics. Frances read them the Bible, and they attended Mass weekly at Knoxville's Church of the Immaculate Conception and regularly made confession.

Sandy always loved animals. Bonniefield was home to a long line of dogs—Mack, his favorite, Duff the sheepdog, Jo Dick, and later a slew of hounds whose puppies he trained for bird hunting—cats, and homing pigeons, not to mention the snakes, toads, and lightning bugs he captured in the nearby woods.

When he was ten, Sandy became passionate about photography. He constantly pointed his No. 2 Kodak Automatic Brownie at his sisters and baby brother Gordon, his pets, the house and surrounding lands, and friends, especially his favorite boyhood companion Shirley Spence (a boy). His photo albums reveal an early charisma, theatricality, and sense of humor: carefully posed shots of him preparing to dump a bucket of water from a hayloft onto his "unsuspecting" sister, or "stuck" in a coal chute while Margot prepares to paddle his rump, mincing with a parasol. His sisters and mother laughed at his performances, and even stodgy, serious Alex Bonnyman couldn't help breaking a smile at his antics.

"He has always been such a lovable boy and there will always be much of the boy and a sheer joy of living in him," a family friend observed.[7]

Sandy traveled to Europe twice by the time he was twelve, and the wounds of The Great War were still fresh when the family sailed aboard the *New Amsterdam* and *Iles de France* in 1920 and aboard White Star line's *RMS Adriatic*, sister to the doomed *Titanic,* two years later. Visiting recent battlefields in France, Italy, and Belgium, Sandy photographed landscapes still scarred by battle.

"On this hill more than 2000 French and American soldiers were killed in less than 2 min.," he scribbled beneath a photo of a barren, blasted hillside that had been covered in blood in the Battle of Marnes. "It was taken by the Germans and when the Allies made an attack they blew it up."

Sandy matured into a strikingly handsome young man with golden hair, penetrating blue eyes, and his father's dignified, straight nose. By age twelve he had already surpassed Alex in height, on his way to becoming the only six-footer in a family of men for whom five-foot-eight was an achievement.

As a teenager Sandy learned his lifelong love for fishing and bird hunting while traveling with Shirley Spence's family to the hills of Tennessee and the great lakes of Michigan and Minnesota. He always returned with photos of himself with his quarry—duck, pheasant, a toothy pike—in one hand and a shotgun or rod in the other. Having long outgrown his pony, he loved to ride sleek

Thoroughbred horses in jodhpurs and tall black boots. He took up tennis and soon was competing with some of Knoxville's top junior players, including city youth champion Kyle Moore.

He also began to reveal a wild side that troubled his sober father. As soon as he was able to drive, he began to stay out late. Alex tried to ground him, going so far as to drain his Ford Model T's gas tank, but Sandy just slipped out through a window, siphoned gas from other vehicles at Bonniefield, and drove off into the night, drawn into a wider, wilder world he could never resist.[8]

As he matured, Sandy began to develop a reputation around town as something of a lothario. His sister-in-law, Isabel Ashe Bonnyman, described him as "the most devastatingly handsome man" she'd ever seen, and her prominent Knoxville family was at first reluctant to allow her to date Gordon, fearing he shared his brother's wild ways.[9] Mary Tate, who spent years working as a housekeeper for the Gordon Bonnyman family, heard many stories about my grandfather, who was "flamboyant . . . a lover, a playboy" and perhaps a little spoiled.

"Granny (Bonnyman) couldn't do a thing with him," Tate said. "She always knew he would have his way."[10]

Sandy's Berry blood seemed to overpower his father's cultured European ways, and he fit the archetype of Southern masculinity, displaying honor, self-reliance, faith, virility, and martial prowess. But like so many of Faulkner's tragic white men—like Faulkner himself—he also shared another, less honored, aspect of traditional Southern manhood: hard drinking.[11]

So it was no surprise, perhaps, when Alex sent his strong-willed son away to attend the Newman School, a Catholic boarding institution in Lakewood, New Jersey, at age sixteen. There, well north of the Mason-Dixon Line, Sandy fell in love with one more staple of modern Southern manhood: football. Starting at left offensive guard in 1926, he got to shake President Calvin Coolidge's hand as a member of the 1927 squad.[12] Long before it became a multi-billion dollar spectator extravaganza, football engaged what William Phillips called "the most primitive feelings about violence, patriotism, manhood," for fans and players alike.[13] The game thrummed with martial metaphor and Sandy possessed the size, fearlessness, and drive to make him a captain worth following.

Upon graduation, Sandy became the first in a long line of Bonnyman sons (and recently, one daughter) to attend Princeton University, where he studied engineering. He had earned enough college credit in prep school to enter as a sophomore in 1928, and he made the first string of the Tigers football team at guard that fall. He proved indomitable on the field, refusing to leave a 1929 game with Yale even after a 200-pound opponent had cleated his hand and he could no longer see out of one bloodied eye.[14]

Football brought out more than just his iron will and physical courage. My grandfather's charisma and ability to rally the troops inspired fierce loyalty from his teammates, who made him their captain. "I thought the sun rose and set on Sandy as did, I believe, everyone who knew him," wrote one.[15]

But Sandy had never liked—and never would like—sitting at a desk, and in 1930 he was summoned to the dean's office to account for his poor grades.[16] We'll never know whether he really sealed his fate, as legend has it, by punching the dean, but when they heard that their captain was being booted out of school, the rest of the Tiger players converged on the dean's office to protest, *en masse*. Their ploy didn't work—nor did pleas to the university president from his aunt Martha Berry, founder and head of Georgia's Berry College—and that was the end of my grandfather's college career (though Princeton now proudly claims him as a member of the class of 1932).

Having failed out of college, but leery of working for his father, Sandy found mining and construction work in the mountains of

Virginia, where he gained real-world experience in demolitions, carpentry, surveying, mechanics, and engineering. Eventually, if a little reluctantly, he accepted a job with Blue Diamond, and his father put him in charge of one of its principal mines in Virginia.[17] But it wouldn't last long.

Though grooming his son to take over the company some day, Alex had, for the present, no intention of relinquishing the slightest control. And despite the prospect of rich rewards for continued obedience, Sandy Bonnyman simply wasn't cut out for the role of dutiful son. By 1932, he'd had enough. He handed his silver spoon back to his father and headed west to seek his own fortune.

"He was a restless spirit," his father would later admit ruefully. "He always had to have adventure."[18]

FIVE
RENDER UP THE BODIES
2500 BC-AD 1992

Although most people who heard about my upcoming travel to Tarawa were intrigued, many were puzzled that the US government would spend tens of millions of dollars to retrieve the earthly remains of men who had lain undisturbed, and mostly forgotten, for so many decades. Some found the whole enterprise distasteful.

"May they rest in peace and not be disturbed as a result of political posturing by stupid members of the Congress of the United States of America," said the late Col. Ed Bale, who as a first lieutenant on Tarawa commanded the medium Sherman tank *China Gal*. "I just think after all the years let 'em lie where they are buried. I think if I were among them, that is where I'd want to be."[1]

Bale had good reason to be skeptical. He had personally buried two marines after the battle, and while serving as a marine recruiter during the Korean War was assigned to inform families in person when a family member had been killed.

"So many of them felt they should not be shipped back to the US. It would open wounds that were just beginning to heal," he said. "I can specifically recall two men who were shipped back and whose families regretted it later."[2]

Ed's views were also informed by a chance meeting in 1948 with the caretaker of a British military cemetery at Souda Bay on the Greek island of Crete, where sailors from a cruiser and two destroyers sunk during the recent war were buried.

"He said, 'You know, we British never ship our dead home. The first thing is, we don't have all this land like you Americans do. The policy has always been, we bury them where they fall,'" Ed recalled. "I like that. I think remains should be left to rest in peace."[3]

Katherine Davis Moore, widow of Navy Lt. Cmdr. Kyle Moore —my grandfather's teenage tennis partner—who went down with the USS *Indianapolis* in 1945, wanted her husband's remains to be left sleeping in the deeps.

"When the people who discovered the *Titanic* went off to the Pacific to find the *Indianapolis*, oh, my heart was so torn," she said at age ninety-five. "The *Indianapolis* is down in the deepest part of the Pacific, at fourteen thousand feet, where I hope nobody ever finds it."[4]

(On August 19, 2017, a team sponsored by late Microsoft co-founder Paul Allen located, mapped, and filmed the *Indianapolis* lying 18,000 feet deep; Katherine Moore died November 14, 2015, at the age of one hundred.)

"Leave the guy alone," Robert Kossow, ninety-three, said of his cousin, Pvt. William Edward Rambo, a marine reported to be buried in the same trench as Sandy Bonnyman. "Let him rest!"[5]

And as the search for Tarawa's missing began to ramp up in 2010, even my mother was ambivalent about the prospect of finding her father's remains.

"I know my grandparents would have adored having him returned," Fran Evans said. "But sixty-five [*sic*] years is a long time. I have no illusions about how wonderful it would be to find him. But since people are going to all the trouble, it would be nice, I suppose, to be able to find some of his remains."[6]

But such doubters are in the minority. Most family members I contacted on behalf of History Flight were thrilled about the possible recovery of long-lost relatives—occasionally brothers, but because most of Tarawa's dead were too young to have families, mostly more remote relatives, second cousins or great-nieces. Many embraced the solemn duty of closing a painful chapter, not for themselves, but for people long dead.

"It was always my grandmother's and my mother's wish that he be brought back home, probably to be interred next to his parents in Chatham, New York," said David Silliman, whose uncle, Pfc. George Harry Traver, was killed on the first day of fighting at Tarawa and recorded as interred in Cemetery 27.[7]

There was never any doubt how Sandy's parents felt. The Catholic belief in the physical resurrection of the body has long inspired pilgrims to travel thousands of miles to venerate a splinter of bone believed to be the earthly remains of a saint. Until 1963 Catholics were even banned from choosing cremation, which the church deemed blasphemy against the doctrine of physical resurrection. Alex and Frances Bonnyman wanted nothing more than to bring their son's body home for burial.

"I do want my son's remains returned to Knoxville, Tennessee. . . . If any further or additional request or advice is needed to insure (*sic*) his remains being returned to me here, I shall appreciate your writing to me," Alex wrote to newly minted Marine Commandant Lt. Gen. A.A. Vandegrift just days after receiving news of Sandy's death.[8]

Many governments in the Western world now routinely invest tens of millions or even billions of dollars on bringing lifeless bones home for burial. As of 2020, the US Defense POW/MIA Accounting Agency (DPAA) had a $145 million annual budget to locate and repatriate any and all missing war dead (technically classified as MIA, missing in action, though most were confirmed dead).

Germany's War Graves Commission now spends some $45 million a year on recovery efforts and has repatriated 30,000 sets of remains from two world wars, driven by public demand. Even Great Britain now offers families the choice of repatriation instead of letting soldiers lie where they fell.

Reverence for the dead, especially those slain in battle, is a universal trait of human cultures, expressed in the world's oldest and most enduring literature, from the ancient *Epic of Gilgamesh* to the writings of Thucydides and Homer. Yet for purely practical reasons, the world's great empires, from Greece to Britain, found it too expensive and unwieldy to repatriate every imperial soldier killed on a faraway battlefield, choosing instead to bury or cremate them far from home.

For most contemporary Americans, the idea that the federal government has an obligation to account for and return all overseas dead seems unremarkable.[9] But in post-Enlightenment Europe and North America, the kind of attachment to physical remains that would drive a grieving king between clashing swords to retrieve his lifeless son—as in Homer's *Iliad*—was seen by many as a distasteful, even ghoulish obsession.

Writing in the April 15, 1921, *New York Times*, Owen Wister, author of *The Virginian*, pondered the gruesome realities of exhumation after World War I: "Out of these holes were being dragged— what? Boys whom their mothers would recognize? No! Things without shape, at which mothers would collapse."[10]

Americans were long content to leave their war dead buried far from home, and many churches vocally opposed exhumation of battlefield remains, deriding it as a "costly pagan venture" and "a basic misconception of our rapidly changing bodies, which on earth have been but the vehicle or vestment of immortal spirits."[11]

But something began to shift in the wake of the mechanized mass slaughter of World War I. British Maj. Gen. Fabian Ware, appalled by hasty burials and the neglect of British graves overseas, established the Imperial War Graves Commission in 1915. Soon, investigators were venturing boldly beyond the trenches and into the blasted, haunted moonscapes of no-man's land to painstakingly record the identities and burial locations of British war dead, thus saving them from becoming "known only to God," a phrase coined by Rudyard Kipling, whose own son John's remains were never found.[12]

After the war, the United States mounted its own campaign to locate dead and missing soldiers from cemeteries and hastily dug graves across Europe. Nearly a thousand investigators eventually identified an astonishing 98.8 percent of the 116,000 Americans who died in the war. Once identified, the dead were reinterred in fifteen cemeteries in France to await the War Department's decision on their final disposition.[13]

But where upper-crusters like Wister and former President Teddy Roosevelt—who publicly declared his wish that his own son Quentin "continue to lie on the spot where he fell in battle"—a wave of plainspoken, grieving mothers begged to differ, making their case in letters to military officials, politicians, and newspapers.

"You took my son from me and sent him to war. . . . My son sacrificed his life to America's call," one Gold Star mother wrote to Secretary of State Robert Lansing, "and now you must as a duty of yours bring my son back to me."[14]

Undertakers, unsurprisingly, soon organized the Purple Cross to lobby for—and cash in on—the return of the dead.[15] Finally, on October 29, 1919, the War Department announced that it would pay to bring the dead home for burial upon request. In the end, the families of forty-six thousand World War I dead opted for repatriation.

Having abandoned its historic reluctance, the United States would eventually become the worldwide leader of a post-post-Enlightenment attachment to, even veneration of, the remains of war dead and extravagant, expensive efforts to bring them all home.

With a tally of some 407,000 deaths, American losses in World War II were greater than those of any other conflict in American history except for the Civil War. But compared to much of the rest of the world, they were slight. Just 0.32 percent of the nation's population died in the war, compared to an astonishing fourteen percent in the Soviet Union, eight percent of Germans, four percent of Japanese, three percent of the Chinese, and nearly one percent of the British (not counting colonial fighters).

By the 1940s, the US military had developed more efficient strategies to keep track of its dead. Even while the fighting raged, the Army Graves Registration Service swept in behind the troops, doing its best to locate, identify, and temporarily inter the dead with the intention of exhuming and repatriating them after the war.

Even so, due to the truly global nature of the conflict and high numbers of air and naval casualties, perhaps seventy-eight thousand personnel—nearly twenty percent of all Americans killed in action—remain technically missing in action more than seven decades later, and another ten thousand are still identified only as "unknown." Around half of the missing are believed to rest in Davey Jones' locker, leaving some forty thousand that are potentially recoverable.

Within weeks of the atomic bombing of Hiroshima and Nagasaki in August 1945, hundreds of teams were roaming quiescent battlefields across Europe, Asia, Africa, and countless islands dotting the Pacific Ocean. Eventually, they would recover and identify seventy-five percent of those killed in the fighting.

The World War I policy allowing American families to choose whether they wanted remains interred in overseas cemeteries or returned home for burial in a national or private cemetery remained in place. Yet only about a quarter of families elected to have a son, brother, or father's body exhumed and brought home for burial, less than half the rate from the 1914–18 war.[16] The establishment of resting places that were virtual works of art, such as the 170-acre Normandy American Cemetery and Memorial, with its green grass and nearly ten thousand gleaming white crosses and stars, and the equally well-tended Manila American Cemetery and Memorial, home to some seventeen thousand dead, surely persuaded many families that their loved ones were truly resting in peace. There also had been a smattering of coverage, mostly in the disapproving foreign press, recounting the grisly realities of forcing young soldiers, many of whom had seen comrades die during the war, to engage in what amounted to an officially approved form of grave robbery.

"Everywhere we searched we found bodies, floating in the rivers, trampled on the roads, bloated in the ditches, rotting in the bunkers, pretzeled into foxholes, burned in the tanks, buried in the snow, sprawled in the doorways, splattered in the gutters, dismembered in the mine fields, and even literally blown up into the trees," the writer Paul Fussell quoted one World War II graves-detail grunt as saying.[17]

Faced with such challenges, in the autumn of 1947 the Army Quartermaster General established the Central Identification Laboratory at Schofield Barracks on Oahu, Hawaii, or CILHI, for short.

"Our government has undertaken to return the recoverable remains (approximately 300,000) to American soil, should such be the desire of the next of kin," wrote Mildred Trotter, a Washington University (St. Louis) School of Medicine anatomy professor who took a leave of absence to work at CILHI from 1948–49, where her duties included sorting out the remains of sailors recovered from the USS *Arizona*. "If the next of kin wishes interment overseas, the remains are interred in American-owned cemeteries in Holland,

England, France, Italy, Luxembourg, Tunis, the Philippine Islands, Hawaiian Islands, Alaska or Puerto Rico. When a remains [*sic*] is exhumed and positively identified the next of kin is notified and given a choice of disposition; either burial in a private cemetery or in a National Cemetery."[18]

But by the end of the 1940s, the government's efforts to recover the dead were rapidly petering out. By the mid-1950s, there was just one Graves Registration team assigned to the entire Pacific region.[19]

Perhaps not surprisingly, America's most divisive war since Appomattox supercharged the nation's appetite for recovering war dead. Vietnam created a political and cultural shift that would result in the expenditure of billions of dollars to reclaim the missing.

Having won concessions from North Vietnam at the Paris peace talks in 1973 that would allow the United States to search for remains of missing soldiers, the Army set up a branch of the CIL in Thailand. But the program went off the rails after several team members were killed in an ambush in North Vietnam, and appeared doomed until an American military transport plane carrying Vietnamese "war orphans" to the US for adoption (Operation Babylift) went down in South Vietnam in 1975, killing 78 of the 243 children aboard. Media played up the fact that remains were taken for processing to the lab on the Thai coast, igniting public support. A year later, the CIL's mission and budget were expanded to recover remains from all previous wars, not just Vietnam.

Just as important, perhaps, was the arrival of Johnie Webb to supervise the laboratory immediately following the Operation Babylift disaster. The former Army colonel led the nation's first effort to find World War II remains in New Guinea in 1978 and began to add expert historians, archaeologists, forensic anthropologists, and odontologists—specialists in identifying dental remains—to the staff.

Politics also played a crucial role. Following the end of the war in Vietnam, many Americans, from hawkish veterans groups to

President Richard Nixon, accused the victorious North Vietnamese Communists of holding thousands of American captives.

Despite repeated Congressional investigations that found no basis for the claims—"No Americans are still held alive as prisoners in Indochina," a House committee concluded in 1976—the rumors continued to gain steam, creating a thriving industry of hucksters pitching tales of live sightings, phony dog tags, and doctored photos purporting to prove that Americans were still being held prisoner. To date, the silver screen is the only place living American POWs have ever been found, in films such as the hugely popular *Rambo: First Blood Part 2, Uncommon Valor,* and *Missing in Action.*[20]

These movies portrayed the effort to recover "forgotten" POWs as a middle finger to an ungrateful public that turned against not just the war, but also the soldiers themselves. In *Uncommon Valor,* Col. Cal Rhodes, played by Gene Hackman, tells his men, "You are thought of as criminals because of Vietnam. You know why? Because you lost. . . . That's why they won't go over and pick up your buddies." John Rambo asks before going in to take care of the problem all by himself, "Do we get to win this time?"

While the movies catered to the idea that living Americans were still being held captive, the now-familiar black flag featuring the silhouette of a blindfolded prisoner in front of a guard tower over the words "You are not forgotten" was emblazoned not just with the letters POW, but also MIA—missing in action. The term applies to all unrecovered remains, even in cases where the subject is known to be deceased. On the heels of Ronald Reagan's highly successful effort to revitalize public support for the military following Vietnam, Congress gave its official imprimatur to the POW/MIA flag, still the only banner to be so recognized besides the Stars and Stripes.

In 1992, Congress created the Joint Task Force-Full Accounting (JTF-FA), specifically to focus on Vietnam. A year later it authorized the creation of the Defense POW/MIA Office (DPMO), to provide "centralized management of prisoner of war/missing in action (POW/MIA) affairs within the Department of Defense."[21] The CIL and JTA-FA were merged in 2003 as the Joint POW/Accounting Command (JPAC).

There was never any mistaking that Vietnam catalyzed all this renewed attention. Despite the fact that MIAs from World War II and Korea outnumber those from Vietnam by twenty to one (not even including those believed lost at sea), most of the attention was focused on the latter conflict. Though tasked with accounting for the missing from all of America's wars, as of 2013, JPAC had identified 0.6 percent of the thirty-five thousand remains deemed "recoverable" from World War II and 2.9 percent of those from Korea, compared to 16 percent of MIAs from Vietnam.

It shouldn't have surprised anyone that a sibling rivalry developed between DPMO and JPAC. The two organizations constantly schemed and skirmished over turf, influence, reputation, and funding, resulting in inefficiency, redundancy, and a failure to meet goals set by Congress for the recovery of tens of thousands of remains.[22] It would take more than a decade for the Department of Defense to separate the squabblers, or rather, bring them together.

But while they squabbled, private, non-governmental organizations such as the BentProp Project, Pacific Wrecks, MIA Hunters, and History Flight were quietly stepping into the breach, setting the stage for a sea change in how America searches for its missing war dead.

SIX
FIRST LANDING
AUGUST 2010

I was thrilled when the day for my departure for Tarawa finally arrived. But soon enough, my excitement would turn to bafflement as I found myself caught in the crossfire of dysfunction that characterized JPAC.

As my plane rose from the runway at Denver International Airport on August 8, I pondered my grandfather's much more convoluted journey to Tarawa: trains from Albuquerque to Phoenix to San Diego; sailing to New Zealand; first combat on Guadalcanal; steaming toward Tarawa; a gut-jarring ride on a crowded Higgins boat across lagoon and reef; and finally, sloshing through chest-deep water into a hellscape of smoke and flying ammunition. As my stomach churned with excitement and anticipation, I imagined those same emotions were among the many he felt during those last, tense hours before landing. He was, after all, a US Marine, and this was exactly what he'd been seeking when he left his comfortable life behind to fight the enemy.

More than twenty-four nearly sleepless hours later, I was pressing my face to the window of a creaky Air Pacific 737, peering down at the pale emerald waters of the lagoon enclosed by the narrow necklace of Tarawa Atoll, which was surrounded by the dark cobalt expanse of the open Pacific Ocean.

Clusters of children and teenagers waved from the edge of the long, unfenced runway as we taxied to the terminal. Bonriki International Airport wasn't officially "international," lacking, among other attributes, anything resembling perimeter security. Whenever planes were not landing or taking off—which was almost always; the only traffic was twice-weekly Air Pacific flights from Fiji and arrivals and departures by Kiribati Airways' island-hopping commuter flights every couple of days—kids played soccer, mobs of teenagers flirted, families picnicked, and dogs trotted across the convenient concrete expanse of runway.

During a seven-hour layover in Fiji, I had met two CNN journalists and an independent videographer who were headed to Tarawa to document the renewed search for the missing marines. CNN's Ted Rowlands, tall and sandy-haired, with the mandatory chiseled good looks of a TV reporter, was skeptical and drily witty; his cameraman John Torigoe had the build of an outdoor athlete and frequently flashed a broad, white smile. Marc Miller, a videographer working for Los Angeles-based Rogin Entertainment, was dressed all in khaki, as if headed out on safari. Not eager to spend seven hours in the tiny, stuffy confines of Nadi International Airport before our flight to Tarawa, I persuaded Ted and John to join me in hiring a taxi to find a beach. At First Landing, a half hour from the airport, we watched the sun rise, swam, and ate a leisurely breakfast while bathing in a soft, warm, flower-scented tropical breeze.

Stepping off the plane on Tarawa some ten hours later was an entirely different kind of tropical experience. The brassy equatorial sun sizzled the top of my skull as we walked the short distance to the terminal, where a throng of smiling Kiribati people (they call themselves i-Kiribati, pronounced ee-KIDH-uh-boss) pressed against a chain-link fence, waving and shouting. Inside, slow-swooping fans did little more than stir the rank odor of sweating bodies; everyone stinks on Tarawa, including you, but you quickly get used to it.

I shouldered my backpack as Ted, John, and Marc collected huge piles of equipment, then breezed through immigrations. Outside, children shouted, "i-Matang," or "foreigner," as I passed. The air, humid and soft, almost doughy, carried the scent of the sea, laced with dust, smoke, and the occasional whiff of a pigpen. Despite the heat, my skin prickled as I thought, *I am the second Bonnyman ever to set foot on this place.*

After Ted, John, and Marc had piled their equipment on the sidewalk, a beefy, bald i-Kiribati wearing a golf shirt, shorts, and a floppy yellow terry-cloth hat seemed to appear out of nowhere. Kautebiri Kobuti, History Flight's local fixer, had the look of a retired Samoan football player. He introduced himself in choppy, but understandable, English, and directed the others toward a rental car and flatbed truck. I stepped up and introduced myself.

"Bunnymin?" he said, tugging a small notebook from his shirt pocket. "No . . . Mark say you coming next week—seventeenth."

Mark Noah, through Kautebiri, had kindly made a reservation for me at the "King's Hotel" on Betio after Steven Barber had withdrawn his invitation to find a place for me at the convent.

"No," I said. "I'm here."

As Kautebiri whipped out a cell phone and strode away from me, I pondered my options. I could try the convent myself; though a lapsed Catholic, I'd slept on many floors, cots, and beds at monasteries and abbeys around the world. Nighttime temperatures virtually never dropped below eighty degrees and my friend Kelle, who had served in the Peace Corps in Kiribati, had said crime wasn't a concern, so if worse came to worst, I could probably shack up on a beach somewhere. But soon, Kautebiri returned and waved me toward the waiting convoy.

"Iss OK, iss OK," he said. "You come with us."

It was the first display of the man's wizardly problem-solving abilities. *Guess that's why they call them fixers,* I thought as I climbed into the back of Marc's rented blue Toyota for the slow, bumpy ride to Betio. It was just ten miles, but it would take nearly an hour.

Seeking to escape the mildew-scented, tepid air blowing from the car's air-conditioning vents, I rolled down the back window and thrust my face into a tropical breeze, mesmerized by the shallow, pellucid water stretching across a shallow reef toward foamy breakers. There were hints of the atoll's less presentable side—scabby, skinny dogs trotting down the road, heaps of garbage baking in the sun, tires and other flotsam dotting the reef—but the downtown area of Bairiki, home to government offices and the president's residence, was as colorful and charming as any Mexican seaside village I'd ever seen. It wasn't until we were almost across the two-mile long Nippon Causeway between the islets of Bairiki and Betio—built by Japan in the 1980s; prior to that, most people walked across at low tide—that the smell of raw sewage and sunbaked rot punched a hole in my reverie.

"Phew! Roll up your window!" Marc barked from the front.

That smell was my introduction to Betio.

Marc paid the forty-cent toll (Kiribati uses Australian currency) and we continued along the eastern tail of the island—whose contours somewhat resemble a deceased bird, lying on its back. We passed a park studded with Norfolk Island pine trees, where I saw my first, exhilarating reminders of the battle that took my grandfather's life: the skeletal remains of two massive eight-inch British guns. Numerous concrete bunkers, pitted, stained, cracked, and choked with weedy growth, wallowed in yellow sand, slowly being reclaimed by the sea.

The "King's Hotel" was named after its owner, a local Taiwanese immigrant named King Kum Kee, but the sign out front read "Betio Apartments." Within a few years King would expand it into three-story blocks of rooms, rename it Betio Lodge, and open a second multi-story hotel down the street, Betio Lodge II. But for now, it was just a crushed coral courtyard shaded by coconut and breadfruit trees, with two long, wooden buildings containing five rooms each, and a broad, thatch-roofed patio with a microwave oven, television, and DVD player. My room was spacious and comfortable, featuring red-tile floors, an air-conditioning unit, a king-size bed, and a small kitchen. Despite a faint sulfurous odor and a trickle of deep-blue fluid bleeding from the base of the toilet, the bathroom and showers seemed more than adequate. Hell, I'd stayed in worse places in Wyoming.

Before he left, I reminded Kautebiri that I hoped to rent a bicycle.

"Bush bicycle?" he said (or maybe it was "push" bicycle; I was never quite sure). "Shuh, shuh, I bring you tomorrow."

As the sun sank in the west, Marc Miller chauffeured the four of us back across the causeway to eat at Mary's Hotel at the western tip of Bairiki, where the team from the Joint POW/MIA Accounting Command was staying. It was, we'd been told, a decent place for dinner, and I was anxious to touch base with Maj. Ramon Osorio, the public affairs officer for the mission, whom I'd spoken to before leaving.

The menu at Mary's featured simple entrees of white rice and chicken, fish, or vegetables in Asian-style sauces. Warned against eating local fish due to the presence of ciguatoxins in the water, which can cause vomiting, diarrhea, numbness of extremities, mouth and lips, chills and fever and muscle and joint aches—sometimes for months, with no antidote available—I went with vegetables.

As we waited for our food, clean-cut members of the JPAC team began to filter out from a two-story stack of cinder-block rooms. The young men nodded respectfully in our direction before dragging out black trunks that were packed with genuine American fare—Ruffles, Chips Ahoy, Milk Duds, Power Bars, Gatorade, Cheetos, and just about any other irresistible sugar, salt, or fat hit you might want. They spun up a DVD and started watching a Jean Claude Van Damme movie on the white wall.

After dinner we knocked on the door to Osorio's room. Tall, slightly stooped, and paunchy, he answered with a towel wrapped around his neck and flecks of shaving cream clinging to pink cheeks. A round of hand shaking ensued.

"Now, who you're with again?" he said, nodding at Marc Miller.

Marc produced a letter from Osorio's superior in Hawaii to his employer, Rogin Entertainment. But the major said he hadn't been apprised of Marc's visit.

"And you two are attached?" he said, wagging his chin at Marc and me.

Surprised that he'd forgotten, I reminded Osorio of our most recent phone conversation and reiterated that I was traveling, on my own, to represent my family and research a book about my grandfather.

"Well," the major said, "it's my understanding you two are attached."

For whatever reason, Osorio was playing dumb: Just four days earlier his boss, Lt. Col. Wayne Perry, had emailed him to confirm that, "A Camera crew working with Mark Noah will be heading over on Sunday, as will Clay Evans, freelance author and family relative of Medal of Honor winner Marine Lieutenant Bonnyman. A CNN news crew from Los Angeles will arrive on Tuesday to capture a few days of activity for news reports."[1]

"I just remember him looking like he had seen a ghost," Marc recalled later. "Then he kind of backpedaled a little and told us to show up the next morning for a briefing."[2]

My wristwatch buzzed me awake at five o'clock the next morning. After melting the small plastic coffee pot I'd brought with me—

outlets on Betio run 240 volts, twice as hot as standard American juice—I pulled on a tank top, shorts, and a pair of running shoes in near throwaway condition, and headed east on the road toward dawn.

It was still dark, but the air was warm and humid. Unseen birds chittered in the trees and Tarawa's ubiquitous "island cat" mini-buses were already clattering along the bumpy, potholed road as I loped past the tollbooth and out onto the causeway. Once free of Betio, a breeze blew clean ocean air past my face, and by the time the red sun melted over the horizon I was crossing the lone small culvert through which water flowed between the lagoon and open sea. I was slippery with sweat and giddy with endorphins by the time I reached Mary's Hotel on Bairiki.

Returning was less idyllic. As I approached Betio the breeze delivered the scent of burning plastic, sewer gas, and Betio's dead and rotting reef to my nostrils. Trash-strewn weeds filled the spaces between squat cinder-block structures and makeshift shanties, and I gave a wide berth to an eager cluster of skinny dogs jockeying for access to a pitiful bitch in heat. Schoolchildren in colorful uniforms and women offered shy smiles as I passed, though the men's faces were uniformly stony.

I didn't realize it, but in less than an hour, I had experienced a microcosm of Betio, an island of indescribable beauty, shocking squalor, and warm welcome.

It was oppressively hot even in the shade at Mary's when we sat down to watch a brief informational video about JPAC the next morning. The field team had already rolled out for the day, located in a small, scruffy cemetery just up the road from our lodgings. Osorio ticked off our rules of engagement for the dig site: Stay away from the edges of holes, lest they collapse and compromise the soil profile; cameras and recorders must be turned off on request, no questions asked; and most emphatically, we were not to speculate openly about any particular MIA, including my grandfather.

"This process takes a long time," Osorio explained. "We don't want to cause any confusion for families back home."

He paired the CNN team up with Lee Tucker, a civilian JPAC public-affairs officer, and sent them off to the site. Then he turned to Marc Miller and me to explain that we were free to follow, but would be restricted to a "designated area" beyond the perimeter. He also said that we would not be allowed to join the CNN crew that afternoon at a "turnover ceremony," during which JPAC would take custody of two sets of remains found by locals. Between the CNN team, a videographer for the Armed Forces Network, and filmmaker Steven Barber—with whom, Osorio explained, JPAC had an exclusive contract[3]—there would simply be too many people to manage.

"For today, that's the way it's got to be," he said, but promised to "get you guys offline so you can understand where your opportunities are going to be."[4]

Puzzled, I asked the major what was going on, since he and his boss had told me just days earlier that I would have full access to the sites.

"I am a straight shooter, Mr. Evans, I'll always look you in the eye and tell you the truth," he said. "I don't have any reason to think you are anything other than a fine, upstanding American. But it's my understanding that you are attached to Mr. Miller."[5]

In so many words, he was accusing me of lying. But he *knew* I was coming and knew Marc was filming for History Flight (which even I didn't even know until Marc told me), so even if we had been "attached," why would that have been a problem? It suddenly struck me how odd it was that Mark Noah himself wasn't there, given that JPAC was excavating sites based on his organization's expensive, painstaking research.

"I don't get it," I said. "Does this have to something to do with Mark Noah?"

"Mr. Evans," Osorio replied with mild exasperation, "I assure you this has nothing to do with someone else's food fight."

Marc took the snub with more aplomb than I did, counseling patience. As we drove back across the causeway I stared out across the jewel-hued lagoon, wondering if I'd come halfway around the world for nothing.

If you were to dig at random anywhere on Betio, chances are about ten-to-one that any bones you found would be of Japanese rather than American origins. Almost the entire Japanese garrison of more than 4,800 had been buried permanently on the island, compared to the four or five hundred American personnel that had been left behind.

The Japanese have never mounted an organized effort to locate and repatriate their fallen from Tarawa. The Kiribati government has turned over remains to Japan over the years, along with maps and other information about burial locations. On Tarawa, as elsewhere, when Japanese remains are unearthed from foreign battlefields, they are cremated and deposited in Tokyo's Yasukuni Jinja Shrine, created after World War II to honor the spirits of those who died fighting for the emperor between 1868 and 1945.

Where Americans revere and lionize the likes of Audie Murphy, John Basilone, and Sandy Bonnyman for individual acts of courage and heroism, the Japanese focus more on the virtues of the collective. Tarawa does not loom large in Japanese history books, but when the battle is noted, the entire Betio garrison is praised for its collective heroism, honor, and selfless devotion to the emperor; occasionally, Admiral Keichi Shibasaki, commander of Japanese forces on Tarawa, is singled out for mention.[6]

Despite the fact that the US Army Graves Registration Service (AGRS) officially closed its books on Tarawa in 1950, a steady trickle of American remains have turned up in the intervening years. British foreign-service officer Ron Summer dug up eight sets of remains in the 1960s while installing underground electrical cable, but was informed by US embassy officials in Fiji that "we have graves for these men in the states already."[7] British construction crews discovered thirteen sets of remains, including dog tags, in 1963; all but one were buried as unknowns at the Punchbowl in Hawaii. Australian workers in the 1970s unearthed several American skeletons, including one found in a buried amphibious assault vehicle; three were later identified, and the rest were buried as unknowns in Hawaii.[8] Sewer-project supervisor Louis Eickenhout exposed two more sets of remains in 1979; Japan reclaimed one and he reburied the other at the site of the New Zealand Coastwatchers Memorial on Betio after being told by American officials that, "the US has accounted for its war dead."[9]

Although at least ten other likely American skeletons were turned over to JPAC between 1999 and 2007, only one had been positively identified by 2010. In 2002, local workers installing a light pole on the north side of Betio came upon a virtually intact skeleton. A Peace Corps volunteer collected the remains, which were later taken back to JPAC's Central Identification Laboratory on Oahu. But it would be another nine years before the agency identified the remains as those of Pvt. Herman Sturmer.

Mark Noah had always been intrigued by that 2002 discovery, because it had been recovered from general area of the island where Cemetery 27 had been located. After History Flight board member Paul Dostie posted an inquiry on a Facebook page for former Kiribati Peace Corps members, someone sent him a photo not just of the 2002 Peace Corps volunteer, but also the local workers who had dug up Sturmer's remains. Mark gave the photo to Kautebiri, who tracked down the locals, who led him to the exact spot where they'd dug up the skeleton, in a shipping yard some one hundred feet from the boat basin. Comparing a Google map of the location with a post-battle aerial photo, Mark realized that the remains had been found in the vicinity of a long-gone monument listing the forty dead buried in Cemetery 27.

Mark immediately flagged the area as the most promising location of the long-lost burial trench where my grandfather had lain buried for more than sixty-six years.

Lt. Col. Perry in the JPAC public affairs office had told me the team would be digging on the north side of Betio, where my grandfather was buried, during my visit. But archaeologist Gregory Fox had instead set up the first dig in the dowdy little cemetery on Betio's south side, in the shadow of a shiny steel memorial honoring twenty-two British and New Zealand coastwatchers beheaded by the Japanese on April 15, 1942 (reportedly in reprisal for strikes by an American warship and planes[10]). That's where Australian worker Eickenhout had told Mark Noah he'd reburied the American remains he found in 1979, even providing a photo of himself standing on the exact spot.

By the time Marc Miller and I arrived that morning, the team was busy shoveling out a neat, five-foot-deep trench in the wet, heavy coral sand. Crewmembers took turns shoveling and sifting the sand through makeshift screens. Anything anomalous was tossed into a galvanized steel bucket to be examined by Dr. Fox, the scientist in charge of the Joint POW/MIA Accounting Command's first full-scale mission to Tarawa.

The archaeologist looked more like an aging Deadhead or North Shore beach bum than a member of a military recovery team. He wore grimy cargo pants, sodden, threadbare t-shirts, and a sweaty do-rag to restrain his profusion of thick, red-gray hair. He had the ruddy complexion of a man who has worked outside for much of his life.

Fox served in Vietnam as a member of the US Air Force from 1971–75. He earned a master's degree in anthropology in 1982 from the University of Nebraska-Lincoln and a PhD in anthropology from the University of Missouri-Columbia ten years later. He spent the first part of his career working as a cultural-resource management specialist for the National Park Service's Western Archeological Center in Tucson, Arizona.

He began working as a contractor with the Department of Defense on Southeast Asian recovery missions in 1995 and in 2000 formally joined JPAC's Central Identification Laboratory in Hawaii. In his thirty-seven-year career he had led recovery teams around the world, from the deserts and Great Plains of North America to Germany, Belgium, and remote battlefields in Vietnam, Cambodia, Laos, North Korea, Kwajalein, and Alaska.

Of all the places he'd worked, Fox found Tarawa to be one of the most challenging. With some twenty thousand residents crammed onto less than four hundred acres of coral sand, the island of Betio is one of the most densely populated areas of the world. There are numerous dwelling places and businesses, and a loop of paved, rutted road, but much of the island is covered with low shanties assembled by island residents from bits of flotsam gleaned from the beach or ubiquitous trash piles, covered by thatches of grass and dried breadfruit leaves.

"We haven't worked in this kind of confused, busy landscape out here. And we don't even know how deep (any remains) may be," Fox said while working at the team's second dig site on the island.[11]

And, he noted, every one of the possible locations of Cemetery 27—where my grandfather and thirty-nine other men were believed to be buried—near the port on Betio's north side posed even greater challenges.

"One is in a yard that is extremely packed down," Fox said. "One has a concrete slab on top. One of them is on the road into the pier. And one is at an intersection of roads in a back neighborhood."[12]

From the moment I met him, JPAC's team leader seemed doubtful that this much-publicized mission would locate anything other than what he called "dry holes."

The activity at the first dig site drew a huge crowd of mischievous kids dressed in cast-off Western t-shirts, shorts, and flip-flops, though some sported only a shirt, or nothing at all. Boys dangled like mischievous monkeys from the branches of a spreading breadfruit tree, a maneuver that allowed them to violate the carefully patrolled perimeter while dangling well above the annoyed Americans. Some wriggled in beneath orange hurricane fencing to snatch empty plastic water bottles, shouting in triumph and receiving high fives whenever they successfully completed a mission. High palms swayed in the sultry morning breeze while a boom box thumped alternately with hard rock, country, and Christian contemporary music.

Although Osorio had assured me that I would be "postured in order to get some decent material," there was little to see from outside the barrier and nothing to hear but murmurs as Ted Rowlands interviewed Fox on camera. But Lee Tucker, the other public affairs officer, took pity, motioning for Marc and me to step inside the perimeter. We could stay, he whispered, so long as we remained well back from the hole and didn't talk to the team.

Fox spent much of his time perusing detailed maps tacked up between two slender palm trees, cigarette in hand. Any time a shovel struck an anomaly in the hole, everything stopped until the archaeologist could climb down and have a look. Fox would carefully brush away sand until he could determine if the target was "osseous material" or an artifact of interest. Mostly, the items weren't significant—pig bones, nails, lumps of encrusted black metal—though the team did accidentally exhume the remains of a local woman who had been buried in a long-decayed wooden coffin.

As much as he tried, Fox could not conceal his irritation at being in the media spotlight and, especially, his disdain for any outsider who got up in JPAC's business.

"We encourage people to provide us information. In fact, we have an area on the website [for that]. We just hope that is as far as they go. Looking around is no big problem, but any excavation has the potential to compromise evidence," he said.[13]

He seemed particularly prickly on the subject of History Flight.

"The work of Mark Noah is a starting point," he snapped. "That's all."[14]

JPAC's third leader on the ground on Tarawa was Marine Capt. Ernest "Todd" Nordman, who commanded a team of nine men who did the hard labor: US Navy Medic Jeff Cavallo; Army staff sergeants Jordy Anthony and Tyler Green; and six marines, Staff Sgt. Adaeus Brooks, Sgt. Andrew Pateras, Staff Sgt. Kurtis Witt, Cpl. Joe Mejia, Cpl. Svyatoslav Nemenko, and Lance Cpl. Matthew Nesting.

Short, fit, and businesslike, Nordman, twenty-eight, proudly hailed from Cape Girardeau, Missouri, hometown of conservative talk-radio superstar Rush Limbaugh, and had worked as a counselor at a Young Life Christian camp in Colorado. He served one tour in Iraq before coming to JPAC in 2009.

Nordman expressed admiration for the men who took Tarawa, as well as doubt that his fellow marines would have the discipline and toughness to win that kind of brutal, bloody fight today. Today's corps, he said, is "coddled," thanks to political correctness. The team under his command here, he said, were mostly "voluntolds" who had been sent to JPAC as "diggers" after underperforming in previous assignments.[15]

Nordman was clearly unenthusiastic about Betio, which he considered the armpit of all assignments. At least when searching for Vietnam-era remains, teams got periodic R-and-R in Bangkok, which still shimmered with decadence and the ghosts of legendary Vietnam-era escapades. Tarawa, a hot, stinking, crowded atoll overloaded with poor people, pigs, and stray dogs, offered little in the way of drunken revelry or close encounters with the exotic human offerings of Bangkok's notorious Patpong Road.[16] (Though Tarawa, like anywhere, isn't immune from prostitution, as I learned early one morning when a couple of drunken, giggling working girls mistakenly banged on Marc Miller's door.)

The only member of the team who approached me was Navy Petty Officer First Class Justin Whiteman, who was filming the mission for the Armed Forces Network. He introduced himself, shook my hand, and said he'd read about Sandy Bonnyman.

"I hope for your family's sake that your grandfather is found," he said.

In mid-afternoon, a small, blue sedan pulled up next to the dig site. A short, brush-haired guy with a shadow of fashionable stubble tumbled out the passenger door. Whipping out a flipcam, he stepped over the hurricane fencing and made a beeline toward the trench. A tall guy in shades emerged from the driver's side, stretched, and drifted over to the perimeter fence. He introduced himself as Matthew Hausle, a cameraman working for Steven Barber, the filmmaker hired by JPAC to document the mission, whom I had alienated when I refused to be "embedded" with him.

When Barber finally spotted me a half an hour later, he immediately launched into a litany of complaints about JPAC. He and Hausle had hitched a ride from Hawaii on military transports, but a pallet loaded with his gear had not been transferred from a C-17 on Kwajalein to the C-130 continuing on to Tarawa, and it was now back in a hangar in Honolulu. John and Ted from CNN took pity and let Barber borrow memory cards and other equipment, though they soon regretted the impulse, later complaining to JPAC that the videographer had treated them, "as disposable fools to be utilized as a free resource whenever he had problems."[17]

The crew knocked off early that afternoon so they could go back to Mary's and clean up for the turnover ceremony at 1600 hours. Tucker agreed to let me to tag along, so long as I didn't take any pictures or notes, but Marc Miller was still a no-go.

The ceremony was held in an air-conditioned government office building on Bairiki that looked like any other cubicle warren around the world. The crew, wearing clean khakis and shirts emblazoned with the JPAC logo, crammed into a small room alongside smiling Kiribati officials. One official stepped forward and peeled back a black sheet to reveal a box containing a crisscross of white and brown human bones recovered by local residents. Nordman spoke a few brief words, signed some papers, and it was over. Marc hadn't missed anything.

"Well," Ted said when we reached the parking lot, "at least now we can say we saw some bones."

It would turn out to be the high point of JPAC's two-month mission, and though I didn't know it at the time, they had History Flight to thank.

When we got back to the hotel I found a pink-and-white ladies' bicycle tilted against a coconut palm in courtyard.

"Sweet ride," Ted said.

"Hey," I replied, "wheels are wheels."

SEVEN
DISILLUSIONMENT AND DOUBT
AUGUST 2010

Dr. Fox declared the first dig site a "dry hole" on the third day of digging and ordered the excavation refilled. The rest of the team moved up the road to begin digging another site where History Flight researchers had detected sub-soil anomalies that might indicate the presence of human remains.

Halfway across the world, Mark Noah was going crazy. He could see from photos transmitted by Marc Miller that the team was digging outside the concrete border of the coastwatchers' monument, despite the fact that Louis Eickenhout had buried the remains he found in 1979 *inside* the border, immediately adjacent to the monument itself. Mark also believed that the second site was likely to turn up empty, due to a potential discrepancy in the respective GPS systems used by History Flight and JPAC. He frantically emailed JPAC headquarters in Hawaii to notify them of the problems, but either the message wasn't conveyed to Fox, or the archaeologist simply didn't care.

I didn't know any of that at the time, though I was becoming ever more curious about why Mark wasn't there to help. After all, he was the person most familiar with the History Flight data JPAC had relied upon to identify its six potential dig sites. When I asked about Mark's absence, Marc Miller said he'd heard he couldn't get off work. That seemed ludicrous to me, given the time and money he'd sunk into this venture already. Something was rotten on the island of Betio; I just didn't know what.

Later that day, as I yawned with boredom while watching the team dig the second hole in front of a low-slung blue house, a shiny new SUV rolled up behind me. Ray Osorio rolled down a window, his eyes concealed behind aviator sunglasses. He called me over.

"Mr. Evans, I'd like to remind you of the ground rules," he said. "There's to be no mention of any names in relation to these MIAs."

"Yeah, I haven't forgotten."

"Well, it's my understanding that you've been throwing your grandfather's name around," he said.

"What? I literally haven't even mentioned his name to anyone on your team except your cameraman, and *he* was the one who asked *me* about him," I said. "If that's 'throwing his name around,' you guys have some crazy high standards."

Osorio gave me that PR-guy smile of his.

"I'm just relating what I've been told by headquarters. So, if you would, just remember our ground rules moving forward," he said. Then, sliding his sunglasses down his nose, he ticked his chin to my right. "That's a pretty nice bike you've got there. Did you have that shipped down here from home?" Someone snickered in the back seat.

"Yeah, Ray," I said. "I had my pink ladies' bicycle flown eight thousand miles because I just can't bear to be away from it for a week."

In hindsight, I should have been grateful for Osorio's snark, since it led to an epiphany that saved my first trip to Tarawa: *Archaeology is not a spectator sport.* I hadn't come halfway around the world to be treated like an enemy spy, take juvenile insults, and watch people digging holes all day. These guys were just grunts doing a dirty, tough job in a place they hated; I was here by choice, on a deeply personal quest to find the grandfather I had admired my whole life. I didn't need JPAC and I owed them nothing. I wasn't on anybody's leash and I had a whole island to explore on my pink ladies' bicycle.

Demonstrating his seeming superpower for perfect timing yet again, Kautebiri Kobuti, History Flight's local agent, pulled up in his car to the second dig site moments after Osorio drove away. He wanted to know if Marc Miller and I would like to meet two local men who had unearthed what was believed to be an American skeleton earlier in the summer.

We certainly did. I climbed in Marc's car and we followed Kautebiri north on Betio's looping main road.

During my stay, I had noticed that the JPAC team seldom interacted with the local population. Other than going to work or venturing out, en masse, to a restaurant for dinner, the team sequestered itself inside a mini green zone where they ate American snacks and watched American movies.

History Flight took a different approach.

"Our most promising source of information is talking to locals," Mark Noah had told me. "We get all kinds of potential leads from the local population, which knows so much more about the location of skeletons. Sometimes they've known about a burial site for years, having dug up bones by accident and thrown them away."[1]

We pulled in behind Kautebiri on a dirt road leading into a cluster of small cinder-block houses, not far from the island's west-facing beaches. Marc and I followed him into a yard where a large sow grunted contentedly. A skinny young man dressed in saggy black slacks and a pit-stained button-up shirt emerged from the house, followed by a man with watery blue eyes, short-cropped silver hair, and a face deeply etched with wrinkles. They were Temoana

Tabokai, twenty-three, and his father, Tekinaa. The old man languidly smoked a reed-thin local cigarette as his son pointed toward a slight depression in the yard, speaking rapidly. That's where the men had been digging a hole for garbage when they found the bones. They'd been certain the remains were American.

"When people die in Kiribati, we put them in a coffin. We found no coffin here. And we knew this is a marine, because this bone," Temoana said, tapping his thigh, "Japanese shorter. I-Kiribati shorter. Americans much longer."[2]

The old man was the first person I'd met on the island with direct experience of the battle. He didn't know when he'd been born, but recalled that he was nine or ten when the Japanese came to Tarawa, so he was probably in his late seventies.

The Japanese takeover was frightening to the inhabitants, he said. They mostly left the people alone until August 1942, when they forced the women, children, and elderly to abandon Betio and walk across the reef to Bairiki. Able-bodied men, including Tekinaa's father, were pressed into unpaid labor clearing the jungle for the airfield, digging trenches, and hauling heavy supplies and tools for the construction of bunkers.

A few people made friends with the Japanese, Tekinaa said, but most feared them because they carried guns and entered houses uninvited to take whatever they fancied.[3]

"The Japanese were very cruel," Tekinaa said. "They whipped the men and said they not work hard enough. They threatened them but they did not kill them."[4]

When construction was complete, most of the men were sent across the reef to Bairiki to rejoin their families.

The islanders were both elated and terrified when American planes began bombing Betio in isolated raids starting in September 1943. When the final battle commenced on the morning of November 20, they watched in awe from Bairiki's western beaches. Tekinaa remembered the sun rising into a sky choked with thick gray smoke, the smell of burning rubber and metal, ear-shattering explosions, and the crump of shells as they smashed craters into the sand and reef. The sickly odor of burning flesh drifted all the way across two miles of water to where they stood.

The people were fearful of what might happen next, Tekinaa told me. But the Americans were different, promising to pay the men who helped them rebuild the battered airfield. Tekinaa remembers that his father returned from his first day of work and told his family the marines were not their enemies.

"The Japanese threatened us and we hated them. We feared them. But my father wanted to help the Americans because he knew they were our friends," the old man said, turning to me. "We were very grateful. We saw that marines gave their life to save the people of Kiribati. So I thank you for your grandfather."[5]

Over the next days, I conducted myself on a grand tour of Betio. I started with the broad, fringing reef on the lagoon side, hoping to gain some perspective on just how far the marines had been forced to walk into withering Japanese fire that first day.

When I reached the crumbling seawall west of the pier, the pale, mucky reef lay exposed at low tide, littered with tires, tangles of fabric, diapers, mangled appliances, and distant hulks of grounded vessels. Just offshore, children played around the turret and barrel of the medium Sherman tank *Cobra*, remarkably well preserved but still jammed into the shell-hole where it foundered during the battle.

As I prepared to walk out to the farthest edges of the reef, a young guy wearing a golf shirt, shorts, and Keen sandals approached, obviously an American.

"What brings you here?" he asked.

I gave my well-practiced thirty-second elevator speech.

"Wow. You're Bonnyman's grandson."

He introduced himself as Jeremy Shiok, a thirty-four-year-old writer from Alaska. Like me, he was trying to trace his grandfather's steps during the war. Two grandsons of Tarawa marines had come to walk the infamous reef at the same moment, wearing the same shoes and even sporting the same camera. We scrambled down the seawall and began sloshing through the hot, ankle-deep water.

The reef at low tide looked and smelled as dead as it was. The only visible life were humps of sickly brown seaweed, a few small, drab fish, sea cucumbers coated with muck, and a handful of starved-looking white birds.

About twenty minutes later, we were standing in hip-deep water about thirty yards from where the reef dropped away into deeper, darker water. It had been a hot, slow slog in sandals and shorts; how much worse it must have been to slosh through chest-deep water wearing heavy herring-bone cotton twill utilities and lugging fifty pounds of gear while being raked by fire from machine guns from six hundred yards away.

Walking back to the beach, I learned that Jeremy had been completely unaware of JPAC until he'd checked in to Mary's. Since then he'd been eating, drinking, and hanging out with the team, and Major Osorio had given him *carte blanche* to visit dig sites and take photos. I told him my reception had been a little different, so far. He also told me that when he'd asked Dr. Fox about the possibility of locating the remains of my grandfather, the archaeologist barked, "Fuck Lt. Bonnyman. I'm not out here to find a Medal of Honor winner."

"I can see where you'd be pissed off at being treated like you're some kind of outsider or suspicious plant," he said. "You're a family member of someone whose remains are still buried on the island somewhere; they should treat you like one."[6]

The truth is you can see just about all the interesting remnants of the battle in a day's wandering around Betio. But I took my time, walking every beach, climbing atop the big guns, and snooping out three surviving steel pillboxes and the remains of amphibious vehicles. I started to enter several concrete bunkers, including Admiral Shibasaki's command post, but quickly abandoned my exploration when it became apparent they were used as a public latrine. I even went out to the Our Lady of the Sacred Heart convent. Mother superior Sister Margaret Sullivan, who had lived there for fifty-six years, showed me wartime letters from nuns and the ominous warning to locals posted by the Japanese when they arrived in 1941.

"You'll have to sign our book before we eat," she said. "Now we can say that Bonnyman's grandson came to visit us. People know that name, you know."[7]

All that was interesting, but from the moment I decided to follow my grandfather's footsteps on Tarawa, there was no doubt what I most wanted to see: the enormous concrete blockhouse where he'd been killed, which was known as Bonnyman's Bunker. John and Ted from CNN wanted to be there to capture my words and expressions as I explored, so we drove there one evening before dinner.

In November 1943, it stood about thirty yards inland from the lagoon, perhaps three hundred feet east of the Japanese pier. Fifty-six feet by forty-nine feet, its three-and-a-half-foot-thick, steel-reinforced concrete walls were fifteen feet high. The entire structure had been shored up with coconut logs and railroad ties, then covered over with hundreds of tons of sand, turning it into a nondescript mound that betrayed no hint of what might lie beneath to passing Navy bombers. Only after the fighting did the Americans discover it housed the island's main power generator.

Today, thanks to landfilling, the blockhouse lies about a hundred yards from the seawall. Its sand covering and other fortifications long gone, the lichen-blotched walls jut straight up from the coral sand, so it appears far more imposing than it did during the battle. A seven-foot-wide passageway runs the length of the east-facing wall, leading to a heavy iron door, behind which lie the huge, high-ceilinged generator room and two smaller administrative rooms on the north side. There are no windows, but a ragged hole gouged from the west wall, now covered with a heavy metal grate, was the conduit for cables that delivered electricity throughout the Japanese fortress on Betio. The building was never intended to house troops, but by the third day of fighting, some 150 desperate Japanese *rikusentai*, many injured, had taken refuge inside while battle raged outside.

Today, if you don't know where to look for it, you might never know it's there. It lies hidden in the shadow of a sprawling bread-fruit tree behind a tidy blue building housing a Betio Police sub-station. Before Ted had even come to a complete stop, my door was open and I was tumbling across the street, my heart racing.

"Wait!" John shouted. "I have to get the camera."

With John on my tail, I monkeyed up a twisted ficus tree on the north side (too impatient to realize that there was a much easier way to get on top, at the bunker's western wall). The top was covered with sand, scrubby grass and spindly trees, not to mention a good deal of garbage and many unpleasant splotches of human feces. John trailed along behind me, camera rolling, as I went from corner to corner and peered over each edge, craving, maybe even expecting, some visceral sense of my grandfather.

(Bill Niven, a key catalyst for JPAC's 2010 mission, had mounted the bunker during his only visit to Tarawa in 1989, also hoping to encounter some resonance of the battle. It was much harder to climb back then, and he had to stand on his guide's shoulders to get on top. Once there, he found what he said were casings from strafing US Navy Hellcats and .30-caliber shells from M1 marine rifles, along with many footprints in the crusted sand. Climbing up had been so difficult that Bill believed he was the first person to walk there in more than forty-five years: "I can't prove it, but I believe those boot prints in the sand had to come from the marines who were up there during the battle," he told me.[8] Chalk it up to wishful thinking; rain and wind would have erased all traces of the marines within weeks, or even days, of the battle.)

If I found the top of the bunker disappointing, the interior was even more disheartening. There was little light, but I could see that it was being used as a dump of sorts. Reams of office paper spilled across the floor and plastic buckets teetered in stacks of forty or fifty between cobweb-draped bicycles and spears of rusted rebar that had fallen from the crumbling ceiling. A faint, foul order drifted out from the shadows. There was nothing here to illuminate what had happened the day my grandfather died.

When we emerged from the passageway, a smiling young woman in a checkered police cap was waiting for us. She politely inquired about our interest in the bunker, in excellent English. I zipped through my elevator speech.

"Oh yes," Constable Mareta Hinokua said excitedly. "I know this story. Your grandfather killed one hundred Japanese. He went inside and shot them all." It was the first of many Rambo-ized versions of the legend I would hear from local residents over the next several years.

Then, as casually as if she were offering us a glass of water, the constable said she'd be happy to show us some "American bones" they'd been keeping at the station, if we were interested. We certainly were. A few minutes later, we were peering down at a jumble of brown, white, and gray bones—femurs, ulnas, vertebrae, pieces of skull. Mareta informed us that a man and his son had come across them while digging a trash pit a couple of months earlier—these were the remains discovered in July by Temoana and his father, Tekinaa. The police had been expecting the Americans to collect them for weeks, but they had not come.

"Perhaps you would like to take them?" she offered sweetly.

I briefly imagined the thanks I'd receive from the JPAC team as I handed them over before coming to my senses. They already thought I was—what? A spy, a plant, a meddling interloper?—and I could just imagine what Ray Osorio would make of my gesture. I told Mareta that I'd report the remains to JPAC, and surely they'd pick them up in no time.

Before we left, we walked out to the concrete seawall, perhaps not far from where Sandy Bonnyman came ashore. The eastern sky was now deepening to purple as wind-driven wavelets rolled in from the turquoise lagoon. John quietly lifted the camera to his shoulder and Ted asked if I could sense anything of my grandfather's presence, here or at the bunker where he'd been killed. I really wanted to, but what had I expected? A ghost?

"No," I said. Then, after a pause: "I do keep thinking about what it must have been like for all of them, not just my grandfather, as they plowed toward the island under heavy fire and hunkered down by the seawall . . . But you can't know what that's like, unless you live through it. There's no way."

It wasn't going to make CNN Headline news, but it was the truth.

That night, we arrived at Aboy's Chinese restaurant in beautiful, downtown Betio just as the JPAC crew was leaving. I told Lee Tucker about the bones at the police station, and he led me over to a new SUV so I could tell Capt. Nordman and Dr. Fox in person. They weren't exactly appreciative.

"We know already. We're working to coordinate with the police for transfer," Nordman said tersely. "Please just leave this to the team."

"For fuck's sake," I fumed as they drove away. "How was that not 'leaving it to the team'? And who needs 'coordination'? I could walk over there right now and they'd 'transfer' those bones to me, no questions asked."

"Sorry about that. I don't know why they acted that way," Tucker said. "But you did the right thing."

I learned later that History Flight also had done the right thing: When Kautebiri heard about the bones through the coconut telegraph, he reported it to Mark, who instructed him to take them to the police. Mark promptly emailed JPAC to let them know the remains were waiting for pickup and provided GPS coordinates for the gravesite. "Thought you would want to know about it before they disappear like so many others have," he wrote, alluding to remains he'd had to rescue from a local resident's porch.[9]

He offered to have Kautebiri show the team the exact spot where the bones had been found, as well as the location where Mark had found two skeletons in April.

But JPAC waited until near the end of the two-month mission to collect the bones from the police station. The team never sought out Kautebiri or laid an eye on the sites where three sets of likely American remains recently had been unearthed.

As my time on Tarawa began to dwindle, Lee Tucker approached me to apologize for the way I'd been treated, which he blamed on what he called "bad intel" from headquarters in Hawaii. "Someone," he said, had given his superiors the impression that I was working "undercover" for Mark Noah.

"But why would Mark Noah *need* a spy?" I asked.

Tucker said he couldn't say anything more.

Mark Noah and JPAC had, so far as I knew, enjoyed a cooperative relationship. But I would soon learn otherwise.

Mark had met with officials from both JPAC and DPMO in March, April, and June to discuss History Flight's research in advance of the August-September mission. During a June meeting with civilian administrator Johnie Webb and archaeologist Fox,

Mark had raised concerns about a possible "9-meter range of error" in his coordinates, due to discrepancies between the different GPS systems used by History Flight and JPAC. With the agency's blessing, he obtained the necessary permits from the Kiribati government and planned a June trip to resurvey his sites on Betio.[10]

But shortly thereafter, the Deputy Secretary of Foreign Affairs of Kiribati abruptly revoked the permits.[11] Mark was put on a "no land" list at the airport and he was told that if he showed up, he would be forced to return to Fiji.[12]

"I cannot see the point of having a private organization meddling with our procedures saying they should be here because they prepared an outstanding report," a Kiribati official wrote in an email.[13]

But History Flight was hardly "meddling." Mark had dutifully respected JPAC's authority for years, openly sharing the fruits of his privately funded research. History Flight had repeatedly protected remains found by locals, turning them over to the government until JPAC could collect them. And less than a week before my departure for Tarawa, Mark was receiving emails from a JPAC scientist proposing that they co-author a paper for presentation at the American Academy of Forensic Sciences in February 2011.[14]

Then, inexplicably, he had been declared *persona non grata* and banned from the island, and JPAC's public affairs office began seeing plots where there were none. Ironically, it was only after Osorio declared his suspicions to me that I began to email Mark Noah about what was happening.

Mark did not go gently into exile, and unbeknownst to me, he had been emailing JPAC leaders, demanding to know why Osorio had made things difficult for Marc Miller, whom they'd approved to film the mission, and why they'd decided to treat a family member of a Tarawa MIA—me—as some kind of suspicious intruder. He also wanted to know why Dr. Fox had allegedly barked, "Fuck Lt. Bonnyman," in response to a question from Jeremy Shiok. (JPAC did not respond to several requests to interview Fox, but other staff members have told me that he made the remark.[15])

Mark's emails, in other words, not anything I said, had somehow been interpreted by JPAC as me "throwing around" the name of my grandfather.

After two months on Betio, the JPAC team flew back to Hawaii with the remains received at the August 11 turnover ceremony and the bag of bones from the police station, all previously reported to JPAC by History Flight, and a skeleton unearthed by Betio resident Petis Tentoa in his garden, which he'd lovingly stowed inside his thatched-roof home for more than a year. ("To us," he said, "he was like family.")

With little to show for the reported $500,000 mission, Osorio publicly blamed an unnamed "private group" (History Flight) that had provided faulty site coordinates.[16]

Mark Noah wasn't the only one to wonder if JPAC had actually *wanted* the mission to fail all along, to shake off a pesky "avocational"—professional archaeology's term for non-professionals who dabble in the field—and escape unwanted attention from Congress and the media. CNN reporter Ted Rowlands initially accepted JPAC's claim that History Flight's research was not up to snuff, but later came to see the whole mission as a farce, perhaps even a deliberate misdirection.

JPAC, Ted said, was "spending millions of dollars a year flying around looking for jawbones in Cambodia when you've got this gold mine on Tarawa. . . . Why wouldn't they go for the mother lode? I'll tell you: They didn't like the congressional mandate, being told what to do."[17]

Ted also believed that JPAC had violated Mark Noah's constitutional rights.

"They absolutely prevented him from entering the country while they were there. The net ramifications are that taxpayers spent millions (*sic*) on that trip, which yielded nothing, just because they didn't want him there to take credit," he said. "But they were happy to use (History Flight's 2009) report, including the GPS coordinates, even as they went out of their way to . . . take away the rights of a U.S. citizen."[18]

JPAC may have hoped that a high-profile failure to recover American remains from "several sites publicized by History Flight"[19] would be enough to discredit and discourage Mark Noah. But they just made him mad—and more determined than ever.

I enjoyed that first trip to Tarawa. But what I'd seen of JPAC left me feeling disillusioned and doubtful that the lost marines of Tarawa would ever be found.

EIGHT
ROUGH AND READY
1930–1942

Having jumped the silver-plated tracks of an Ivy League education and the lucrative career his father had prepared for him, my grandfather went in search of action and adventure.

On December 8, 1931, he passed the entry examination for the US Army Air Corps, and on June 28 the following year he was enrolled as a cadet in pre-flight school at Randolph Field outside San Antonio, Texas. Sandy had always been what we now call an "adrenaline junkie," and learning to fly military aircraft in 1932 offered plenty of thrills and danger. That year, 50 fliers, most of them trainees like Sandy, were killed, and 89 were injured in 423 crashes.[1] Still, as one family friend remarked, Sandy was "so steady of nerves that he ought to make a grand pilot."[2]

But adventure was only part of what drove him to try to become a pilot.

"I joined the Air Corps because I thought we were going to fight the Japs," he wrote in 1943. "Everyone thought I was crazy to say in 1932 that such an insignificant people would dare tackle the mighty United States.... Ten years preparation and if we had had to do this job at all we would at least be able to see the end of it in sight."[3]

But less than two months after beginning his training, Sandy was busted back to civilian ranks. According to oft-repeated family legend—it's the kind of tale that's just too good *not* to be true—he was dismissed from the Flying Cadet Detachment for "buzzing the towers" during training flights. "He was," wrote Joseph Alexander, who repeated the story in *Utmost Savagery*, "too free a spirit."[4]

It's not a stretch to think a man of my grandfather's irreverent tendencies might pull such a stunt, and the story is certainly in keeping with his fearless, swashbuckling side. But it's probably apocryphal, an exaggeration, at best. Exhibit A: Sandy was honorably discharged, "By reason of flying deficiency," and his character was listed as "excellent."[5] That's the kind of assessment you'd expect for a solid candidate who just didn't have the skills to make a good pilot, not for an insubordinate cadet who put lives and valuable US Army property at risk. Besides, any pilot who could demonstrate the kind of control required to buzz the tower probably wouldn't have been bounced out as "deficient."[6]

But Sandy had found much to like in Texas, including Josephine Virginia Bell, a local girl he'd met at a debutante party. He was so smitten with Jo that he stuck around and took a job washing dishes at the famous Frenchy's Black Cat Restaurant in San Antonio just so he could court her.[7]

Jo was born in San Antonio on July 13, 1912, to Blanche Browne Bell, an amateur artist whose roots reached all the way back to John Rutledge, second chief justice of the US Supreme Court, and Andrew Jackson Bell, a circuit judge who had traveled by horse to conduct trials in rural west Texas. Jo had one sister, Blanche, six years her elder. Though not especially wealthy, the family was socially prominent and spent summers at a second home in Boerne, thirty miles northwest of San Antonio in the Texas hill country.

It's no wonder that my grandfather was drawn to Jo. She was elegantly attractive, with wavy dark hair, high cheekbones, and a small, angular nose, and partial to padded shoulders, white gloves, and two-tone high-heel shoes. Something about her smoldered.

Yet Jo was also something of a tomboy, a crack shot with a rifle who shared Sandy's love of bird hunting. She was an excellent rider—as a girl, she showed off by doing her morning calisthenics on the back of a pony—and was locally competitive in the sport of equestrian cart driving. Like Sandy, she played a mean game of tennis, and both enjoyed a good party.

Jo also had the advantage of being related to her sister Blanche, who had married Henry Sanford, whose father owned a ranch in Coahuila, Mexico. Sandy and Henry became friends and made many three-hundred-mile trips in a Model T to go bird hunting at Rosita Coahuila.

Sandy was a catch for Jo. But Alex Bonnyman wasn't a fan of the match, going so far as hiring a detective to sniff around San Antonio for dirt on her (though he found no hint of scandal). No family members were present when Sandy and Jo were married by a judge on February 15, 1933.[8]

After the wedding, Sandy swallowed his pride and returned to Knoxville to work for his father at Blue Diamond. This time, putting his son's natural charisma to work, Alex put him on the sales team—not what Sandy wanted, but a savvy business move.

"We always heard he could sell coal to people in Appalachia," said his nephew Robert McKeon.[9]

On May 4, 1934, Jo gave birth to their first child—my mother— Frances Berry Bonnyman. Though Sandy was immediately smitten, Jo had little passion for motherhood. She would come to think of her children as a "life long problem,"[10] and child rearing was mostly delegated to paid staff or relatives.

Now responsible for an infant daughter, Sandy did his best to please his father. But he wasn't cut out for working inside or wearing a suit and tie, and they clashed. Recalling bitter memories of retrieving his alcoholic father from the seedy taverns of Louisville, Alex fretted that Sandy and Jo's drinking and socializing would reflect poorly on the family's good name.

Ironically, it was to Louisville that my great-grandfather sent his son shortly after the birth of his first daughter. Somewhat to their surprise, Sandy and Jo loved it. They lived in tiny Harrodsburg, the oldest permanent American settlement west of the Appalachians, where they rode horses while dressed in matching jodhpurs and boots, played tennis, and quickly developed a circle of friends who loved a party as much as they did. After the birth of their second child, Josephine, or Tina, on June 3, 1936, Sandy began talking to his mother about buying a horse farm and really settling down.

He also gave an early demonstration of the kind of selfless courage that would later earn him the Medal of Honor when he commandeered a skiff to rescue several stranded people when the Ohio River flooded in 1937.[11]

Those brief days in Louisville would turn out to be the happiest of my grandparents' lives together.

In 1937, Alex appointed his son assistant superintendent for Blue Diamond for the Lake District of Minnesota and the northwest, which meant relocating to Minneapolis. Sandy and Jo hated it from the start. There was no riding in the great white north for most of the year, no tennis, no garden parties. They missed their friends in Kentucky and Jo was repelled by the dowdy midwestern home-bodies who, she complained, so desperately wanted "to get her in the basement to do canning."[12]

Unsurprisingly, drinking became an even greater focal point in the couple's lives during their winter of discontent. The parties were wilder than ever, but somehow less fun, more desperate. Sandy broke a man's jaw in one drunken brawl and young Fran recalled seeing one inebriated guest tumble down the stairs and smash through a plate-glass window.

My grandfather had managed five years of obedience to his father, but Minnesota proved too much. In 1938, Sandy quit Blue

Diamond for the last time, packed up his family and headed for the untamed promise of Mexico, Texas, and the Southwest.

"I am certain it was a mistake to exile him out here to the west after he left his father's company," my grandmother later complained. "Sandy was very restless, the years he was out here. I'm sure that's why he decided to join the Marines."[13]

Sandy first made for the ranch in Mexico where the Sanford clan raised cattle and horses while playing the role of benevolent patrons to the local community. Jo was no fan of this rustic life, but like her father, young Fran was immediately at home in the wide-open desert landscape where she and her cousin Ann rode ponies, chased chickens, and skinned many knees.

Sandy had come to Mexico to seek advice from Henry Sanford, who managed a nearby plant for El Paso-based American Smelting, about buying his own mine. Henry made some inquiries and told his brother-in-law he might want to take a look at a small copper mine he'd heard about near Santa Rosa, New Mexico, nine hundred miles north.

The eighty-acre mine site near the tiny village of Pastura was located just a mile from the Chicago, Rock Island and Pacific Railroad's Guadalupe station. Bought in 1925 by I.J. Stauber, the mine—which featured several shafts and pits, as well as houses, outbuildings, and its own small rail line to move tons of ore—produced some five million pounds of copper worth nearly $800,000 (about $12 million in 2018 dollars) before Stauber ceased operations due to low market prices in 1930.[14]

But Sandy, convinced that war was on the horizon, was sure demand for copper would soar. In 1939, he secured a lease on the property with a $5,000 loan (about $93,000 in 2020) from the Blue Diamond Investment Co., whose directors graciously overlooked his lack of collateral on the good word of the company's founder: Alexander Bonnyman Sr.[15] Incorporating as the Guadalupe Mining Co., he contracted with Jose and Joaquin Campos, brothers from Santa Rosa, to haul copper ore to the railroad station, began hiring local laborers, and commenced operations.

My grandmother, put off by a reported lack of indoor plumbing, refused to relocate to Santa Rosa. Instead, she took the girls to stay in the graceful Alvarado Hotel in Albuquerque to look for a place to set up house. But she found the state's largest city dusty, sprawling, and lacking in charm, hardly better than Santa Rosa.

Then she saw Santa Fe, perched below the southern reaches of the snowcapped Sangre de Cristo Range, sixty miles to the north. Settled by the Spanish empire twenty-two years before the pilgrims scratched "1620" on Plymouth Rock, New Mexico's small capital city has long exuded exotic culture, history, charm, beauty, and ineffable magic. Jo knew immediately that's where she wanted to live.

Sandy soon rented a small adobe house at 570 East Garcia Street for Jo and the girls. Because Santa Fe had a reputation as a "wild and woolly town," he insisted that Jo sleep with a pistol in her bedside table.[16]

Sandy spent five or six days a week working the mine. He lived in a small rented cabin on the outskirts of Santa Rosa and commuted three hours over rough, unpaved roads every weekend to spend time at home. His hard work began to pay off quickly. By 1940, the mine was turning an annual profit of $40,000 and he was earning the equivalent of more than $600,000 a year in inflation-adjusted dollars. It wasn't the Kentucky horse farm he'd been dreaming about, but it beat the hell out of wearing a tie and peddling coal in grim, wintry Minnesota.

Sudden prosperity made life hospitable, even for Jo. Perched at seven thousand feet above sea level, Santa Fe's winter nights were bone-cracking cold, and there were occasional desert snowstorms, but its piercing blue skies were clear more than 320 days a year. She once more took up tennis and riding, and in spring and summer,

Sandy sometimes took time off to drive his family into Pecos hills for trout fishing and picnics.

As always, Sandy and Jo were quick to form new friendships, and it wasn't long before they met James Hobart "Jimmie" Russell, a tall, silver-haired charmer with a perpetual tan who could pass for a poor man's Cary Grant. Jimmie's past was obscure, though he was rumored to have Cherokee Indian ancestry. Born in Oklahoma, he'd left home at age fourteen and never lived anywhere but New Mexico for the rest of his life. He worked for years as the chief bookkeeper for the American Metals Company in the tiny community of Terrero northeast of Santa Fe. When the mine closed in 1939 he joined my grandfather's Guadalupe Mining Co., managing finances from Santa Fe. Restless, adventurous Sandy and calm, coolly competent Jimmie may have seemed an odd couple, fire and ice, but by all accounts made excellent business partners. Sandy was soon calling Jimmie his best friend.

On November 28, 1940, Jo gave birth to a third golden-haired daughter, Alexandra. All three girls were usually left in the care of nuns, teachers, nursemaids, or a local woman of Spanish descent, Cassamira, hired to do the shopping, cooking, and cleaning. Every summer, Jo and the girls boarded the Super Chief to Chicago on their way to Knoxville, where the girls would spend the next three months with their Bonnyman grandparents.

But over time, and despite all their good fortune, cracks were developing in Sandy and Jo's marriage. Now, when he came home, Sandy spent more time in his own pursuits, training bird dogs, haunting the city's taverns rather than hosting parties for friends, even taking up the seedy pastime of cockfighting; fueled by alcohol, he and Jo began arguing and fighting more often.

Meanwhile, down in Santa Rosa, Sandy quickly earned a reputation for drinking and troublemaking alongside his employee, Jose Campos.

"They were good friends," said Joseph Campos, then-mayor of Santa Rosa and owner of Joseph's Café, opened by his father in 1956. "And they were hell-raisers."[17]

While my grandfather had not, as family lore claimed, been "shot in a bar fight in Santa Fe," I learned that he *had* been shot in a gas-station parking lot in Santa Rosa. At 5:30 a.m. on Saturday, March 8, 1941, a mysterious, simmering feud with a local rancher, A.A. Mack "Eck" Walker, exploded into violence outside the Squeeze Inn on the banks of the Pecos River.

"The two men engaged in an argument . . . and shortly thereafter Walker left and got in his car," reported the *Santa Rosa News*. After Walker was "again accosted by Bonnyman," the rancher fired a single round from rifle at point-blank range, dropping my grandfather instantly to the ground.

My mother always believed he'd been shot in the leg, but in fact the slug tore through his "left upper thorax" less than half an inch from his heart and pierced his lung.[18] He was "rushed" to the nearest hospital—three hours away in Santa Fe—accompanied by a local doctor named Von Pohle.

"Bonnyman has survived this long and reports today are that he will probably recover," the paper reported, "though no hope was held at first for his life."[19]

Walker turned himself in to the sheriff. He was charged with assault with a deadly weapon, and released on $10,000 bond. Sandy sued the rancher for $13,918 and on March 16, 1942, a jury awarded him $5,000 ($80,000 today).[20] Yet just a month later, a jury in the criminal trial found Walker not guilty, "at which the courtroom was filled with whistles, indrawn breaths, sighs of relief, and handclapping."[21]

"Details of the fracas were vague," according to initial reports, and the origins of the feud are now lost. It's not clear why locals would cheer Walker's acquittal, but even some Bonnyman family members described him as a "mean drunk."[22]

Whatever happened, three-quarters of a century later Guadalupe County proudly claims Sandy Bonnyman as one of its greatest heroes.

"What really matters," said former county superintendent and historian Daniel Flores, "is that he survived. He could have used that injury or the fact that he had a copper mine as an excuse not to go to war, but he wanted to serve his country."[23]

Three decades earlier, I had angrily doubted the cousin who had first related his garbled version of the shooting incident. But now, as the impossible myth I'd known as a boy continued to unravel, I felt kinship. I was no hero, but it was somehow comforting to know that my grandfather also had fought with his father, dropped out of college, upended family expectations, impulsively sought adventure, chosen unapproved women, and drunk too much.

Alarmed by the news of his son's brush with death, Alex Bonnyman dispatched a deputy from Blue Diamond, Fred E. Gore, to Santa Fe that spring in an effort to put Sandy on the straight and narrow. Gore lectured my grandfather that he could lose it all—his wife, children, and business—if he didn't stop his carousing, fighting, and other unsavory pursuits. He also presented an offer from the elder Bonnyman to take Sandy back at Blue Diamond for a third chance.

But this time, he didn't need to go home again. He didn't need to live life to please his father—and he knew he'd always have his mother's unconditional affection and support. He had broken free.

For all his wild ways, my grandfather dearly loved his daughters. Whatever went down on Saturday night, he was always to be found in the pews of Santa Fe's majestic Cathedral Basilica of St. Francis of Assisi on Sunday morning, young Fran perched beside him, feet swinging (Jo was an Episcopalian). Afterward, he would take her over to the Capitol Pharmacy for a treat.

Though she was just seven years old at the time, three-quarters of a century later, Fran Evans vividly remembered one particular

Sunday—December 7, 1941. An Associated Press bulletin first broadcast the news at 12:22 p.m., Santa Fe time.

"We were in the Capitol Pharmacy when we heard it," she said. Once home, her father "was very agitated, he was pacing, very upset about the whole thing."[24]

Sandy and Jo spent the rest of the day listening to crackling radio updates and calling friends and relatives.

A married father of three young children and owner of a business critical to the coming war effort, Sandy Bonnyman was thrice exempt from military service. But he'd never been one to shy from a fight. As the scion of a wealthy, well-connected Southern industrialist, he surely could have had his choice of plum roles in any branch of the service. But Sandy didn't want a cushy stateside job, and on February 8, 1942, flush with pride and patriotism, he signed papers to join the US Marine Corps. At thirty-one, the recruiter warned, he was too old to go straight to officers' training school. He didn't care. He wanted to be a marine, to fight on the front lines, and if he had to start at the bottom alongside teenaged recruits, so be it.

My grandfather's patriotic decision to become an enlisted marine has always been foundational to his legend. But as with all legends, it's more complicated than that. Despite his outward success, Sandy had grown restless for adventure after years of hard work at the mine and "troubles at home."[25]

"One of the many great appeals of war for men," wrote the late Christopher Hitchens, "is that it legitimizes flight from domestic entrapment."[26]

NINE
DIGGING DEEPER
2010–2012

Despite my disillusionment over the prospects—perhaps even the wisdom—of finding my grandfather's remains, walking in his footsteps on Tarawa had inspired me to begin a long-overdue excavation of his life.

I began by reading (or rereading) every history of the battle I could find: Alexander's *Utmost Savagery*, Eric Hammel and John E. Lane's *Bloody Tarawa*, Michael Graham's *Mantle of Heroism*, Robert Sherrod's *Tarawa: The Story of a Battle*, *One Square Mile of Hell* by John Wukovits, *Line of Departure: Tarawa* by Michael Russ, the Marine Corps Historical Section's detailed official 1947 account, *The Battle for Tarawa*, and a gung-ho 1944 retelling by combat correspondent S.Sgt. Dick Hannah, *Tarawa: Toughest Battle in Marine Corps History*. I also obtained the Second Marine Division's official 1943 after-action report.

And I embarked on what I thought would be a simple process to get copies of my grandfather's official military records from the National Personnel Records Center (NPRC) in St. Louis, Missouri. A month later I received a letter explaining there were no records on anyone named Alexander Bonnyman, Jr.

I knew that a 1973 fire at the center had destroyed an estimated sixteen to eighteen million military personnel files, but also that no marine files had been destroyed. So I wrote the NPRC again, noting that Lt. Bonnyman was a Medal of Honor recipient and well known in Marine Corps history. Four weeks later, I received the exact same form letter: "We have been unsuccessful in identifying a military service record for the above-named individual."

When I called the people who signed the letters, they kicked me upstairs to other staff members, who all gave me the same maddening answer. At their suggestion, I contacted the Marine Corps in Quantico, Virginia, which bounced me back to St. Louis.

Over the course of the next two years I continued to write and call the records center, always receiving the same Kafkaesque reply—no records—until I met Katherine "Katie" Rasdorf. Katie, a marine veteran and master scuba diver from Virginia, had thousands of hours of archival research for Pacific Wrecks, BentProp, and History Flight, as well as JPAC and the DPMO, under her belt. Within a week of our first phone conversation, I received a fat FedEx envelope containing 275 pages of records from Sandy Bonnyman's personnel file.

Evidently, the staff members who processed my multiple requests hadn't bothered to check a special archive for PEPs—"persons of exceptional prominence"—where my grandfather's documents were kept, by virtue of his Medal of Honor. I was utterly baffled that people paid to process public requests apparently didn't know it existed.

"You have to understand," Katie said, "most of the people answering requests at the NPRC are just minimum-wage workers. They have no idea what they are doing."

Over the next few years, Katie Rasdorf would become indispensible in my efforts to fill the gaps in my grandfather's story.

Almost as soon as I returned from Tarawa, the most remarkable sources of information began to open up, thanks to John and Ted's stories on CNN. Men who'd been in the battle, or their relatives, contacted me to share their memories.

"My dad always spoke so highly of your grandfather, and they were good friends," said George Clerou, son of Sandy's commanding officer, Capt. Joseph Clerou. "He always talked about how he didn't have to be there. He was there when (Sandy) died and he never forgot it. He was one of the men who recommended him for the Medal of Honor."[1]

In waiting so long to undertake the quest to know my grandfather, I had lost the opportunity to interview many men who had fought beside him. So I was deeply gratified to begin hearing from men in their late eighties or nineties, members of the rapidly dwindling population of Tarawa veterans, who eagerly shared their recollections of the battle—and often, Sandy Bonnyman.

There were many over the years, including: Marvin Sheppard, a private in intelligence with Headquarters Company of the 2nd Battalion, 8th Marines (2/8, in shorthand), who had stood at the back of the bunker and cheered on the assault; Norman Hatch, the intrepid cameraman whose film footage became part of the 1944 Oscar-winning documentary, *With the Marines at Tarawa*; Ed Bale, tank commander; machine gunner Max Clampitt, long-time mayor of Hobbs, New Mexico; Japanese translator Robert Sheeks; Dean Ladd; Elwin Hart; Victor Ornelas; Roy Elrod; and others.

"He was just fearless," said Sheppard, who said he, too, recommended Sandy for the Medal of Honor.[2]

I began to contact Bonnyman family members, seeking any and all documentary evidence of my grandfather's life, and soon began receiving scrapbooks and letters. I mined my mother's basement— an invaluable, if maddeningly disorganized, archive of trunks, files, and boxes—which yielded a steady stream of precious gems in the form of letters, photos, and newspaper clippings.

Fortunately, the Bonnymans were not only prodigious letter writers, but also dedicated savers of correspondence that illuminated every part of my grandfather's life, from his childhood to his Princeton days, life in New Mexico, and the eighteen months he spent in San Diego, New Zealand, Guadalcanal, and Tarawa. I began reading dozens of letters sent to the Bonnymans by my grandfather's marine comrades, the beginning of a long and maddening paper trail of the family's quest to learn how my grandfather died and bring his remains home for burial.

Yet this rich vein of information raised as many questions as it answered: What really happened that day Sandy was killed? And what about the startling fact—I'd never heard it before—that he was initially awarded the Navy Cross, the second-highest honor bestowed on marines, despite being recommended for the Medal of Honor—and why was that decision later reversed? And of course, what really happened to his remains?

I had spent most my life content to know little about the grandfather I so admired. Now, the more I learned, the more I had to know. We might never recover his bones from the sepulchral sands of Tarawa, but I was more determined than ever to exhume him, his life, his story, from the tomb of legend.

Mark Noah wasn't the kind of guy to let a bunch of bureaucrats interfere with his own quest to bring home Tarawa's missing marines.

In the weeks following my departure from Betio, JPAC had begun to backpedal from its inexplicable treatment of Mark while the team was still on Betio, going so far as to invite him to attend a September 20 repatriation ceremony in Hawaii for the remains recovered during the mission.[3]

At the same time, the agency soured on its relationship with filmmaker Steven Barber: "We are still on with Steven Barber but just enough to facilitate his end product. . . . Continue to stress that we are in no way affiliated with Steven Barber," the public affairs office wrote, instructing staff not to interact with the filmmaker in any way.[4]

This swift reversal of fortunes led Mark Noah and others to wonder if the filmmaker had somehow been a factor in JPAC's ill-advised attempt to freeze out History Flight. Certainly, the two men did not get along. Mark had granted Barber an on-camera interview years before, but publicly criticized the filmmaker when he posted video footage that not-so-subtly implied that he had conducted History Flight's field work on Tarawa. In retaliation, Barber continually trashed Mark to JPAC and others, calling him "sick and disturbed," "a certain deranged UPS pilot," and worse.[5]

And JPAC couldn't have been happy when it learned that Barber had surreptitiously agreed to film the agency's 2010 mission on behalf of an MIA charity called Moore's Marauders for $30,000.

"JPAC must think that I am on my own and totally independent of the Marauders, Mark Noah, Steven Spielberg, Tom Hanks . . . I AM STEVEN BARBER. . . . So let me make perfectly clear. I AM A MARAUDER!!! But I am a COVERT MARAUDER . . . A STEALTH MARAUDER . . . I will deny any involvement with the Marauders or ANYONE so I can film at JPAC headquarters and in the field!!" Barber wrote in an email to Ken Moore, leader of the group. " . . . My LOYALTY is with the guy who writes the check—110%!!!!!!!!!!!!!"[6]

In the first half of 2012, Paul Freeman, a freelance Hollywood writer/editor—basically, a guy who rescues projects in trouble— managed to mold Barber's footage into *Until They Are Home,* a follow-up to *Return to Tarawa* that focused on the mission to recover remains. Narrated by former *Cheers* star Kelsey Grammer—Barber's claim to "have (Matt) Damon on the hook" with Clint Eastwood "right behind" having evidently fallen through[7]—the film never found the audience of its less calculated predecessor.

"It was better than I expected it to be but . . . in the end I was not moved," said History Flight videographer Marc Miller,[8] who saw the movie at a May 28 screening in Los Angeles (as did Maj. Gen. Stephen Tom and civilian administrator Johnie Webb, shepherding JPAC's ill-starred partnership with Barber to the bitter end). A reviewer for the *Hollywood Reporter* wrote, "It feels downright unpatriotic to criticize *Until They Are Home*, a well-meaning but pedestrian documentary. . . . Even with its scant 66-minute running time it feels overextended."[9] The *New York Times* called it "just plain boring."[10]

As soon as he was back in JPAC's good graces, Mark Noah returned to work on Betio. In February 2011, he assembled an eleven-person team to conduct History Flight's sixth trip to the island, including geophysicists, historians, and two top archaeologists with expertise in clandestine grave detection, Jennie Sturm and Dr. Chet Walker. The team used magnetometry, ground-penetrating radar, and soil analysis to survey some fifteen sites around the island.[11]

Among the sites examined were the yard of Petis Tentoa, who had kept American remains in his home until turning them over to JPAC in 2010; the area around a housing project built by the Taiwanese government, where the two skeletons given to JPAC in the 2010 turnover ceremony had been found; the center of the campus for Kiribati's Marine Training Center, where a historical map indicated that six bodies were buried; and an area believed to be Cemetery 25 that had lit up History Flight instruments like nuclear Christmas trees.

Mark even agreed to try out a new member of the team: a big, friendly black Labrador retriever named Buster, trained in the detection of human remains.

"He was skeptical of the dog, so when we went down there he did some double-blind tests on us," said Buster's trainer and handler Paul Dostie, a former police investigator with the city of Mammoth, California.[12]

Mark observed while Buster sniffed around sites where bodies had been recovered and sites where there were known to be no remains. The dog didn't miss a beat, dropping to his "alert" position on each site where remains had been found, and ignoring the others. Buster paid no attention to pig bones littering the subsurface soil.

"He was impressive," Mark admitted. "We let him search where we knew there were remains and exactly where they were to test him, and he was dead on."

Buster came to Tarawa sporting his own "bone" *fides*. Credited with solving numerous crimes, sniffing out some two hundred sets of remains, and sporting a thick portfolio of media stories, he was arguably the biggest celebrity on the team. Dostie first trained him to be an avalanche rescue dog. He later became interested in forensic work and began to train Buster in dilapidated Nevada cemeteries.

"Decomposing bones give off a unique chemical signature that rises up through the soil, and Buster can detect it even after they have been buried for decades," Dostie said. "Most cadaver dogs are only trained to detect soft tissue, but I have trained Buster to alert to much older remains."[13]

In his illustrious career, Buster had been brought in to search for Americans shot down in the Battle of the Bulge and victims of the Charles Manson family, and to search the home of a long-dead man suspected in the eerie, unsolved, 1947 murder of twenty-two-year-old Elizabeth Short in Los Angeles, the infamous Black Dahlia case.

On Betio, Buster alerted near a two-story, tin-sided building used to process copra (dried coconut), not far from the pier. Mark had interviewed locals who helped build the plant, who said they had dug up human remains, leading him to believe that Cemetery 27, where my grandfather was supposed to be buried, might be nearby. Buster sniffed out the whole area, alerting around a large cistern, as well as on the concrete pier, where the workers said they had deposited dirt containing human remains. All that was encouraging, but Mark gently reminded me that the odds against finding Sandy Bonnyman were immense.

"If we are ever able to excavate there at all, we might find a complete, forty-person cemetery, or we might find traces of a cemetery that was carved up and dumped into fill," he told me. "Maybe your grandfather really is one of the unknowns buried in the Punchbowl."[14]

In September 2011, Mark got a call from JPAC civilian administrator Webb, who wanted to know if a History Flight team might arrange to be on Betio October 5 and 6 because, as Mark put it, "Hint, hint, there might just be some important people from JPAC there at the same time." Webb asked that the whole thing be kept on the down low.

"He was a real positive force. He realized that we knew more about where the graves are than they did," Mark said. "He was interested in getting that information and doing it in a way that didn't involve all the factions in the pointless battle constantly going on at JPAC. We said we'd be there, but I said, 'Please don't send Dr. Fox.'"[15]

They didn't. Instead, they sent archaeologist Jay Silverstein. Silverstein earned his PhD from Pennsylvania State University and had been with JPAC since 2002. He was an expert in geographic information systems with a long interest in military archaeology and ancient Greco-Egyptian and Mesoamerican societies. As an adjunct faculty member at the University of Hawaii, he was co-leader of a team that discovered a 2,300-year-old temple built by Ptolemy II in Philadelphus, Egypt.

Silverstein had in recent years found himself on the wrong side of factional fighting at the Central Identification Laboratory and JPAC. He had been scheduled to lead the 2010 Tarawa expedition and met with Mark Noah in April to discuss possible excavation sites. But he returned from that meeting to find that he'd been replaced by Fox. Silverstein's advocacy for History Flight's work would have him in the doghouse with some higher-ups for years to come.

During the October 2011 mission, Mark, Chet Walker, Paul Dostie and Buster, and volunteer land surveyor Paul Schwimmer spent twelve to fourteen hours a day sweating under the merciless equatorial sun, trying to cram in as much work as they could in just a few days. They checked out a couple new sites and went back over sites JPAC never got to in 2010, including the area around the copra plant. Mark advised JPAC that he thought a shipping yard on Betio's north side, where the remains of Herman Sturmer had been found in 2002, was a prime candidate for exploration.

The joint mission left Silverstein determined to convince his skeptical colleagues that History Flight wasn't made up of weekend warriors or unethical bone hunters, but rather, serious professionals. After making his case to JPAC boss Maj. Gen. Stephen Tom that the agency should send teams to work jointly with History Flight on two sites, including a possible location for Cemetery 27, he told Mark Noah that he expected it to happen by April 2012.

Despite Silverstein's advocacy, JPAC still wasn't giving Betio the attention it deserved. A group of children found a skeleton in an area just south of Betio's "Bird's Beak," where the team unearthed a substantial pile of human remains in a trash pit. They turned the remains over to local police, where they languished for many months before they were finally picked up by JPAC; higher-ups nixed Silverstein's request to further excavate the site.

The team also surveyed a site where a local man said he had dug up a skeleton in his yard, which he believed to be American, based on a canteen found with the remains. When they plotted GPS coordinates, they found the site was right in the center of the original Cemetery 25 location. The Army Graves Registration Service had repatriated dozens of remains from the area in 1946, but four marines listed as also having been buried there were never found.

History Flight spent much of 2012 conducting successful recoveries in Europe. Mark had taken particular interest in the *Hunconscious,* a B-26 that went down in Belgium with a six-man crew that were still MIA, after reading *The Dead of Winter* by Bill Warnock. Mark sent a reconnaissance team in June 2011 to examine a crash site found by a German forestry worker in the forest of Ardennes. In April he led a team to excavate the site. They were a long, long way from the heat and squalor of Betio.

"We encountered rain, fog, ice pellets, and snow," Mark said. "The guys wet-screening the debris wore heavy-duty rain gear. I thought wearing a leather bomber jacket would do, but I ended up contracting pneumonia."[16]

The work yielded seven sets of remains, which were duly turned over to JPAC. But Mark was once more beginning to lose his patience with the agency.

"They've totally let the World War II ball drop. They spend four or five or six million recovering a fighter plane wreck from Vietnam, but when I asked them how many missions they'd sent to Europe, they said three," he said. "And it literally took an act of Congress and political arm twisting to get them even engaged on Tarawa."[17]

In October 2012 JPAC sent a team to Tarawa, led by anthropologist Dr. Bill Belcher, a fourteen-year agency veteran and one of its most respected archaeologists. Belcher earned his doctorate in anthropology from the University of Wisconsin-Madison, with a focus on the fishing economy and trade among ancient Indus peoples in southwest Asia. Since coming to JPAC he had led recovery missions in

England, Cambodia, Laos, Vietnam, Papua New Guinea, Palau, and North Korea. By the time he first met Mark Noah on Tarawa, he had risen to deputy director at the Central Identification Laboratory.

Like most of his colleagues, Belcher had long been skeptical of non-agency personnel hunting for MIAs, especially when it came to World War II remains.

"I'm leery of people who aren't trained to do forensic archaeology. There are a lot of people out there who are basically ambulance chasers, who do it for the notoriety or because they think it's a way to get a lucrative contract from Uncle Sugar," he said. "Some are after artifacts to sell, and most of them don't have the right training or the right perspective."[18]

But like Silverstein, Belcher had concluded that History Flight fell into none of those categories. Mark Noah had not only raised more than two million dollars in private funding—$869,000 in 2010 alone—but also had sunk hundreds of thousands of dollars of his own money into the project. He was smart enough to know what he didn't know, and, like the nonprofit organizations BentProp and Pacific Wrecks, paid top experts and professionals to do his field-work. After four years it was clear to Belcher that Mark wasn't in it for fame, glory, or riches, and he wasn't a grave robber bent on selling bones and artifacts on eBay.

The October 2012 joint mission looked like it might be the beginning of a beautiful relationship. JPAC recovered three sets of intact remains, as well as partial remains, beneath a pigsty in the area associated with Cemetery 25—right where History Flight's research, and Buster's nose, had predicted they'd hit pay dirt.

Belcher also conducted exploratory excavation at all five sites History Flight had identified as potential Cemetery 27 locations. His team found no indication of human remains near the copra plant, but three shallow trenches in the shipping yard, adjacent to where remains had been recovered in 2002, turned up human arm and hand bones, shreds of marine poncho, a spoon, and a canteen cup.

Mark was excited by the finds, but when he urged Belcher to "throw a wider blanket" and dig deeper, at least down to the water table, the archaeologist demurred. "There's nothing here," he said, according to Mark. "You're just showing me empty holes."[19]

Belcher "categorically" denied using those words.

"I was just saying, 'There needs to be more (survey) work done here. Otherwise we are just chasing our tails,'" he told me.[20]

Whatever was said, it's inescapable that when History Flight teed up a site that would have thrown many an archaeologist's heart into joyous palpitations, one of JPAC's top scientists simply walked away. Assuming Belcher knew best, Mark turned elsewhere in the search for Cemetery 27, Betio's most elusive burial site and the final resting place of my grandfather.

TEN
PROUD TO CLAIM
THE TITLE
JUNE 1942-NOVEMBER 1943

Those close to Sandy Bonnyman were torn about his decision to join the Marine Corps in the winter of 1942.

"I knew he would unquestionably make a good soldier," his father said, "but I did not like to see him enter the marines at thirty [*sic*] years old as a private, leaving a copper mine that was paying him $30,000 to $40,000 a year . . . and leaving a comparatively young wife and three girls, the youngest of whom was only one year old when he enlisted."[1]

My grandmother Jo "admired him for wanting to fight for his country," but considered the Marine Corps "practically a Suicide Squad. . . . I would not have minded a safer branch of the service."[2]

Sandy hoped the war would not go on for long. But he shared President Roosevelt's conviction that unconditional surrender by the Japanese was the only sensible conclusion, and he knew that would take time. He was busy with the mine during the spring of 1942 and my mother didn't recall seeing him at all after April. But he went to great lengths to ensure that his family and business would be taken care of in his absence.

On June 29, my grandfather signed a partnership agreement that gave his best friend Jimmie Russell sole management of the Guadalupe Mining Co. He would continue to own fifty percent of net assets, receive half of all profits, and would be liable for just ten dollars in debts or obligations.[3]

Upon hearing of the proposed partnership, Alex Bonnyman hired a local attorney to nose around about Russell's reputation (much as he had done with my grandmother before her marriage to Sandy). Ultimately, Alex "thoroughly approved" the partnership, citing Russell's "very fine brand of honesty and splendid character," business knowledge and "pep and energy."[4]

Sandy initially set Jo up with a monthly allowance of $400— nearly $6,500 today—though he would later have to raise the amount more than once: "I had hoped that she would do on her $500 [$8,000], but which [sic] is not happening."[5]

Alexander Bonnyman, Jr. boarded a train in Albuquerque, bound for Phoenix, on June 28, 1942. The next day, he completed his paper- work—including forms certifying he had never been convicted of a crime and a sworn affidavit that "there is nobody dependent upon me for support beyond my ability to contribute beyond the pay of a private in the U.S. Marine Corps"—and was inducted in the US Marine Corps Reserve. On that day his income dropped from $3,000 a month to just $183.34.

On July 7, Pvt. Bonnyman was ordered to board a Southern Pacific Railway train to San Diego and, likely because of his age, put in charge of three other new recruits. Arriving twelve hours later, he herded the men aboard buses that would take them to the depot at Marine Corps Base, San Diego, where all recruits from west of the Mississippi were being sent for training (on Sept. 25, President Roo- sevelt would dedicate a new facility, named Camp Pendleton after World War I Gen. Joseph H. Pendleton). Two weeks after arriving, Sandy was appointed acting corporal, the first of many promotions he would receive over the next fifteen months.

At thirty-two, he was very much the "old man" to the mostly teenage recruits enduring boot camp with him. Sandy's age no doubt also paved the way for his highly unusual friendship with forty-nine-year-old Col. Gilder D. Jackson Jr., the highly decorated commander of the Sixth Marine Regiment. The corporal and the colonel became so close that Sandy visited him and his wife Vesta in their home many times, and when Jo came to San Diego to see her husband for the last time, the couple spent an evening with the Jacksons at the Hotel del Coronado. Jackson declared that he'd never had a marine in his command "that I was any more devoted to on such short acquaintance."[6]

It took less than two weeks of boot camp to disabuse my grandfather of any romantic notions he might have had about being a grunt ("An enlisted man's life would grow a little monotonous," he wrote[7]). He had helped train his first platoon after an instructor became ill, and was kept behind when his unit was shipped overseas to be a drill instructor. He didn't love the assignment, especially having to attend "school" from 1500 to 1630 every afternoon, but it was an importance showcase for initiative and leadership.

"I took the assignment as a stepping stone to Officer's Training School or OCS or whatever the correct term is," he wrote his mother. "It is supposedly not possible for me to go there until I am a Corporal . . . although I have the same responsibilities and duties of a regular Cpl."[8]

Ironically, maturity and success put Sandy at a disadvantage when it came to being commissioned as a marine officer. The upper age limit to join officer's candidate's school as a recruit was twenty-seven and regulations specifically excluded married men and those without college degrees (unless they had earned credit for, or taken an examination in, ten of fourteen tough classes, including differential calculus, physics, and "rhetorical principles").[9] Meanwhile, field commissions were generally reserved for recent college graduates or non-commissioned officers who had served for more than a year.

Nonetheless, Jo and his parents were thrilled by his change of heart, convinced that serving as an officer would be safer than as an enlisted marine. But time was a factor, and Alex immediately began pulling strings. He wrote to his friend Francis Biddle, Attorney General in the Roosevelt administration, to ask for advice. And through a mutual acquaintance, he arranged a meeting with retired marine Maj. Gen. Hugh B. Matthews, who had received the Navy Cross while fighting with the Second Marine Division in France in 1918. The general concurred Sandy was "just the type of man they wanted as an officer." (Alex wrote his son, "Maybe this was brought about by your father's, shall I say eloquence?—or salesmanship?"[10]) Matthews wrote Maj. Gen. Clayton B. Vogel, commanding general of the Marine Amphibious Corps in the Pacific, on October 7, urging him to take a close look at Sandy Bonnyman. To the disappointment of all, Vogel never replied.

But Sandy might not have needed such help in the first place. Jackson had seen his potential and placed him in the Officers' Candidate Class, which "put him in a status for commission later, provided he made the grade."

"After seeing him in my home and having him in my Regiment, I was never in doubt as to the eventual outcome," the colonel later wrote.[11]

Sandy wasn't the only one in his family to show leadership potential. Before he even became a marine his brother Gordon, nine years his junior, had graduated from the US Army ROTC program at Princeton and was commissioned as a second lieutenant. Promoted to first lieutenant on February 1, 1942, he was sent to India on October 31, where he began instructing Chinese troops in the use of field artillery. In April 1943, Gordon was promoted to captain and sent to Burma as a liaison to the Chinese army.

On October 19, 1942, Sandy boarded the USS *Matsonia* as part of Headquarters Company, 6th Marines, arriving in Wellington, New Zealand, on November 4. Wellington was about as close to home as a marine could get overseas, reminding many of San Francisco with its wharves, hills, and temperate climate. When the marines weren't training, they enjoyed milk shakes and ice cream sodas at the city's many "milk bars," ate hearty meals of fresh lamb, beef, and eggs, and drank Waitemata beer and eye-opening Australian "jump whiskey," a "villainous, green Mexican distillation."[12]

On November 25, Sandy was promoted to corporal and appointed to F Company, 2nd Battalion, 18th Marine Regiment, "to take full advantage of his talent and ability . . . (as an) Engineer."[13] His experience in the mining business had prepared him well for such a role, and he was excited to be "back in my old trade."[14]

The *New York Times* editorial page wrote admiringly of combat engineers: "They are masters of many trades, men-of-all-work as well as men-at-arms. . . . They lay and unlay mines, dig trenches, run railroads and railroad shops, make bridges, roads, fortifications, airports, bomb-proofs, gun emplacements, barracks, anything buildable. They map and camouflage. They are photographers and cinematographers. They incinerate, refrigerate, disinfect. They are first-class plumbers. They attend to the water supply. They are expert handlers of explosives and all tools, including a rifle and a bayonet. One of their favorite sports is tossing a flame-thrower at a pillbox. . . . They are real Yanks of the Yankiest kind."[15]

Sandy's 18th Engineers, aka Pioneers, were among some 3,800 marines billeted alongside the Third Wellington Regiment of the New Zealand Army in the Judgeford Valley, a bucolic farming community north of Wellington. He boarded the USS *President Jackson* December 24 and spent Christmas at anchor in Wellington Harbor before sailing for the Solomon Islands to mop up after the First Marine Division, which had been fighting—and winning—

the grinding jungle campaign on Guadalcanal since August. He made landfall on January 4, 1943.

Engineers were jacks-of-all-trades on the island, serving as everything from infantry to demolitions experts to bridge builders. Sandy Bonnyman's most notable task in his six weeks on "the canal" was supervising construction of a pontoon bridge over the Toha River. His team labored from daylight until dark and bivouacked on the river, where Japanese artillery or machine gun fire kept them awake half the night. In the morning they breakfasted on scalding coffee and hardtack before getting back to work.[16]

"It was due to Sandy's energy, ingenuity, and his personality that he was able to have his men erect this bridge in record time," Col. Jackson recalled.

Bonny, as his friends now called him, made little fuss over his first taste of combat, when he and a reconnaissance team surprised eight Japanese fighters, killing three.[17]

Stories of a dramatic jungle ambush and bridge building make good copy. But on Guadalcanal, as it would be on Tarawa, it was Sandy Bonnyman's leadership and work ethic that won the respect of his fellow marines. As Jackson wrote, "He was always cheerful, ready to work twenty-four hours a day without rest, and was always to be found in the front line trying to do some job that would make the Infantry advance a little bit easier."[18] Jackson's gambit and Sandy's hard work paid off, and on February 7, 1943, he received a commission as a second lieutenant. His commanding officer, Capt. Joseph Clerou, recommended that he be given command of a company once the Second Marine Division had finished up on Guadalcanal. Seven months after entering the Marine Corps as a private, against the odds, my grandfather was an officer in the US Marine Corps.

"Obviously your confidence in Bonnyman's ability is justified," a secretary for Gen. Vogel wrote Maj. Gen. Matthews—five months after the Bonnymans thought the retired general's efforts had gone nowhere.[19]

The family was elated, and with good reason. At Guadalcanal enlisted men of the First Marine Division had been killed at nearly twice the rate of officers, a ratio that would be matched at Tarawa.

On February 19, the marines handed Guadalcanal over to the Army and 2nd Lt. Alexander Bonnyman, Jr. sailed back to New Zealand aboard the USS *President Adams*. Having tasted combat, he was eager for more.

"When we do get another chance," he wrote Jo, "I believe we will do a good job. We certainly pray and hope so because the First Division certainly gave us a mark at which to shoot."[20]

But it would be nine long, difficult months before the Second Marine Division engaged the enemy again.

During his second stay at Camp Judgeford my grandfather forged close friendships with numerous officers—2nd Lt. Barney Boos, 1st Lt. Paul Govedare, Capt. Clerou, Capt. John Murphy, Capt. Bert Watson, Capt. Don Farkas, 1st Lt. Tracy Griswold, and others.

"There's so much a fellow could write about Bonny and it wouldn't even cover half the man he was," wrote Boos, one of the few who also had "come up through the ranks" to become an officer.[21]

Though eager for action, Sandy enjoyed New Zealand. He served as F Company's athletic officer, tasked with keeping the men in fighting trim. He frequently went to the horse races and shopped for his daughters, even placing an order at a local harness shop for a custom English saddle for Fran that he would never see completed. While other marines took jaunts to such places as Rotorua, the "valley of geysers," and Christchurch on the country's South Island, Sandy took his two weeks of R&R in March in a "Scotch town"—perhaps Dunedin on the South Island—where he slept between soft sheets and enjoyed eating "anything that wasn't G.I. cooking."[22]

With thousands of young Kiwi men deployed overseas in Africa and Europe, many of the marines found local women receptive to their charms, and many ended up marrying them. Competition between the Americans and New Zealanders occasionally erupted into violence, as with the April 3 "Battle of Manners Street," a tavern brawl that began at the Allied Service Club when a group of drunken Southern marines refused to let dark-skinned Maori soldiers enter. More than a thousand American and New Zealand troops and hundreds of civilians, some armed with belts and knives, were embroiled in the melee for four hours before the police could restore order.[23] (There is no indication that my grandfather took part in the fight.)

Rumors persist among family members that he fathered a child with a Kiwi girlfriend, but according to 23andMe, at least, I have no Bonnyman relatives in New Zealand.

Malaria was a scourge of Guadalcanal, and many marines came down with the debilitating disease after the battle. Sandy stayed healthy for months, attributing his immunity to, "hard work, and lots of it."[24] But on April 26, complaining of headaches, chills and malaise, he reported to a Navy doctor and learned that he had not escaped the pestilential mosquitoes after all.

"The So. Pacific islands," he noted ruefully, "are a far cry from Hollywood's portrayal of the Tropical Paradise. No Hedy Lamarrs, no dusky Belles, just mud, bugs and bad smells."[25]

Placed on bed rest for a week, he began treatment with quinine sulphate and Atabrine. The latter was despised by the troops, not just because it turned their skin a waxy yellow, but also because it was rumored to cause what former US Senator Bob Dole would one day call "erectile dysfunction."

Released under treatment, Sandy was back at the doctor's office on June 16, battling a fever of 102 degrees, and was readmitted to the hospital. He weighed just 157 pounds, having lost 41 pounds since his first marine physical. The next month was better, but after hard maneuvers he was in the hospital again on July 31, this time with a 105-degree temperature. All told, he spent more than thirty days in the hospital or on bed rest, but when he was discharged on August 7 the disease had finally run its course.

"I have gotten back some of my pep and zeal," he wrote to Jo. "We have been working hard and my appetite is like a horse's so that I look like 'Porky Pig.'"[26]

Sandy Bonnyman was widely admired by his men, not just for earning his lieutenant's bars the hard way. He was daring, competent, hard working, even keeled, and generous, going so far as to share his officer's whiskey rations with his men.[27]

"No matter what happened and we did have some rough times, on maneuvers, landing exercises, troop movements, etc. Sandy would never lose his temper or his perspective," Tracy Griswold recalled. "He was always very even tempered, and could always see the humorous side of any situation, no matter how tense it seemed at the moment."[28]

Sandy genuinely enjoyed the company of the men in his command, seeing in each a unique character. His three-page homage to the men he commanded on Guadalcanal reads like a character sketch for a Hollywood war epic:

"There were the Bird brothers from La. (the swamp country) . . . neither yet 20 and they have three more brothers in uniform; 'Tommy' Thompson from Mississippi is the wit of the company; Two Spanish boys, Vaca and Vasquez, always quiet, never hurrying but always working and both with [skills] that must be inherited from their Conquistador ancestors; Raw-boned lanky Doug had been a miner and a cowboy from Montana [who] drove the truck and got us through mud that no one else could; 'Hillbilly' Austin sometimes known as 'Governor' because he wants to be governor of Tennessee; Entwhistle (yes that is his name) is the faithful sheep dog of the outfit, the one to catch the little uninteresting routine jobs and who does them uncomplainingly; My right arm . . . is Henry Watson from near Brownsville, Texas (who) left a fine job with the telephone company to join the Marines . . . I have yet to find anything he can't do and do well; There were others who worked for us and all of them good men who stuck to the job day in and day out in spite of heat, wind, insects, timber rash, hard work and three Jap snipers."[29]

Having spent time as an enlisted man, Sandy was a tough but fair officer, recalled Victor Ornelas. Victor volunteered for the marines as a teenager after the Army told him he was too young, arriving at Camp Pendleton in September 1942. He and Sandy both sailed aboard the *Matsonia* for New Zealand in October, but they didn't meet until they pulled KP duty at the same time in Wellington. Victor spent the next week being entertained by the tall Tennessean's wild and woolly tales life in exotic New Mexico.

Months later, Victor was driving a jeep loaded with ammunition on Guadalcanal when he accidentally ran over a wire fence, which dragged behind him as he passed a group of officers. One yelled for him to stop.

"'Hey, you son of a so-and-so, stop! You're pulling up all that wire!'" Victor recalled. "I stopped and turned around to see who in the heck it was, figuring the worst he could do was bust me to a civilian. Well, who do I see coming up but your grandfather? He'd gotten his commission as a second lieutenant. I think he was really going to tear my head off, but when he saw it was me, he just gave me a smile and said, 'Don't do it again!'"[30]

Sandy also befriended Father William O'Neill, a Navy chaplain who would help oversee burial of the dead on Tarawa and return after the war to search for their graves. Sandy not only received communion from "the Padre," but also joked with him about their mutual acquaintance, New York Archbishop Francis Spellman, prelate for all Navy chaplains. The Southern rebel and the rugged priest, both fearless and eager for action, would themselves have made a pretty good duo in a war movie.

"When the Padre wasn't up in the front he was charging all over the muddy Guadalcanal roads in a truck with no windshield top or brakes on it," Sandy wrote. "He would drive from the front ten and twelve miles so that the boys in the rear areas could go to Mass."[31]

With the same theatrical flair that had so entertained his sisters when he was a boy, Sandy also regaled his men with tales about life in the rugged West, fishing and hunting expeditions, and his drinking exploits.[32]

My grandfather seldom passed up a chance to play games of chance, whether Acey-Deucy—a variant of backgammon—or poker, until long after midnight. On the decks of the USS *Heywood* the night before landing on Tarawa, he famously refused to accept payment for a $10 drinking debt incurred by Capt. Joseph Clerou, joking that if the captain were killed, he'd be happy to accept his brand-new combat boots as payment.[33]

Somehow, he always seemed to balance such easy camaraderie and playful spirit with his role as a leader and his deep understanding of the war's gravity.

"I found him a man of rare intelligence, understanding and compassion," wrote Richard W. Johnston, a United Press International correspondent who received a Marine Corps commendation for bravery on Tarawa. "He seemed to me one of the relatively few Americans in the Pacific war who fully comprehended the meaning of the war and the meaning of his own country."[34]

In light of his accomplishments and the widespread respect of both officers and enlisted men, it was no surprise when Sandy Bonnyman was appointed to the rank of first lieutenant in the US Marine Corps Reserve on September 1, 1943. It had been fourteen months since he'd arrived at boot camp as a buck private.

ELEVEN
BITTER PILLS

1942–1943

The deeper I delved into my grandfather's past, the more I realized how completely whitewashed his life had become since his death. Google "Bonnyman," and the Wikipedia article about Sandy always pops up on top. The information there isn't exactly wrong, but it's so shallow that it's closer to meme than man. Peering into shadows my family didn't even know existed, I was slowly chipping the plaster from St. Sandy. I'd always admired my grandfather, but only now was I beginning to mourn him.

The Second Marine Division had a long break from combat between Guadalcanal and Tarawa, in part because most of New Zealand's defense forces had been shipped off to fight in the Africa campaign.

But there was plenty to do, as men trained to operate new medium Sherman tanks, engineers refined the flame-throwing skills they'd first tested on Guadalcanal, and all worked hard to stay in fighting trim. Finally on September 15, 1943, the division was attached to the Fifth Amphibious Corps, a harbinger that they would soon be in action again.[1] They just didn't know where.

Plans to take Tarawa back from the Japanese had been brewing in earnest since March. Even before the fight for Guadalcanal had been wrapped up, marine and navy commanders were pondering next moves in the Central Pacific. With the Caroline and Marshall islands too far from ground-based bombers stationed in the Ellice Islands, the airfield at Tarawa soon became the next logical step in the island-hopping campaign.[2]

Commanders believed an assault on Betio would be a relatively pain-less way to achieve several goals, including capturing an airfield that would be able to provide critical support for successive campaigns and eliminating a potential threat to crucial shipping lanes between Hawaii and Australia. Just as important—maybe even more so—the marines had been looking for a laboratory to test men, equipment, tactics, and strategy in a full-scale amphibious assault on a heavily defended beach-head. Moving north toward the Japanese home islands via a series of enemy-held atolls and islands would be all but impossible without amphibious capabilities, and Tarawa was to be a high-stakes experiment.

By mid-October, the second interlude in New Zealand finally came to an end. Marines began boarding sixteen transport ships in Wel-lington Harbour, informed that they were going to conduct exer-cises at Hawkes Bay on New Zealand's northern tip. But that was a ruse intended to foil Japanese spies, as well as prevent marines going AWOL to remain with Kiwi brides or girlfriends. In fact, they were headed to Mele Bay on the island of Efate in the French-British administered New Hebrides islands some 1,800 miles to the north, where they would begin practicing amphibious landing.

Sandy boarded the *USS Heywood* on October 13, along with the rest of the 2nd Battalion, 18th Marines (or 2/18) Pioneers, which had been attached to Maj. Henry P. "Jungle Jim" Crowe's 2/8. Built in 1919, the *Heywood* had sailed between San Francisco and New York as the City of Baltimore for Panama Pacific Lines before being acquired by the Navy in 1940. A massive convoy finally departed November 1. Most of the men would never see New Zealand again.

"Along the rails the Marines watched Wellington, warm and gray and soft with remembered delights, slowly drop astern," wrote UPI reporter Johnston, who stood beside them. "And in many of the homes on Wellington's steep hills, moist-eyed girls waved unseen farewells."[3]

Despite his enviable record of achievement in just over a year as a marine, the war's seesaw between action and sheer boredom had taken its toll on my grandfather. He missed his wife, children, and mother, and his old domestic life now didn't look so bad.

"I would never make a peace-time soldier . . . I have great respect for the discipline and thoroughness of the Marine Corps methods, but it is definitely a grind and of a great sameness," he wrote. "In action it is all different, one has to deal with the unexpected and things move along fast so it is easier to forget how terribly lonely you really are, lonely even when you can't turn around without bumping into a Marine."[4]

Despite all appearances of success in business and the military, Sandy felt burdened by life and feared how he would be affected by the war.

"I have had to (at least in my own mind) swallow a lot of bitter pills in my thirty-three years. I guess in a way these things, these uncertainties, these disappointments have hardened me," he confided to Jo. "My recent life has not been one to soften up a person and the eventual results I often wonder about. I do believe Jo that no matter what turns up now I can keep my sense of values. I hope so."[5]

His regrets were many, from struggles with his father to his sometimes-volatile marriage. But he remained a devoted son, husband, and father, writing letters home almost weekly. Though stiffly formal when addressing both his parents as "Father and Mother," his frequent letters to his beloved Mumsie were relaxed and warmly conspiratorial.

Alex Bonnyman struggled with his talented son's rebellious, reckless streak. But Frances almost seemed to live vicariously through Sandy's high-spirited embrace of life and refusal to live according to anyone else's expectations. My great-grandmother was herself a non-conformist who scandalized neighbors by inviting poor families to have lunch at posh Bonniefield and attending services at a neighboring synagogue to the outrage of a sniffy local Protestant minister. She not only let her son have his head, but also constantly assured him she was on his side; she even promised to help him buy the horse farm in Kentucky he dreamed of when the war was over.[6]

Though work at the mine had kept him away from his daughters before the war, Sandy now desperately missed them. His letters to the girls were mostly cheery and chatty, emphasizing school, Catechism, helping their mother, and physical fitness. But with Fran, the only one old enough to read, he could be more vulnerable: "Daddy is expecting his big girl to look after everything while he is gone"; "I hope Alix doesn't forget her real Dada by the time I get home"; "I thought of you when I went to Mass this morning Baby and realized how much I would have loved taking you to Easter Mass at the Cathedral."[7]

Sandy's letters to his wife were full of love and longing, liberally sprinkled with terms of endearment—*Baby; my dearest Darling; my favorite gal.* Alas, my grandmother was not the best correspondent. "Mail call has not been good to me lately, Jo," Sandy wrote a few weeks before his death, noting that he had not received a letter from her since summer.[8]

His mother had been writing since the spring that Jo was "distracted" and paying little attention to the girls. He seemed to know all was not well in Santa Fe and understood that that his business partner and erstwhile best friend, Jimmie Russell, was the cause of the trouble. But rather than fume or rage, he and his mother devised a plan, by letter, to lure Jo away from Russell. In June, without judgment, Sandy began urging her to leave the house on East Garcia Street and move in with the Bonnymans in Knoxville for the duration of the war, so she would have more help and "the Babies" would be "one hundred percent on the playlist. . . . I honestly believe you will find the move very constructive too."[9]

My Granny Great had always loved Jo, treating her with kindness even as she recognized her deep insecurities. It was with politely controlled fury that she wrote "My Dearest Jimmie" warning him not to take advantage of Jo's vulnerability.

"While my son is on the other side of the world, having been sent by his Country to kill the betraying little yellow men, do you find what you are doing akin to betrayal? Whatever his shortcomings & faults may be, he, his brand of honor would never permit him to do the thing that you are doing," she wrote. "You are among those fortunate young Americans who will never know the horrors of this war & who can enjoy in security the peace and plenty of our beloved land. For this you must be very grateful. Could you not in your blessed security make a little sacrifice and let Jo alone while her husband is far away defending this very security? She could then go her way, coordinate her life, put out the Confusion you have brought into it, settle down and give a mother's thought and care to the little children who need it so profoundly."[10]

Sandy's campaign may have given Jo courage to end the affair. In June she left the girls in Tennessee as usual, but when she returned in August she informed them that they weren't going back to Santa Fe. The girls, and the Bonnymans, were thrilled.

But the plan to stay in Knoxville didn't last long. Jo spent the next couple of months in Florida with baby Alix and her nurse Rosa Dee while Fran attended school in Knoxville and Tina was cared for at

Bonniefield. In November, Jo retrieved Fran and took her to live at Mooney Cottages in Fort Lauderdale, leaving frail Tina behind.

Jo's attempted geographic cure had seemingly ended her affair with Jimmie Russell. But it didn't quiet her gnawing neediness, and she began bringing sailors and soldiers home "to entertain" while living in Florida.[11] Her tragic anxiety about living life without a man beside her would continue to shatter lives for decades to come.

Trouble had also been brewing with the Guadalupe Mining Company. The copper mine had made Sandy Bonnyman a wealthy man, but problems were already bubbling to the surface before he had finished training in California.

Despite enthusiastic reports from Jo—whom Russell had appointed as his bookkeeper despite her lack of experience—the operation was grinding to a halt. The heirs of I.J. Stauber, who owned the property leased by my grandfather, were dissatisfied with ten percent of declining profits and were clamoring to sell off the land, and one thousand tons of low-grade ore was sitting unsold because the market had collapsed.[12] In October, Sandy arranged to begin providing Jo's income from one of his New York bank accounts because receipts from the mine were no longer adequate.[13]

And despite nearly four years of impressive profits, Sandy had never started repaying his $5,000 loan from the Blue Diamond Investment Company. Russell finally made the first payment of $1,000, on July 1, 1942,[14] but the mine shut down in December and he stopped paying on the debt. Not long after, Frances Bonnyman quietly retired her son's obligations, which amounted to about $60,000 in today's dollars.

"Mumsie," Sandy wrote from New Zealand, "paying off my Blue Diamond note was the most wonderful thing for you to do."[15]

And there was one bitter pill that Sandy never revealed to his family. On July 23, 1943, he was arrested in Wellington for "rendering himself unfit for duty by excessive use of intoxicants." In punishment, he was immediately suspended from all duties and confined to quarters from July 27 to July 31.[16]

The arrest clearly had a sobering effect on my grandfather, and he began to see his alcoholic excesses in a new light. "It is amazing," he mused, "what extremes one goes to in this life to fool himself into thinking that he is having a wonderful time."[17]

The Marine Corps treated the incident as a minor blip on the record of an otherwise excellent officer, but it would taint my grandfather's legacy long after death.

The marines of the Second Division had no idea where they were headed on November 8 when they arrived at Mele Bay. But almost from the moment they anchored, they were practicing assaults on the beach with Higgins boats—wood-bottomed transport vehicles made in New Orleans—rubber rafts with oars, and seventy-five brand-new "landing vehicles, tracked," or LVT-1 amphibious tractors (aka amtracs), dubbed Alligators. Unfortunately, a shipment of new, rubber-wheeled LVT-2 tractors, known as Water Buffaloes, which had been specially adapted for use in Pacific combat, arrived late in the game, leaving the marines without an opportunity to try them out in the water.[18] Gen. Julian C. Smith, commander of the Second Marine Division, was unhappy with the results of his marines' first practice landings and ordered them onto the beaches over and over until there was simply no time left.

One pivotal development at Efate would greatly influence the coming invasion of Tarawa: Smith replaced Col. William M. Marshall with thirty-nine-year-old Col. David M. Shoup as commander of the 2nd Marine Regiment.[19] Though twenty years younger than

Marshall, Smith and other officers felt more confident in Shoup's ability to command.

After six days at Mele Bay, the massive convoy of troop transports, destroyers, support vessels, minesweepers, and carriers known as Task Force 53 steamed away from the New Hebrides. Even then, the marines knew only that they would be attacking a strongly defended atoll, and rumors that they were going to retake Wake Island spread like a virus throughout the convoy. They were gung-ho about that mission, relishing the chance to avenge Maj. James P.S. Devereux and the rest of the marines who had valiantly defended Wake before surrendering to the Japanese on December 23, 1941.

Had anyone bet on the actual destination, the tiny islet named Betio on an unheard-of atoll called Tarawa, his wallet would have been fat indeed on the eve of battle. "Wake," journalist Johnston wrote, "might have been easier, at that."[20]

But after nine months of boredom interrupted by bouts of malaria, loneliness, and an embarrassing arrest, Sandy Bonnyman was eager to get back into the fight. Lt. Ed Bridgeford, a navy corpsman sailing aboard the *Heywood* as it zigzagged along a north-westerly course toward Tarawa, "had never seen Sandy so happy or more excited and there was never a more enthusiastic Marine. . . . He raved over the Corps, his three blondes, and Santa Fe."[21]

Roy Holland Elrod, who would later retire from the Marine Corps as a lieutenant colonel after a long career, was a first lieutenant with the 8th Marines weapons company who got to know my grandfather during their twenty-six days together on the *Heywood*. At twenty-four, Elrod was also considered an "old man" by most of the marines.

"We were both sort of outsiders, so we fell in and did a lot of talking," Roy said at age ninety-six. "I found out he roamed around northern New Mexico and southern Colorado, and so had I. We'd even been to some of the same Navajo turquoise mines. . . . He told me he was a real, old-time prospector."[22]

Sandy was hopeful that the coming battle might be the Second Division's last before respite in Hawaii and maybe even a trip home for Christmas. Navy Capt. Harry Price, a doctor and family friend from Knoxville who had visited my grandfather in the hospital that summer, had assured him that officer rotations all but guaranteed him a trip home within three to six months.[23]

"I am counting like everything on Christmas '43 at home and can already taste that ham and hominy," my grandfather wrote his Mumsie.[24]

On November 14, Navy Adm. Harry Hill sent a message to the transports in Task Force 53: "This is the first American attack of a strongly defended atoll and with northern attack and covering forces, the largest Pacific operation to date." The transmission included maps of a bird-shaped island, code-named Helen, with landing beaches designated Red Beach No. 1, Red Beach No. 2, Red Beach No. 3, Green Beach, and Black Beach.

Five days later, Sandy took Communion and made his last confession on the decks of the *Heywood*. While they lay on their bunks late that night, he told his friend 1st Lt. Tracy Griswold that "a lot of shooting" had shown him that he "hadn't been as good as possible to all his family."[25] After the war, he said, he was going to change his life.

"Baby, there is a day coming when we can make up for the unnatural lives we have been living," he had written to Jo, "when we can relax and really feel some deep emotions besides hate, fear, anger."[26]

"I can't imagine . . . that Sandy ever did a mean thing in his life, but then, we all have our moments of remorse," wrote Griswold[27] (who was to become a tiny footnote to history years later, when a researcher offered evidence purporting to show that he had exhumed the bones of Amelia Earhart on Saipan).[28]

The first shift for the marines' pre-battle "breakfast"—by tradition, steak and eggs, though that wasn't always the case for everyone—arrived at ten o'clock on the night of the nineteenth, and there was little time for sleep. At 0320 on D-day, marines aboard the twenty transport ships of Task Force 53 anchored a mile beyond the narrow channel into Tarawa's lagoon assembled on deck. They descended hemp nets to waiting Higgins boats and LVTs as another seventeen fire-support vessels prepared to move into position.

Since November 13, heavy bombers from bases in the Ellice Islands, carrier-based fighter planes, and light bombers had been doing their best to "soften up" Betio's defenses, dropping some six million pounds of explosives on a square kilometer of sand.[29] Many marines were relieved to hear their officers' assurances that the engagement would be over quickly: "Before we started it was great fun. We grinned and chortled. We said, 'There won't be a Jap alive when we get ashore.'"[30]

"The Navy . . . made it sound pretty simple, so many tons of naval shells, aerial bombs, straffing [sic], Destroyer support and so on," Griswold recalled. "The night before we landed I can remember our tactical meeting in the wardroom and Col. Bill Amie [sic; Amey, commanding officer of 2/2] telling us that he'd see us across the island in three hours after the landing."[31]

First Lt. Alexander Bonnyman, Jr. was eager to fight the enemy he'd seen coming from a decade away, get back home and turn over a new leaf. With the brilliant spray of the Milky Way overhead and the Southern Cross tilting on the horizon, my grandfather swung over the edge of the *Heywood* and climbed down to Higgins boat No. 374, bobbing on the black sea below.

TWELVE
BONE SHOW
APRIL 2013

After JPAC's Bill Belcher declined to further excavate the site Mark Noah had considered most promising in his quest to locate long-lost Cemetery 27, Mark initiated excavations at his number-two site, the copra plant west of the shipping yard.

Mark was willing to try anything to find Cemetery 27, which some described as the "holy grail" and "lost ark" of Betio's many mysteries, because, alone among the island's numerous named or numbered cemeteries, no trace of it had ever been found since 1943. Mark even requested a sample of my mother's hair, for use in an experimental "episio-electric" device that Arpad Vass of the Oak Ridge National Laboratory—a well-known but controversial figure in forensic circles—claimed could detect a DNA match to any sub-surface human remains.

"It was pure science fiction," Mark said later.

For more than five years, Mark had rigorously maintained public deference and cooperation with JPAC officials, in the firm belief that the surest way to find the missing marines and bring them home was to stay in the agency's good graces. But he didn't have a true advocate at the agency until he met JPAC anthropologist Jay Silverstein in 2011.

"Mark had put together a crack team," Silverstein told the *New*

York Times. "They were innovative. They were open to new ideas. Tarawa is one of the most complex battlefields we have, and Mark was using the right composite of scientific members to piece together that puzzle."[1]

But Silverstein's efforts to bring JPAC together with History Flight for a full-scale recovery effort on Tarawa only managed to put him on the outs with more senior members of the agency, including Thomas Holland, then-scientific director of the Central Identification Laboratory.

Believing that Belcher, deputy director of the CIL, had promised to involve him the next time JPAC worked on Tarawa, Mark was surprised to learn in early 2013 that a JPAC team had been conducting excavations on Betio. After an exchange of testy emails, Belcher ended a heated phone conversation by telling Mark never to contact him again.[2]

Long frustrated by the agency's glacial pace and lack of progress, inept public relations skills, internecine squabbling, and reluctance to give credit where due, Mark Noah finally decided he was done playing the good soldier.

"The CIL is so far away from the objective, and our experience dealing with them had been so negative, we finally decided there was no point to trying to work with them," he said. "We decided, 'Hey, we have this great opportunity, let's not waste it.'"[3]

He quietly converted a small room behind the Betio Town Council hall into a lab, stocking it with shovels, picks, five-gallon buckets in Home Depot orange, wheelbarrows, and enough lumber and hardware to build sand screens. He then began approaching owners and heads of households of property on Betio where anomalies had been detected, offering to pay them $50 a day for permission to dig, ten times the average daily wage on South Tarawa. He hired archaeologists Drew Buchner and Eric Albertson from Memphis, Tennessee-based Panamerican Consultants, Inc.; flew in

willing grunts like Vietnam marine veteran Glenn Prentice and
Harlan Glenn, a Los Angeles-based researcher who advises film
companies on World War II artifacts; and recruited local men to do
heavy labor. Crucially, he also persuaded the New Zealand High
Commission on Tarawa, which has considerable influence with the
Kiribati government, to give him a letter of support in exchange for
help in locating the seventeen Kiwi and five British coastwatchers
beheaded by the Japanese in 1942.

History Flight's gang of archaeological outlaws started working
in February 2013. Working ten- to twelve-hour days, seven days a
week, the team failed to uncover any significant American remains
for the first several months. But there were plenty of other items
of interest, including a buried bunker containing Japanese remains
and hundreds of small human bones and war-era artifacts.

Once the operation was up and running, Mark called and asked
if I wanted to come down back to Tarawa and get my hands dirty.
Of course I did.

I had more than my fill of archaeology's apparently negligible thrills
and chills during all those hot, dull hours hanging around JPAC
digs in 2010. The antidote to such tedium, I learned not long after
returning in April 2013, was working the end of a shovel, hauling
buckets of wet sand, and endlessly shaking crude sifting screens
beneath a relentless tropical sun. The work was exhausting, filthy,
sweaty—and deeply satisfying.

By the time I arrived, Drew and Eric had systematically gridded
out and conducted the excavation of several neatly carved "units" in
a 500-square-foot sandy yard between two ramshackle family com-
pounds. This was the former site of Cemetery 25, just a few feet
from where JPAC had recovered three marines the previous fall,
based on History Flight research.

Sporting marine-like camouflage pants, an olive drab t-shirt, rough-out boots, and a camouflage boonie hat, Harlan Glenn spent most of his time in the lab cleaning up artifacts and remains. And videographer Marc Miller was back for the first time since 2010, hired to shoot video of History Flight's illicit excavations.

Ted Somes, a seventy-two-year-old US Coast Guard veteran, also stopped by to help for a couple of hours each morning. He had come to Betio to pay respects to his cousin, Pfc. Arthur D. Somes Jr. Somes's helmet liner had been discovered inside the remains of an amphibious vehicle unearthed by Australian sewer workers in 1979, along with the remains of three marines, none of whom turned out to be Somes. Ted's family had long ago buried remains identified as his cousin's at Arlington National Cemetery, learning of the helmet lining only years later from a newspaper story. Now Ted had come to Tarawa, courtesy of a grant from Wish of a Lifetime, to fulfill his dream of playing "Taps" for his cousin.

"I had a feeling of closeness to my cousin that I had never felt before," he said later. "Maybe it was because I was on the ground where he fought and died. Maybe because there were some of his bones still there. Maybe his spirit needed a family member to come and say thank you, that we care and are not bitter about his death but want to remember his life and sacrifice."[4]

(Arthur Somes is in fact buried at Arlington, according to JPAC. His helmet liner was, for unknown reasons, associated with a skull subsequently identified as that of Pfc. Thomas Scurlock.[5])

Through Ted I met Kantaake Kerry Corbett, a Tarawa native who was serving as his guide, driver, and honorary granddaughter for the duration of his stay (tired of Westerners pronouncing her softly lyrical name *Kentucky*, she introduced herself as Kerry). Then twenty-eight, Kantaake is a rare dual American-Kiribati citizen, daughter of an itinerant California surfer named Chuck Corbett and Toka Rakobu of Bikenebeu village on South Tarawa.

I would learn a lot from her in my next couple of trips to the islands.

Every morning our crew would meet History Flight's steadfast local labor crew, four young men named Aman, Titang, Eru, and Katerak. As soon as we started working, crowds of cheery children would gather from around the densely packed neighborhood and the pervasive odor of pig manure, fish guts, and burning garbage seared our nostrils all day long.

Many days we shoveled and sifted literally hundreds of tons of wet sand (3,200 pounds per cubic yard) and endured the misery of hacking away at indestructible waste in buried trash pits, only to find nothing. But sometimes, things got interesting. Beneath what turned out to be metal-pipe fencing that had bordered Cemetery 25, we came upon five American helmets, blackened and encrusted with coral sand after seven decades in the ground. The surrounding earth soon yielded scores of small hand and foot bones, left behind when Army Graves removed remains in 1946, as well as spoons, olive-drab plastic toothbrushes, glass bottles filled with oily brown insect repellent, ammo clips, and countless pieces of rubberized canvas ponchos.

One morning, Drew let loose a rebel yell and shouted, "We've got a dog tag!" Children, both naked and clothed, joined in our celebratory eruption.

The perfectly legible stainless steel dog tag had belonged to a Lt. Col. D.K. Claude. Back at the lab, Harlan delved into the literature and called on a satellite phone to read a brief passage from Joseph Alexander's *Utmost Savagery*: "Japanese machine gunners killed one observer, Lt. Col. David K. Claude, as he accompanied the 2nd Marines scout-sniper operations against inland strong points."[6] In addition, *Time-Life* journalist Robert Sherrod had noted Claude's burial place in his 1944 book, *Tarawa: A Battle.* It was the most significant find in months of hard labor, a tangible connection to the battle, a name, a history.

"This is the best day I've ever had down here, man," Drew said that evening, holding a dripping can of Fiji Gold as we took our accustomed sunset beach stroll.

One afternoon while sloshing back to shore after exploring some of the grounded vessels on the reef, I spotted a local man spearfishing. As he towed a jury-rigged processing float, his goggled face periodically popped up out of the water. As I waded closer, my shirt damp from a gentle squall that had drifted quickly over the sapphire waters, I eyed his makeshift barge. The man stood up and gave me a huge smile, tugging the mask to his forehead. The salty pungency of blood rose from a stack of gutted silver bonefish, a couple of puffers, and a beautiful green-and-orange parrotfish that lay fading in the sun.

"Where you house?" he said.

"Uh . . . my house? I'm from America."

His grin spread even wider in recognition as he pantomimed digging.

"America?" he said, clapping his hands. "Bone show! *Bone show!*"

I don't think most of the people on Betio understood what we were doing, or why, but the coconut telegraph was buzzing with our presence.

"This is the runway," Kantaake shouted, waving a smooth brown arm toward the tarmac of Bonriki International Airport, where a scrum of kids kicked at a soccer ball in the rain. "You want to drive down it?"

"Absolutely!" I hollered from the back seat.

"Wait!" Ted Somes yelped. "How do you know no planes are coming?"

"Don't worry, my American grandfather," Kantaake said, batting her dark eyes at Ted before swerving to the right.

We were on our way to Tabon Te Keekee, a placid, simple resort owned by Kantaake's family on the islet of Abatao, just north of the airport. Ted was in the front seat and I was hanging my head out the back window, face upturned to the warm rain. The History Flight crew, scheduled to leave the next morning on the same flight as I, was in another car behind us. After a week of sweat-intensive digging at Cemetery 25, we were all ready for a break.

Tabon Te Keekee is one of several businesses owned by Kantaake's entrepreneurial family, including Kiribati Holidays travel agency and the Chatterbox Café near the village of Bikenebeu. The café was a welcome alternative to waiting in the stifling confines of the airport lounge, offering Wi-Fi, excellent coffee, luggage service and check-in, and shuttle rides to departing Tarawa visitors.

At ebb tide, the resort is a five-minute walk across smooth, algae-covered sand from the end of the road on tiny Buota. When the tide is flowing, the channel fills with emerald water and your only options are hitching a ride on a motor-powered outrigger canoe or swimming.

Here, just eighteen miles from Betio (with a local driver like Kantaake, an hour's drive; results may vary), Tarawa is more Gilligan's Island than noxious hellhole. Tucked away in the crook of the atoll's elbow, Abatao is lushly jungled, sparsely populated, and nestled between warm lagoon waters and crashing, deep-blue Pacific waves. There are no cars, feces, or twining columns of toxic smoke; all you smell is jungle and warm sand. Leaf-thatched shelters for lounging and eating and hammocks for sleeping dot the meticulously swept sandy ground in the shade of tall pandanus, coconut, and breadfruit trees. The dogs on Abatao sport shiny coats; some are even neutered.

Driving back to Betio after dark, Kantaake told me about the time she'd spent living in Reno, Nevada, when her expat father, Chuck Corbett, went home for medical treatment after severely breaking an ankle in a surfing accident. Her sister Annie came along, as did the sisters' four young children. Annie stayed, but Kantaake brought the children back to Tarawa after about a year.

"In the US, I could get a job and make money," she said. "But then I would have to leave my children in day care and that would almost be as expensive as the money I could make in my job. And I wasn't raising my own children. Here I have family all around me to help. I don't have to worry about them or pay for child care."

She was also saddened by the insecurity and unhappiness she saw in citizens of the wealthiest, most powerful nation in history.

"They are always so afraid what will happen to them when they are old, that they will not have enough money. Here, I don't have to worry about whether I will be taken care of when I am old. I know I will be. That's how we are. You never have to worry," she said.

She cheerfully acknowledged the laid-back attitude of her people, which so many foreigner visitors have found maddening.

"We're just more here and now," Kantaake said. "We believe in not worrying too much and just being grateful for today."[7]

As I loaded my pack into Kantaake's car for a ride to the airport the next morning, a high-centered red Toyota pickup rumbled into the parking lot at Mary's, raising a cloud of dust. I recognized the two men in the truck as members of the local Australian military detachment, whom we'd met at a sunrise commemoration of ANZAC Day, the worldwide, annual memorial to fallen soldiers of the British Empire, begun in 1916 to honor Australian and New Zealand troops killed in the disaster at Gallipoli.

Ginger-bearded, lanky Chief Petty Officer Scott Dawson of the Australian Defence Force and burly Lt. Commander J.J. Williams of the Royal Australian Navy stepped out of the truck and strode purposefully toward me; I wondered if I was about to be detained for some unknown crime.

"Hello, mate," Williams said. "Is it true you're Bonnyman's son?"

"Actually, he's my grandfather."

"That's right, he was older, wasn't he?" Williams said, thrusting out a meaty paw. "I'd be honored to shake your hand."

I started my well-practiced speech about how I'd earned no honor, which properly belonged to my grandfather, mother, and aunty, each of whom sacrificed . . . .

"Sure, sure, I don't care about all that," the burly Aussie interrupted.

What he *cared* about was Bonnyman.

"You know, without him, that battle goes on and a lot more Americans are killed. He went right up, leading the charge up that big bunker on the other side and who knows what might have happened if he hadn't taken it out?" Williams said. "He's a real hero, your grandfather, not like this crap today where everyone's a 'hero.' You're to be commended in coming down here, and I wish you luck in finding his body."

The whole encounter was over in a couple of minutes.

"Did they really just do that?" Kantaake said. "Your grandfather is still a pretty big deal to some people."

Nothing stays secret for long, and news of History Flight's pirate archaeology soon got back to JPAC. Eschewing the petty tactics it tried in 2010, the agency decided to take a more cooperative approach, and in August, Mark flew to Hawaii to meet with civilian administrator Johnie Webb, who always seemed to remain above the sniping. Mark reported that History Flight teams had filled seven large, watertight Pelican carrying cases with bones from perhaps fifty individuals, as well as scores of artifacts. Instead of excoriating Mark for going rogue, some in the agency noticed once again that History Flight was not some fly-by-night outfit trying to make bank on eBay.

"When Mark decided he was going to do excavation, boom, he did it," Bill Belcher said. "He hired professional archaeologists, dentists, and all that. And we never had a problem with any of that, as long as these groups are professionalizing."[8]

BONA

THIRTEEN
INFERNO
NOVEMBER 20–21, 1943

Since the Japanese expected that any attack would come from the open ocean to the south and west of Betio, the lagoon side was not as heavily defended. At 0441 on D-day, after realizing that the Americans were going to approach the island from the lagoon, the Japanese defenders launched their first salvo, a red-star cluster shell, and cranked their four eight-inch guns around to the north.

A scheduled American airstrike at dawn failed to materialize, which allowed the Japanese to more effectively shell the convoy floating between two and four miles northwest of the island. At 0700, the minesweepers *Requisite* and *Pursuit* took fire as they led destroyers *Ringgold* and *Dashiell* into the lagoon.[1]

As smoke from a burning ammunition dump choked the skies above Betio, the Japanese began to bombard the amphibious LVTs and Higgins boat transports at their departure line more than a mile out into the lagoon, causing Gen. Julian Smith to delay the assault from 0845 to 0900.

As soon as the Second Scout and Sniper Platoon under Lt. William Deane Hawkins and Lt. Alan Leslie reached shore, tasked with capturing a five-hundred-yard-long pier jutting into the lagoon, they reported three alarming facts: The water at the edge of the reef was only three feet deep, not enough to accommodate the four-foot draft of a Higgins boat; there appeared to be plenty of resistance left, despite the navy's bombardment; and LVTs were hanging up on a three-foot coconut-log seawall, unable to move inland. All three problems would contribute to heavy casualties on D-day.

The low tide was no obstacle to the armored LVT-1 "Alligators" and LVT-2 "Water Buffaloes," whose wheels or tracks took over as soon as they hit the reef. But they were also sitting ducks; by the end of the battle, ninety of 125 deployed LVTs had been destroyed by Japanese fire or mines, or knocked out at the seawall.[2]

But marines on LVTs were the lucky ones. Those on Higgins boats fell victim to the "the tide that failed," the shallow water that forced navy coxswains to disgorge their cargo of heavily laden marines some six to eight hundred yards offshore, where some drowned. Those who found footing in chest-deep water had no choice but to slosh shoreward into relentless Japanese fire.

Hundreds of marines were killed before even reaching the beach. Exact numbers are not available, but one chaplain counted seventy-six bobbing in the surf in his sector alone when the fighting was over,[3] while thirty-nine of the seventy men assigned to shore-party duty on Red Beach 1 never made it to the island.[4]

Although some historians have sought to deflect blame for the tide debacle, navy and marine planners were aware that shallow water on the reef could cause problems on November 20. Maj. Frank Holland, a New Zealander who had served as Britain's Resident Commissioner of the Gilbert Islands for fifteen years, warned the Americans that the assault would encounter what he called a "dodging tide" that would doom hundreds of marines to death on the reef. Alas, senior officers said it was too late to rearrange timetables short of calling off the assault, which they weren't willing to do.[5]

Holland was right, though the scientific term is "apogean neap tide," an especially low high tide that occurs when the moon is farthest from the earth; one of Tarawa's two easily predicted neap tides in 1943 led to terrible carnage on on D-day.[6] Some argue, however, that the shallow tide made it easier for the LVTs to reach the shore, since they could move three times as fast once their tracks gripped onto something solid.[7]

Descriptions of the first hours of battle read like infernal visions.

"The island was a mass of smoke, flames of different colors, bright red, gray, black, and stuff was just blowing up like mad. Naval gunfire was coming down on top of us. A lot of marines' entire combat careers lasted only a few seconds. The landing craft ramps went down, and they were shot dead," said Dean Ladd, who was shot in the torso before reaching the beach and taken back to the *Heywood*.[8]

Hawkins and his men were first to reach the pier. Charging up a seaplane ramp, they used grenades, rifles, and flamethrowers to take out a machine-gun position and two structures, which allowed others to reach the pier and make their way to the beach from pylon to pylon. A landing team came ashore on Red Beach 1, the westernmost lagoon assault zone, at 0910, followed by another on Red Beach 3 east of the pier at 0917, and another at Red 1.

S.Sgt. William Bordelon, an assault engineer, one of just four marines to survive a direct hit on their amtrac, landed on Red 1. Once ashore, he took out two pillboxes, then continued to fight even after a charge went off in his hand and he was struck by machine-gun fire. After going back into the water to rescue an injured man, he assaulted another Japanese position before being killed by machine-gun fire. He would later be awarded the Medal of Honor, as would Hawkins, after falling on the second day of battle.

Sgt. Elwin Hart and his two-man radio team followed Hawkins's team into shore, where they took shelter in an abandoned mortar pit just fifty yards from the pier. One of Hart's team, Pfc. Elmer

Mathies Jr., was killed by a gunshot wound to the neck when he peeked above the rim of the pit, and was later buried in Cemetery 27. Hart spent almost the entire battle hunkered down in that hole, where for many hours his Morse code signals were the only communication link between Gen. Julian Smith and Col. David Shoup, earning himself the nickname "the voice of Tarawa."[9]

Those first hours of battle flirted with disaster. At 0959, Maj. John F. Schoettel famously radioed Shoup, "Receiving heavy fire all along beach. Unable to land at all. Issue in doubt." When the colonel ordered him to land on Red 2 at 1015, Schoettel replied, "We have nothing left to land."[10]

A short time later, Schoettel waved down a medium-tank company and ordered it to land, in hopes of softening up the beach. Eight tanks under the command of 1st Lt. Lou Largey, six commanded by 1st Lt. Ed Bale, and three others rolled down the lowered ramps of their transport vehicles and rumbled across the reef toward shore.

On Red Beach 3, only Largey's *Colorado* survived. Bale's platoon, assigned to land at Red Beach 1, ran into all sorts of trouble. Not eager to drive over the bodies of dead marines, he made a split-second decision not to plow through a break in the seawall and instead headed west toward the "bird's beak," Betio's northernmost point. But four of his tanks foundered in shell holes—including the *Cobra*, which remains visible today in surprisingly good condition—and only *China Gal*, commanded by Bale, and *Cecilia*, made it ashore around 1110. *China Gal* soon lost its 75mm gun when a Japanese light tank managed to land a shot right down the barrel, and Bale then took command of *Cecilia*.[11]

Three of Tarawa's four eventual Medal of Honor recipients, Shoup, Bordelon, and Hawkins, were all ashore in the early hours of the fighting. The fourth, Sandy Bonnyman, had been assigned with the rest of his 2/18 Pioneers to shore-party duty, which meant unloading supplies for use at forward positions.

But the chaotic early hours of fighting had blown my grandfather's unit's best-laid plans, and 2/18's lead team didn't reach the pier until 1630 on D-day. Even after they had helped extinguish a fire raging atop the damaged pier, they determined that it couldn't be used to deliver supplies until it was repaired.

At two o'clock on the morning of D+1 (November 21), Sandy's friend 1st Lt. Tracy Griswold crept forward under cover of darkness in search of Col. Shoup's command post. He returned an hour and a half later with instructions to abandon the pier "and return at a time when it would be possible to land supplies without the risk of small arms fire and mortar fire." Some of the 2/18 shore party began evacuating casualties to the USS *Zeilin* while others established security lines at the foot of the pier and on Red Beach 2 to the west. On orders from Maj. George H.L. Cooper, Sandy and 1st Lt. Michael Mosteller assembled thirty marines from their F Company and 2/8 I Company, who spent the first night of the battle holding the security perimeter on Red 2 and retrieving injured marines from forward lines.[12]

At some point early in the battle, my grandfather caught the attention of combat photographer Cpl. Obie Newcomb.

"It was my job to cover the battle as a photographer and . . . I was in the front lines all the time. The reason this Lt. stuck in my mind was whenever there was a job to be done he was the first to volunteer. I can still see him as he went up to the front to bring back a wounded Marine in his deep Southern drawl," recalled Newcomb, who initially believed the officer's name was "Barnaman."[13]

From that point on, Newcomb tried to hover around Sandy. The photographer even let him borrow his entrenching tool to dig the foxhole where he would famously capture him amid his fellow marines as they huddled beneath the shattered, blackened trunks of palm trees, waiting to assault the bunker on D+2.[14]

Despite sustaining heavy casualties, by 1800 on D-day the marines had established footholds two hundred yards in from the "bird's beak" and some four hundred yards inland from the pier, including the northeast-southwest runway of the airfield. That night, dug into their foxholes, the marines anxiously anticipated a counterattack that never came.

Nobody knew it yet, but Adm. Keiji Shibasaki, commander of the Japanese forces on Betio, was dead. He'd been killed while standing in front of his looming steel-reinforced concrete command bunker when an American shell smashed to earth precisely where Shibasaki and his top officers were standing at mid-afternoon on D-day.

According to after-battle accounts by the few Japanese captured, compassion may have killed the much-admired Shibasaki. As the fighting raged, the admiral had allowed wounded *rikusentai*—Japanese marines—to be sheltered in the command bunker.[15] When things started getting too crowded, rather than have them removed, he decided to relocate his command to a smaller bunker on the south side of the island, away from the main thrust of the assault. As his officers assembled in front of the bunker, an unknown American scout apparently saw them and radioed in the fire request that cut the head off the Japanese command just hours into the battle.[16]

The sudden loss of leadership and severe damage to exposed communications wires had left the Japanese utterly rudderless. Had Shibasaki survived, historians surmise he would have mounted a massive counter-attack during that first night that could have proved disastrous to the marines. But thanks to that single, direct hit, the Americans were spared.

Gen. Smith gave orders to step up the fight in the early morning hours of D+1. But as the sun climbed toward its zenith, Shoup radioed, "Situation ashore uncertain."

"From dawn until about 1300, D plus 1 on Betio was like a supplement or extension of D Day," wrote correspondent Johnston, who was hunkered down with the marines. "The fighting was savage beyond belief, the issue was still in doubt."[17]

From his command post in the shelter of a bunker on Red Beach 2, Shoup requested at 0513 that the 1st Battalion, 18th Marines (1/18), commanded by Maj. Lawrence C. Hayes Jr. land on Red Beach 2. The unit encountered heavy machine-gun fire as it waded across the reef, but eventually made it ashore largely intact, where it began to push west to join up with 3/2, which had held the "bird's beak" through the night.[18] Shoup ordered 1/2 and 2/2 to push south from their line in the middle of the airfield and 3/2 to leave its toehold and capture west-facing Green Beach.

Carrier-based navy planes bombed and strafed the airstrip south of the American lines on D+1, allowing elements of 1/2 and 2/2 to clear out several machine-gun positions and drive across the remaining runways to Black Beach on Betio's two-and-a-quarter-mile-long southern shore. LVTs were soon ferrying food, water, ammunition, and medical supplies to the marines holding the beach, returning to the lagoon side loaded with wounded.[19]

Shortly after 1100, 2nd Lt. Thomas N. Greene called in destroyer strikes on Japanese positions south of 3/2's line. Once the dust had settled, Maj. Michael P. Ryan and 3/2 followed the medium tanks *China Girl* and *Cecilia* to Green Beach, meeting minimal resistance. By noon on the second day of battle, the western end of Betio was in American hands. That afternoon, Smith committed the Sixth Marines to the fight for the first time, sending some ashore at Green Beach to push east across the airfield, and others to the neighboring island of Bairiki, to which Japanese troops had begun to flee.

Contrary to some later reports, my grandfather was never idle during the Battle of Tarawa.

Sometime during the day on November 21, Maj. George R.L. Cooper committed the sixty men under Bonnyman and Mosteller "to assault action." But the after-action shore-party report written by Lt. Col. Chester A. Salazar, Sandy's CO, does not give further details.[20] However, when compared to Salazar's report, my grandfather's Medal of Honor citation seems to be in error when it states that he led a group armed with explosives and flamethrowers to destroy "several hostile installations *before the close of D-day*" [21] (author's emphasis); it may be that the citation got the action correct, but misreported the chronology.

Salazar's report lays to rest frequent speculation that Sandy "abandoned" his shore-party duties without orders, and should nullify once and for all Joseph Alexander's assertion that as a shore-party officer, he was "essentially out of a job for the first fifty hours or so."[22] Certainly photographer Obie Newcomb was impressed: "It seemed to me he was the busiest man in the whole battle of Tarawa."[23]

Even as other units had continually pushed forward, Maj. Jim Crowe's 2nd Battalion, 8th Marines had stalled badly on Red 3. Pinned on a narrow beachhead by three machine gun positions firing from a steel pillbox, log wall, and enormous, mysterious sand-covered structure about a hundred yards southwest of the short Burns-Philp pier, the unit continued to take casualties throughout the second day of fighting. When the second platoon of F Company, led by 2nd Lt. George Bussa, attempted to assault the blockhouse from the east, "the enemy laid down such a withering fire that the group was almost wiped out."[24] (Bussa, like Sandy, was recorded as having been buried in Cemetery 27.)

After Bussa's assault failed, my grandfather led an attack on the southern entrance of the sand-covered monolith, "killing many of the defenders before they were forced to withdraw and replenish their supply of ammunition and grenades."[25] (Some accounts have placed these assaults on D-day. However, after-action reports confirm that my grandfather's 2/18 did not land until 0430 on D-day, and the Marine Corps' Historical Division places both attempts on D+1.)

Exposed to constant fire and making no progress, Crowe decided to move his command post back to the seawall in the shelter of the abandoned hulk of LVT 23. A twelve-man patrol sent to protect the short commercial pier killed fifteen Japanese at the expense of just two casualties during the night, but by the end of D+1, 2/8 had made the least progress of any unit on the island. An exasperated Crowe was forced to wait out the night, knowing they'd get nowhere until they knocked out those three Japanese positions.

At 2030 on November 21, Col. Merritt A. "Red Mike" Edson made his way to the island to relieve a wounded Shoup, who had orchestrated the first two days of battle. Having pulled the marines together and taken much of the island despite the disastrous landing on D-day, Shoup was put in command of seven landing teams.

William Deane Hawkins led the charge to clear the pier on D-day, and later took out "three pillboxes before he was caught in a burst of Japanese shellfire and mortally wounded."[26] Engineer William Bordelon also had fallen on D-day.

So when the sun set on the second day of the battle, in other words, the actions for which three of Tarawa's Medal of Honor recipients would be recognized were in the books. The fourth, my grandfather, remained in action, but discrepancies in various accounts—the Medal of Honor citation, photographer Newcomb's recollections, the Marine Corps' official account of the battle, Salazar's report, letters sent to my great-grandparents, and later published accounts—have made it all but impossible to piece together a reliable chronology of his movements prior to his fatal assault on the bunker on November 22.

These actions, at least, are well established: After landing, Sandy and his second-in-command organized a security detail on Red 3, led a team of combat engineers into action, joined up with Crowe, and failed in his first attempt to take the blockhouse.

According to 2nd Lt. J.L. Dent Jr. of Headquarters Battalion, at some point during the early morning of November 21, Sandy "organized a platoon of about fifty men from what there were on the beach, and went forward and posted them in a defensive line for the night. The next morning this group started knocking out pillboxes. . . . He used riflemen to fire into the opening and keep the Japs down, then he would run out, get on top, and throw dynamite or TNT inside and clear it out that way."[27]

At some point, Crowe learned that Sandy was an engineer with extensive mining demolitions experience and began consulting him about taking the hulking blockhouse. Marvin Sheppard, a private in intelligence with 2/8 Headquarters Company, recalled listening in as my grandfather tried to convince the major that the only way to take the bunker was with demolitions.

"I remember Maj. Crowe thought they shouldn't use explosives, because if it was an ammo dump, we'd all get killed," said Sheppard, who contacted me after seeing a news report on CNN. "The first time I ever saw your grandfather he was saying, 'I doubt very much if they would build a weapons building that close to the water.' He said he didn't think there was any danger."[28]

Crowe evidently found that argument convincing enough to send Sandy forward to advise Maj. William Chamberlin on a plan to take the bunker.

By the end of the first day of battle, Betio was a horrific charnel ground. Blistering tropical sun had not only drained the marines of energy, leaving their skin burned, lips cracked and bleeding, but also transformed hundreds American and Japanese corpses into a ghastly mockery of their former humanity.

There was neither time nor equipment to bury the dead during the fighting, and within hours, many bodies had bloated to bursting, leaving splotches of putrid, blackening entrails. The reek of death clung to the marines' hair, skin, and clothing. As Robert Sherrod famously observed, "Betio would be more habitable if the Marines could leave for a few days and send a million buzzards in."[29]

"Even toward the end of the first day, the stench was already bad. There was no breeze blowing at all, we were straddling the equator, and it was about a hundred degrees. Bodies just lay around there, bloating within two or three hours, tearing the uniforms open and releasing the stench," recalled Max Clampitt, a machine gunner with the 6th Regiment who later served seven terms as mayor of Hobbs, New Mexico. "It lasted the whole five days I was there and left a little fog, a kind of haze over the whole island. It sticks with me to this day."[30]

By 1800 on D+1, the marines held the entire western end of Betio as well as most of the airfield, and were gradually drawing the noose around the remaining Japanese forces. Supplies and vehicles were rumbling off the pier and reinforcements made their way to the lines. Before surrendering command to Edson, Shoup offered this famous assessment of where things stood: "Casualties: many. Percentage dead: Unknown. Combat efficiency: We are winning."[31]

The issue was no longer in doubt, but the fight was not yet over, and Sandy Bonnyman was still in it.

Sandy Bonnyman, left, with his father, Alexander Bonnyman, 1912. *Author's collection.*

Sandy Bonnyman at six or seven years old, Knoxville, Tennessee. *Author's collection.*

Sandy and Jo Bonnyman, date and location unknown. *Author's collection.*

Sandy Bonnyman at Camp Judgeford, New Zealand, September 1943. *Author's collection.*

Sandy Bonnyman, second from right, in a foxhole during the fighting on Tarawa, November 21 or 22, 1943. Note the lack of a helmet cover and three stripes indicating shore-party duty. *Obie Newcomb/US Marine Corps.*

Marines swarm up the sand-covered bunker during the final assault on November 22, 1943. Sandy Bonnyman is not visible; he had already been killed at the leading edge of the bunker, out of sight, when this photo was taken. *Obie Newcomb/US Marine Corps.*

Posthumous 1944 portrait of Sandy Bonnyman by Italian artist Arturo Noci.
Clay Bonnyman Evans.

Frances Bonnyman, age twelve, receives her father's Medal of Honor from Secretary of the Navy James Forrestal on January 22, 1947. To Forrestal's right are her mother, Josephine Russell, and grandfather, Alexander Bonnyman Sr. *US Marine Corps.*

Close-up of Sandy Bonnyman's Medal of Honor. *Clay Bonnyman Evans.*

The author stands at the northwest corner of "Bonnyman's Bunker," where his grandfather led the assault, in 2010. The same corner is visible in Obie Newcomb's photo above. *Clay Bonnyman Evans.*

Local children play on the ruins of the medium Sherman tank *Cobra*, which remains stuck in the shell hole where it foundered nearly three-quarters of a century after the battle. *Clay Bonnyman Evans.*

A Kiribati girl poses atop the wreckage of an amphibious vehicle from the battle, surrounded by garbage. *Clay Bonnyman Evans.*

History Flight's Kristen Baker, foreground, left, Paul Schwimmer, center, and John Frye, right, begin the final excavation of Sandy Bonnyman's remains on May 29, 2015. *Clay Bonnyman Evans.*

Kristen Baker brushes away sand, exposing remains in the grave next to Sandy Bonnyman, whose skull is visible behind. Note gold dental work used to identify his remains. *Clay Bonnyman Evans.*

The skull of 1st Lt. Alexander Bonnyman, Jr., uncovered after lying hidden for more than seventy-one years in the sands of Betio island. *Clay Bonnyman Evans.*

Sandy Bonnyman's Zippo lighter, located by the author beneath his remains on Tarawa. *Clay Bonnyman Evans.*

The skeletal remains of Sandy Bonnyman prior to their removal. The helmet belonging to another marine, Ronald Vosmer, is visible to the left. *Clay Bonnyman Evans.*

Members of the History Flight team that contributed to the recovery of Cemetery 27. From left, front row: Hillary Parsons, Clay Bonnyman Evans, Reid Joyce, Paul Schwimmer. Middle: David Senn, Corinne D'Anjou, Mark Noah, Ed Huffine, Glenn Prentice, Rick Snow. Back: Jim Williams, Kurt Hiete, James Goodrich, Katie Rasdorf, John Frye, Kristen Baker. *Jeremy Edward Shiok.*

Retired US Army Lt. Gen. Michael S. Linnington, then-director of the Defense POW/
MIA Accounting Agency, left, with the author, center, and Mark Noah, founder
and director of History Flight, Inc., following a lying-in-honor ceremony for Sandy
Bonnyman in Knoxville, Tennessee on September 26, 2015. *Jeremy Edward Shiok.*

A custom-built caisson transports the remains of 1st Lt. Alexander Bonnyman, Jr. to his final resting place at Berry Highland Memorial Cemetery, Knoxville, Tennessee, September 27, 2015. *Jeremy Edward Shiok.*

US Marine Corps Maj. Gen. Burke W. Whitman hands a folded American flag to Frances Bonnyman Evans at her father's funeral on September 27, 2015. Visible to Evans' right are her sister, Alexandra Bonnyman Prejean, the author, and Margot McAllister, surviving daughter of their late sister, Josephine. *Cpl. Sarah Graham/US Marine Corps.*

FOURTEEN
KALEIDOSCOPE
NOVEMBER 22, 1943

Plans were laid for the third day of battle before the sun rose on November 22. Navy ships were to blast Japanese forces that were holed up on the eastern end of Betio with a barrage of fourteen- and sixteen-inch shells. At 0700, carrier-based aircraft were to make runs over the same area for twenty minutes, repeated at 0830, 0930, and 1030.

Col. Merritt A. "Red Mike" Edson had ordered the 1st Battalion, 6th Marines to push along the southern coast at daylight to meet up with marines holding the south side of the airstrip. Meanwhile, 1/8 was to drive westward at 0700 to eliminate a pocket of resistance on the border between Red beaches 1 and 2. Despite being supported by three tanks, Bangalore torpedoes, thermite grenades, TNT satchels, and flamethrowers, 1/8 was unable to take out three enemy pillboxes. But Japanese forces were in no position to take offensive action. By 1100 the marines controlled most of Betio's southern coast and had almost entirely surrounded the Japanese forces that remained on the western two-thirds of the island.

But over on Red Beach 3, Maj. Crowe's forces had gained no ground, thanks to the interlocking fields of fire from the three enemy positions—a steel pillbox, the L-shaped coconut-log wall, and the massive, sand-covered emplacement some sixty yards southeast of the pier. Roy Elrod, a first lieutenant with weapons company, 8th Marines, recalled that they got a boost when the *Ringgold* fired its five-inch guns from one thousand yards out in the lagoon and struck the bunker, blasting some of the sand from the top.

"It was dangerous to us, because we were only forty to fifty yards away. But what it did do was uncover those air vents on top," he said.[1]

At some point, Maj. William Chamberlin gathered his men and told them he'd decided to lead a charge up the sandy slopes to take the blockhouse. But when he shouted, "Follow me!" only T.Sgt. Norm Hatch, armed with a movie camera, followed.

"Major, where is your weapon?" Hatch shouted when they reached the top of the hill and saw Japanese advancing toward them through the smoke.

"I gave it to a kid and my pistol doesn't work; it got wet," Chamberlin replied.

"[Chamberlin] said, 'We'd better get the hell out of here right now,' and we ran back down the side of the damned thing," Hatch said at age eighty-nine. "It all happened in nanoseconds, though we didn't use that term then. We got back down and the whole goddamn unit was just staring at us wondering what in the hell we were doing. The major held another meeting, which wasn't so pleasant this time."[2]

Sandy Bonnyman had been pondering how to take the big bunker ever since offering his services to Crowe, and seeing the exposed ventilation shafts gave him an idea: If they could take out the gunner on top with flamethrowers and explosives, they could then make a deadly delivery of flaming fuel and TNT down those vents.

"He went back to Major Crowe and said, 'I know how much pressure builds up, and if we can drop explosives down those air vents, it'll chase those people out,'" said Elrod, who contacted me in 2015.

The resulting concussions and inferno would kill many of the Japanese inside and drive any survivors into the open, where Elrod's gunners would be able to take them out from positions facing the east- and south-facing entrances. Chamberlin gave the go-ahead to my grandfather and ordered him to lead the assault.

"Your grandfather drew up the plan," said Elrod, who was sent to cover the south portal with two 37mm machine guns. "The rest of us just went along."[3]

At 0930, Crowe ordered K Company to take out the coconut-log emplacement with a barrage of 60mm mortar shells. At around 1300, Lt. Lou Largey swiveled the turret of the *Colorado* and unloaded his 75mm guns on the steel pillbox.[4] Two down, one to go.

But there was no way to take the hulking blockhouse, which had withstood relentless bombing, from afar. It would require desperate, dangerous close combat by the team of twenty-one engineers and riflemen assembled by Sandy Bonnyman. They dubbed themselves "Forlorn Hope," a British phrase describing a necessary action in which many would die.

"As bright as (Sandy) was," Roy Elrod said, "I'm sure he knew there was little chance he would come off there. He had to know when he went out on top he could be seen by just about every Japanese on the island."[5]

Sometime in mid-afternoon, the men of Forlorn Hope began their dash toward the bunker, covered by 37mm guns and mortars.

"What happened next, though witnessed by hundreds," Joseph Alexander wrote, "remains kaleidoscopic."[6]

It's fair to say that in the chaos of battle, everyone's recollections are probably a little kaleidoscopic. Yet over the years, despite a few counter-historical embellishments, the essential narrative concerning my grandfather's final hours remained remarkably consistent—until the publication of Alexander's *Utmost Savagery* in 1995.

In his exhaustively detailed history of the battle, the retired marine colonel made the curious choice to accord the fifty-year-old recollections of a single eyewitness, Cpl. Harry Niehoff, A Company, 1/18, the status of revealed truth, thereby upending virtually every previous accounting of Sandy Bonnyman's actions on November 22, 1943. Though Niehoff had given a somewhat similar account to Eric Hammel and John E. Lane in 1969[7], *Utmost Savagery* effectively diminished my grandfather's contribution that day.

Doubtful that one man's memory could be trusted to overturn what had seemed to be settled history, I vowed to find the truth, no matter where the evidence led. I spent years tracking down every account of my grandfather's actions I could find, in books, newspaper articles, and letters, even a comic strip. But in the end, it was my conversations with some of the men who were actually there that really made the difference.

There is little dispute over the beginning of the assault: Niehoff began hurling TNT "satchel" charges over the top of the bunker while Pfc. John Borich directed a column of fire from his flamethrower onto the sandy summit, which took out the machine gunner. Sandy led the way up the slippery northwest corner of the mound, accompanied by Borich and Niehoff, a scene captured on film by Norm Hatch and later incorporated in the 1944 documentary, *With the Marines on Tarawa*.

Pfc. Earl "Pappy" Coleman and Sgt. Elmo Feretti soon followed, and once on top, Sandy ordered them, along with Niehoff, to begin tossing explosive charges down three ventilator openings while Borich jammed the nozzle of his flamethrower down a fourth on the north side, spraying the interior of the bunker with flaming diesel.[8] It didn't take long for scores of desperate, screaming Japanese to begin streaming from the blockhouse's east- and south-facing exits, where Elrod and other marines began to mow them down. But those who survived turned to charge up the bunker's east and south slopes to meet the attackers.

The initial assault didn't last long, but Sandy was in constant motion.

"There were three guys going up that bunker. I remember hearing him hollering loud enough to hear over all the ammo and other noises in his Southern accent, 'Fight, you guys! Get over there, you get over here, make sure you kill them as they come out!'" remembered Karol Szwet, a machine gunner with 3/8, at age ninety-two.[9]

Most famously, photographer Newcomb stood at the back of the bunker snapping photos that remain the only known images of a Medal of Honor recipient engaged in the action for which he was cited.

"It was a perfect hell hole and the boys needed a little urging when things started to break," he remembered. "I can still see him waving the boys up over that blockhouse and his Southern voice urging them on. What a wonderful man. A braver man never existed."[10]

Newcomb's famous photos would become a continuing source of confusion, however, when he sent them to the Bonnyman family in 1944. He marked the photos with arrows pointing to a figure he believed to be Sandy amid a swarm of marines. But Newcomb was many yards from the action and numerous sources have discounted those arrows, including Elrod, who witnessed events atop the bunker from his machine-gun position facing the south entrance.

"I have wanted for seventy-one years to tell this story, and I'm probably the only person alive who knows exactly what happened," Elrod told me. "All those pictures you see now, with all the marines on top and coming up, with the arrows, that was *after* your grandfather was killed. No one went up at the time of the initial fighting except those three or four men with him. I saw it all happen."[11]

Elrod, his machine-gun pointed at the south entrance, had a front-row seat as Sandy, a cigar clenched between his teeth, stood alone at the southeastern edge of the sandy mound and continually fired his thirty-caliber carbine at the swarm of enemy fighters coming toward him. Elrod also recalled that Japanese mortar shells were falling all around him.

"I watched the whole thing and I can tell you, he was the only one there, and the one who really turned the tide," said Elrod, who later received the Navy Cross for his actions on Saipan. "I was more impressed with him than anyone else I ever served with. If there was ever anyone who deserved the Congressional medal, he was it."[12]

Pfc. Marvin Sheppard recalled that he and "another kid" from HQ intelligence, whose name he could not recall at age eighty-six, had been drawn to the sound of fighting at the bunker, like many other marines in the area, and watched the assault unfold from the rear. He remembered that they sprinted back to the seawall after hearing Sandy shout for more explosives, but by the time the two young marines returned, my grandfather's voice had gone silent.[13]

In the days, months, and years following his death, the story of my grandfather's last stand would be told and retold countless times, in public and in private, often in contradiction to official records, and occasionally with thrilling, but false, details.

Unsurprisingly, the more remote the source, in both time and space, the more likely the story is to resemble a Hollywood war drama, and Sandy a kind of action figure.

Malaria kept my grandfather's friend and former commanding officer, Col. Gilder Jackson Jr., from fighting at Tarawa, and the non-eyewitness account he related to Jo Bonnyman veered wildly into cinematic melodrama: "He went forward to place the (Bangalore)

torpedo where it would do the most damage and a sniper got him. . . .
(He) turned around and smiled at his men and fell to the ground."[14]

In a breathless 1959 story about Tarawa, the magazine *Saga:
Adventure Stories for Men* reported that my grandfather "shot two
(Japanese), but then the rest were on him. He threw his carbine into
their faces, dived at another and killed him with his bare hands."[15] A
1964 American Armed Forces Features "America's Fighting Heroes"
comic strip depicted Sandy as a Rambo-like superhero defying
gravity, teeth gritted, his automatic weapon spouting fire at swarms
of fang-baring Japanese behind the banner of the Rising Sun.

And then there's the flamethrower myth. In 1968 former head
of the Marine Corps History Division Henry I. Shaw Jr. wrote, "It
was Bonnyman who met the enemy head on, spraying the attackers
with fire from a flamethrower and killing three before he, himself, was shot down."[16] In his vivid 1979 memoir of the Pacific
war, *Goodbye, Darkness*, William Manchester wrote, "Bonnyman
remained standing for thirty seconds, firing a carbine and then a
flamethrower before he fell, mortally wounded."[17] Minus the flamethrower, both accounts are probably quite accurate.

The myth must be laid at the feet of Maj. William Chamberlin,
who erroneously placed the flamethrower in Sandy's hands while
speaking to a Marine Corps historian in 1946 (a detail he did not
mention in his Medal of Honor recommendation).[18] There *was* a
flamethrower atop the bunker, but it was always in the hands of
John Borich.

Historians and fellow marines long gave Sandy Bonnyman
credit for assembling and directing the men of Forlorn Hope,
leading the charge, and, as Maj. Henry P. "Jungle Jim" Crowe
wrote in his Medal of Honor recommendation, leading "his men in
placing flamethrowers [*sic*] and demolition charges" and "standing
at the forward edge of the structure [where] he killed three of the
enemy before he received mortal wounds."[19]

For decades, there was little doubt that my grandfather also schemed out the basic plan of attack. Yet Alexander reports Niehoff's assertion that *Niehoff and Borich* came up with the idea to use the ventilation shafts to deliver explosives and flame, and that Sandy simply "listened to the men."[20] Niehoff also recalled that Sandy Bonnyman had been largely passive during the assault.

But Niehoff's most radical assertion was that he and my grandfather were *jointly* holding off the counterassault, from a prone position, when Niehoff "heard the bullet hit him. He never moved and I knew he was dead." My grandfather's face was so badly damaged, Niehoff reported, that it was unrecognizable.[21] In their 1988 book, *76 Hours: The Invasion of Tarawa*, Eric Hammel and John E. Lane recounted Niehoff's assertion that *he* was the lone marine holding back the Japanese counterattack when my grandfather joined him on his belly, and shortly thereafter "heard the killing shot thud into Sandy Bonnyman's body,"[22] a detail Niehoff first related to the authors in 1969.[23]

Niehoff's own account in 1994 letters to my aunt, Alix Prejean, further detailed that Sandy "turned on his side and rested on his elbow, yelling for some TNT charges to be brought. . . . He had raised his head above the edge of the pillbox and exposed it to fire. . . . I know he never knew."[24] In one letter, Niehoff profusely apologized to my aunt for "using your dad's body as a shield" after he fell,[25] a detail he also reported to Alexander and others. Hammel and Lee reported that Niehoff "leaped across the dead lieutenant's body and wedged himself between it and a dead Japanese machine gunner" just as he saw a grenade tumbling in from the corner of his eye. Lucky for Niehoff, it was a dud.[26]

After repeatedly poring over Harry Niehoff's claims—that he and Borich, not Sandy, had planned the assault and he, not Sandy, had single-handedly held off the Japanese counterassault—I arrived at an uneasy conclusion: If what he'd said was true, then a great injustice had been committed and *Niehoff*, not my grandfather, should have been awarded the Medal of Honor. Or could it be that Harry Niehoff simply misremembered what happened that day? Whatever the truth, I knew I had to find out.

Niehoff first contacted Joseph Alexander at age seventy-one after reading the author's monograph, "Across the Reef," saying he wanted to correct the "very wild and exaggerated view of why (Sandy) won the Congressional Medal. . . . He was too fine a person to have to doctor the story."[27]

After interviewing Niehoff, Alexander wrote a letter to my mother, Fran, describing her father's actions on the bunker as something more like effective management than conspicuous gallantry.

"I have . . . been advised by Mr. Harry Niehoff that events atop the bunker were not quite as melodramatic" as previously described, the author wrote. "Your Dad's conspicuous contributions were more in the realm of organizing and leading a demoralized group of men from scattered units in attacking a seemingly impregnable Japanese strongpoint, one which had stonewalled the 8th Marines for three days. Fine. That does not diminish the significance of his sacrifice at all."[28]

But Niehoff's own words and actions suggest that he may have misremembered what happened that day. For starters, he himself enthusiastically recommended Sandy Bonnyman for the Medal of Honor while bivouacked at Camp Tarawa on the chilly, windswept saddle between two volcanoes on the Big Island of Hawaii.

"We were asked if we wanted to recommend anyone for awards. I happened to be with Johnny Borich at the moment and we both said we wanted to recommend [Sandy] for the Congressional," he wrote. "I am sure it wasn't just us two but I believe others there also wrote him up for the Congressional Medal."[29]

(Documents show that Maj. William Chamberlin recommended Sandy for the medal; several others, including Col. David Shoup, Capt. Joseph Clerou, Pfc. Marvin Sheppard and, according to Sheppard, "the other kid,"[30] also said they put forth his name, and there may have been others.)

In addition, while Niehoff did receive the Silver Star for his "gallantry and intrepidity in action" on Tarawa, the citation simply does not support his version of events: "He attacked and helped destroy by demolitions an enemy pillbox [sic] which held up the advance for fifty hours. Later, he voluntarily carried demolitions and supplies for flame throwers through heavy enemy fire to advance positions."[31] There is no mention of Niehoff planning the assault on the "pillbox" or singlehandedly (or otherwise) firing into an enemy counterattack.

I have no doubt that Harry Niehoff accurately shared what he remembered of that day. But memory is a tricky beast, perhaps especially in combat.

"There is no true narrative in combat; nobody understands what the hell is going on," former combat correspondent Chris Hedges told me. "For everybody who comes through, there is a need or propensity to make it make sense. The fact is, it never does."[32]

The battle of Bonnyman's Bunker was no exception. It was fast, loud, chaotic, and terrifying, from start to finish.

Alexander reported his version of events as fact, but Niehoff himself began to question his memories of the battle not long after giving the interview to the author. Cecil Goddard, a staff sergeant and engineer in Niehoff's outfit who also took part in Forlorn Hope, disputed his old friend's description of a "passive" Sandy Bonnyman, remembering instead that he was "really trying to pump up everyone and running back and forth to check with everyone on our sector."[33] Following a conversation with Goddard, Niehoff wrote a follow-up letter to my aunt in which he worried that, "I have developed greater tunnel vision than I thought."

He acknowledged not just that his memories might be flawed a half-century after the battle, but also his realization that they might never have been correct.

"It is true, when one is in the middle of a war where it was so bad on that first night we knew we were not going to get off that island alive, you think mostly of your own person," Niehoff wrote. "This thinking really separates you from others mentally in a way that you can remember what you were doing clearly but only have a hazy picture of who and what some of the others were doing around you. . . . Your dad was outstanding and age only dims more of the recollections. . . . If this letter rambles it is because my mind is doing the same. As I write of one thing other memories crop up and began to jump around and shift."[34]

I had asked the question of myself honestly, and was willing to follow the evidence wherever it led. In the end, my interviews with living witnesses, which solidly confirmed official documents and contemporary accounts of my grandfather's actions, coupled with the evidence of Niehoff's citation, and his own doubts, reassured me that Sandy Bonnyman had indeed performed the actions that led to his posthumous distinction with the nation's highest military honor.

But my grandfather's story did not end when he fell, and many more unanswered questions still lay ahead.

FIFTEEN
REQUIEM
NOVEMBER 22-DECEMBER 5, 1943

When the fighting was over, nine of the twenty-one marines of Forlorn Hope lay dead on the bunker that would one day bear my grandfather's name. Their names, alas, are lost to history, but their sacrifices had not been in vain.

Scores of Japanese rushing from the hellish confines of the blockhouse had all been cut down by machine-gun and rifle fire as they fled. Marines stood sentry at the two entrances to the bunker until a bulldozer arrived to block them with tons of coral sand, entombing any living Japanese unlucky enough to remain inside. With the last of the three obstacles now taken, the men under Maj. Crowe's command swept through the cluster of Japanese structures on the northern edge of the island, where they found at least a hundred Japanese who had committed suicide.[1] They halted at the eastern end of the airfield, forming a line across the island's eastern reaches with marines that had taken most of south-facing Black Beach.

By the end of D+2, with the exception of one pocket of resistance inland of Red Beach 1, all enemy fighters were dead or trapped on Betio's long, tapering tail, their escape route across the reef to Bairiki cut off. Still, the Japanese mounted three desperate counterattacks, firing machine guns and making suicidal charges into marine lines. Thanks in part to shelling from the *Schroeder* and

Sigsbee offshore, there was almost no resistance left to fight by 0500. By one o'clock the next afternoon, D+3, November 23, fighting on Betio had ended, seventy-six bloody, brutal hours after it had commenced.

In the end, the fighting had taken the lives of more than 1,100 Americans and nearly five thousand Japanese and their captured Korean laborers. Beyond Betio, the US Army's 27th Division wrested Makin Atoll from the Japanese, at a cost of 76 killed in ground combat, 644 died when the Japanese sank the USS *Liscome Bay,* and 44 died in a turret fire aboard the USS *Mississippi.* (In November and December 1999, JPAC recovered the remains of nineteen MIA marines from Butaritari, the main island of Makin Atoll; at the time, it was the largest single recovery since the Korean War.)

"I've been in this business for 30 years," wrote marine Col. Evans Carlson, whose ill-starred 1942 attack on Makin had helped prod the Japanese into fortifying Betio, "and this is the damnedest fight I have ever been in; much worse than Guadalcanal."[2]

Journalist Robert Sherrod wrote, "The story of Tarawa is a saga in which only a few of the heroes have been or ever can be identified." Indeed, the entire Second Marine Division later was awarded the Presidential Unit Citation, recognizing that it collectively had fought at a level worthy of a Navy Cross.

"Sandy Bonnyman's death was no more tragic than any other death," observed former marine Bill Niven. "But he did accomplish things that few others did."[3]

With the end of combat, marines and navy construction battalions (aka Seabees) immediately turned to the task of burying the dead. More than ninety Americans were buried at sea, according to ships' logs, while others had drifted away or sunk in the lagoon. That still left thousands of corpses, American and Japanese, to be buried. Supervised by Sandy's friend Father William O'Neill and Father Francis W. "Foxhole" Kelly, marines buried their dead in at least forty-three locations around the island, doing their best to record the names and mark the graves with sticks, scrap wood, or even ration cans. Just a day after the battle, Betio was already studded with rows of crude wooden crosses bearing dog tags of the dead, with many more to come.[4]

At one of the burial sites, someone set a simple wooden marker inscribed with an apparently original poem, "Requiem: November 1943." Its final stanza read:

> REST, WARRIORS, REST
> AGAINST THE DAY OF JOURNEYING FORTH
> TENDER HANDS SHALL LIFT THEE OUT
> TO HOME SOIL WAITING.[5]

Sometime before sunset on D+3, combat photographer Cpl. Obie Newcomb climbed the captured bunker to visit the spot where the charismatic marine with the booming Southern voice had been killed. He was surprised to find an undamaged helmet perched on the sand, emblazoned with three red shore-party stripes and marked "Bonnyman"; he'd heard Sandy had been shot in the head by a sniper.[6]

"I picked it up and looked at it. I felt so bad . . . As I was leaving the area two Lts. approached me and asked me if I had seen his body. They were his buddies. I told them no," Newcomb recalled.[7] One of the men was probably Sandy's friend 1st Lt. Bernard A. "Barney" Boos.[8]

By that time, Pfc. Marvin Sheppard and the "other kid" had already retrieved the body and taken it back to the seawall near the command post.[9] That fact, recalled decades later, would provide an answer to another mystery: How did my grandfather's remains come to be buried in Cemetery 27 alongside thirty-nine marines, none of whom had been killed in the fighting atop the bunker? All but a handful were killed on D-day, and the only one killed on November 22 was not with a unit associated with the assault.

I was unsuccessful in my efforts to confirm the names of every member of Forlorn Hope. However, records do indicate that eight members of 2/18 and the other two units under Crowe's command that day, 2/8 and 3/8, were killed on the third day of fighting. But we'll probably never know for certain whether they fell taking the bunker or not.

Once the smoke had cleared and the relentless thunder of bombs, mortar fire, grenades, machine guns, and M-1 rifles had fallen silent on Betio, US Navy Adm. Raymond A. Spruance summoned Lt. Cmdr. Kyle Campbell Moore on the USS *Indianapolis*, flagship of the US Fifth Fleet, floating just offshore. He had an assignment for the junior officer.

Moore, thirty-four, had been commissioned as a junior-grade lieutenant in the US Navy Reserve on December 8, 1941, as the ruins of the Pacific Fleet still lay smoking in Pearl Harbor. Kasey, as his shipmates called him, had until then spent almost his entire life in Knoxville, Tennessee, where he was a star running back for the undefeated Knoxville High Trojans football team and two-time city tennis champion in his age group.

He'd entered the University of Tennessee hoping to become a doctor, but the Great Depression forced him to put his plans on hold after just a year. Having been the editor of his high school newspaper, the *Blue and White*, Moore took a job as a reporter for the *Knoxville Journal*. His editors quickly recognized that his real talent lay in photography, and he soon became the paper's sole staff shooter, as well as a southeast region photographer for the *New York Times* and William Randolph Hearst's International News Service. Armed with one of the *Times's* newfangled "telephoto" devices, which allowed him to transmit images by phone, Moore covered President Franklin D. Roosevelt's visits to dedicate Great Smoky Mountains National Park in 1934 and check on the progress of the Tennessee Valley Project in 1940.

Once Moore enlisted, the Eighth Naval District in New Orleans had planned to make use of his photojournalism skills in its public relations wing. But on his insistence, he was sent to the Northwestern University Midshipmen's School in Chicago to train for sea duty, and in July 1942 he was assigned to the *Indianapolis*, where he would remain throughout his wartime service. He married fellow Volunteer and journalism student Katherine Davis just days before reporting for duty in the Aleutian Islands off Alaska's southwest coast.

Aboard the *Indianapolis*, Kasey Moore was promoted to lieutenant commander in April 1943 and placed in charge of damage control and repairs of the ship's thick steel hull.[10]

"As damage-control officer he couldn't go ashore any more. That was a matter of great anguish for him, because he enjoyed being with the marines," his widow Katherine recalled at age ninety-five.[11]

Spruance ended the young officer's shipboard exile at Tarawa. The admiral thought him a "splendid photographer," and needed someone he could trust to document why the navy's relentless, months-long bombardment of tiny Betio that had failed to destroy so many Japanese emplacements, bunkers, and blockhouses, a monumental failure that magnified the death toll in the bloodiest battle in Marine Corps history.

Coming ashore, Kasey Moore watched as navy men used boat hooks to retrieve corpses from the water, and marines performed the ghastly job of burying their comrades. He had just stepped off the Japanese-built pier, camera in hand, when he passed a group of filthy, exhausted marines sprawled on the sand near a burial trench marked with rude crosses assembled from the blasted shards of Japanese structures. Moore happened to overhear the men talking about an officer who had fearlessly led an assault on the hulking bunker he was on his way to photograph.

"Did you say Bonnyman?" he asked. The marines nodded. From Tennessee? Could be, they said; the man had a Southern accent. Bonnyman was a name Moore had only ever heard in Knoxville; surely they were talking about his old friend and tennis partner, Sandy. They'd lost track of each other when Sandy went to college at Princeton, but as teenagers, they had been almost like brothers. Both were rough-and-tumble boys of Scottish descent, adventurous and charismatic. Moore was "an athlete, an avid sportsman, a crack shot, and gentle with his hunting dogs," and he "never lost a friend or forgave an enemy."[12] Much the same could be said of his old friend.

When Moore asked if they knew where the man was buried, the marines pointed to the freshly covered trench.[13] A month later, he recounted the remarkable exchange with his wife while home on Christmas leave.

"I can tell you he had tears in his eyes when he told me that story," Katherine Moore told me. "He never even knew Sandy was in the marines."[14]

Years later, his widow would become a patient of Sandy's youngest nephew, Dr. Brian Bonnyman, in Knoxville.

"Brian told me Sandy Bonnyman had been buried at sea," Katherine Moore said. "I said, 'No, I don't think so,' and I told him that story about my husband on Tarawa."[15]

Like Sandy, Kasey Moore would not come home from the war, and his mortal remains would become lost to history. His bones now sleep forever three miles deep in the watery grave where the *Indianapolis* was sunk by a Japanese torpedo July 30, 1945, after delivering uranium for the atomic bomb that would soon fall on Hiroshima.

By November 25, even as members of the 2nd Battalion, 6th Marines chased down and killed the last couple hundred of fleeing Japanese on Buariki, the northern terminus of Tarawa Atoll, the first transports began steaming away from hell, loaded with marines who had survived the battle. After docking at Pearl Harbor on December 5 to unload wounded, the ships embarked for the Big Island of Hawaii, where the marines would begin construction of their own camp on a windswept volcanic plateau before they could rest, recuperate, and start training for their next deployment (Saipan, in June).

Within a week after taking Betio, all the men who knew where their fallen comrades were buried were gone. On the island they left behind, the navy's 18th Construction Battalion/Engineers, the 74th Construction Battalion, and the 549th Construction Battalion Maintenance Unit set about the task of "reorganizing" the graves and cemeteries—the opening chapter of a mystery that Mark Noah and History Flight were still trying to solve more than seven decades later.[16]

SIXTEEN
SEVENTY YEARS AND COUNTING
AUGUST-NOVEMBER 2013

In the summer of 2013, the Joint POW/MIA Accounting Command quietly decided to follow up on "new leads" developed by Bill Niven, whose archival research had helped thrust the lost graves of Tarawa into the public eye back in 2008.

Like Mark Noah, Niven had been frustrated by the lack of progress in locating the lost graves of Tarawa. But he'd kept the lines of communication open and in late spring he was invited to fly out to meet with JPAC officials in Hawaii to present "updated findings" on the burial locations of dozens of marines at four sites, including one he believed to be Cemetery 27.

"I locate original photographs of the original graves, then locate that spot on current and original maps of Tarawa," Niven told me, describing his research technique. "Photographs don't lie. It's very clear where these men are buried."[1]

As he had previously, the former marine declined JPAC's invitation to make the trip to Tarawa, saying he didn't want to be a distraction. But, he said, "I don't lie awake at night, wondering if my research is right. I expect they will come back with 73 men."[2]

Under the direction of Central Identification Laboratory deputy director Bill Belcher, a team dug exploratory trenches across the road from the copra plant, where Bill Niven believed they would find Cemetery 27 (and about 300 feet west of Mark Noah's preferred site, which Belcher had declined to further excavate in 2012). They found old fire pits and other interesting features, but no signs of a burial trench. Bill complained from afar that the team wasn't digging in the right places, just as Mark Noah had in 2010.

"He'd say, 'I've relooked at the photos, and you need go five meters to the north.' So we'd dig there, and when we didn't find anything, he'd say, 'You need to go five meters more,'" Belcher said. "We were actually chasing this thing to the point where we had moved into the area that was probably Cemetery 26."[3]

But none of the sites yielded any notable remains.

"I like Bill," Mark Noah said. "But he hasn't been on Tarawa since 1989. It looks a lot different than it did in 1943 or 1946."[4]

Earlier that summer, the ongoing scrutiny of JPAC that began in 2009—catalyzed by the lost marines of Tarawa—had become a full-blown public relations nightmare.

The agency lost its fight to quash a damning 2012 internal study, which was published by the Associated Press after it filed a Freedom of Information Act request. The report concluded the agency was "acutely dysfunctional" and possibly headed toward "total failure." Its methods were corrupt, duplicative, and often "subjected to too little scientific rigor."[5] Anthropologist Jay Silverstein, who had alienated some of his colleagues with his advocacy for History Flight, had been the chief whistleblower, blasting his employer for using "poor methods" and failing to "conduct proper scientific work on numerous levels" on Tarawa. He accused team members of using improper excavation techniques, conducting leading interviews with a witness, wasting funds, and other alleged lapses.[6]

The report lambasted the agency for developing too few investigative leads and wasting time and taxpayer money. On JPAC's then-$100 million annual budget, the Central Identification Laboratory made just eighty identifications in 2012—$1.25 million per recovered body. Only thirty-five of those remains were the result of the agency's own investigations; the rest were disinterred from US military cemeteries, or, as at Tarawa, discovered by locals or non-governmental organizations.

The memo also had taken JPAC to task for prematurely declaring remains in Southeast Asia unrecoverable—an echo of Tarawa, six decades earlier—and failing to identify unknown World War II remains in its custody "when evidence suggested they could be identified." Earlier in the year, the agency had declined to exhume and test remains discovered amid the wreckage of an American plane downed in France in 1944 and mistakenly interred in a German cemetery. The French and German governments later stepped up and positively identified the remains as those of Army Pfc. Lawrence Gordon. It was yet another embarrassing PR lapse; one headline read, "The World War II Hero America Abandoned."[7]

Just ten days after the AP story was published, the US General Accountability Office released the results of an investigation that found JPAC and its sister agency, the Defense Prisoner of War/Missing Personnel Office, were inefficient, wasteful, and burdened by ineffective leadership. Among other problems, JPAC and DPMO had for years squandered time and money skirmishing for turf and influence. "Disputes and a lack of coordination characterized the initial response of the missing persons accounting community to the increased accounting-for goal (200 per year)," the report found.[8]

Perhaps most embarrassing, JPAC was forced to admit in October that its touching "arrival" ceremonies at Joint Base Harbor-Hickam in Honolulu—in which flag-draped coffins were solemnly unloaded from aircraft before the teary eyes of family members and other well wishers—were phony. Out-of-service planes were towed into position to pantomime the unloading of coffins that turned out to be empty, all for press and public consumption. Staff had long known about what they called "The Big Lie;" now the public did, too.[9]

In response to all the problems, Congress directed the agency to begin identifying at least two hundred MIAs a year by 2015—and tripled its budget to $300 million a year (with that kind of "stick," who needs carrots?).

Still fighting resistance from many of the top scientists at JPAC, Mark Noah wondered if he could improve History Flight's credibility by hiring experts known to JPAC who would rigorously adhere to the agency's field and lab protocols. He quietly asked Silverstein and others to send any potential candidates his way.

In September, Silverstein invited a young forensic anthropologist, Kristen N. Baker, to have coffee in Honolulu. Kristen had been a contract employee with JPAC from 2008 to 2012, where she had logged hundreds of hours in Vietnam and Papua New Guinea, but had found herself out of work due to a Congressional budget sequester.

"He said, 'Hey, Kristen, if you are looking to continue the type of work you did with us, I think I might know someone to talk to,'" she recalled.[10]

Kristen's resume in forensic anthropology went back much farther than her years with JPAC. Born in Athens, Georgia, in 1985, as a child she was an unusual combination of a nerdy bookworm, basketball and softball player, and rugged outdoors lover. Her father, a lawyer, died when she was nine, and she turned inward, focusing on graduating first in her high school class, attending a top-notch university, and becoming a doctor.

"I wasn't first, but I was in the top ten," she said. "I chose to go to Tulane because it was far away and had a good medical school. Basically, it wasn't Georgia."[11]

While taking pre-med courses, she decided to major in anthropology, with a focus on physical anthropology and forensics; she was still haunted by memories of how long it took medical examiners to officially determine her father's cause of death.

"It was bothersome to me that we had to wait that long," she said. "I had a couple of mean cousins who would say he wasn't really dead, that he'd just run off with another woman."[12]

Upon graduation in 2004, she decided to stay at Tulane to earn a master's degree and study for the Medical College Admission Test. In the summer of 2005, she worked on a 1,500-year-old mass grave in Peru, where researchers recovered scores of decapitated, mummified bodies. Former Presidents Bush and Clinton spoke at her graduation in May 2006, as did a "surprise speaker," Ellen DeGeneres.

After working for a year in cultural resources management, searching Southeast landscapes scheduled for development or roads for historically significant sites, she took a job with the Georgia Bureau of Investigation. She gained invaluable experience in forensic anthropology and met important contacts, but there was little chance for advancement and she didn't like being stuck in a lab. So, shooting for the moon, she applied for a job with JPAC. She was thrilled when Belcher called.

"When I was taking classes, they had been held up as hiring only the best and the brightest, the pinnacle of anthropology," she said. "[Belcher] asked if I was more of a field or lab person and I said field. So I got an archaeology position."[13]

She joined the agency in 2008, and after passing a "mentored mission" with flying colors, spent much of her first year "camping in the woods" in Vietnam. She was later posted to Papua New Guinea, where the United States had lost more aircraft than in any other country during World War II. Kristen relished working out of high-altitude camps in the country's rugged, jungled mountains during three forty-five-day missions.

"PNG is a country of extremes. The lowlands were the hottest place I've ever been. In the mountains, it can be incredibly cold," she said. "I really enjoyed that dichotomy, but it's a really challenging environment to work in. You're always on slopes and you're at altitude for so long your immune system begins to suffer."

When not in the field, she began work on a doctorate at the University of Hawaii. Put off by the "ass-kissing" required in that academic environment—not to mention the fact that her adviser hit on her during a field expedition to Korea—in 2013 Kristen took Silverstein's advice and contacted Mark Noah. The two met for coffee in Honolulu in September and two weeks later she was on a plane to Fiji with two other archaeologists hired by History Flight.

It soon became apparent that Kristen was the only one of the three with the experience, skills, and critically, temperament required to work for the scrappy organization. One of the archaeologists was constantly stressed out and refused further exploration of the shipping-yard site, worried that he'd be electrocuted by cables encountered below the surface. The other was temperamental and openly anti-military and Kristen viewed her methodology as a relic from the 1970s.

"She came over to one dig where I was working [on Betio] and said, 'You're just a kid. You don't know what you are doing,' and refused to help me. She and [the other archaeologist] insisted I was just digging up Japanese remains," Kristen said.

She would soon prove them wrong.

Several years earlier, I had contacted Vicky Reynolds-Middagh of Sausalito, California-based Valor Tours, Ltd., offering to be a leader for one of her company's periodic trips to Tarawa. Started by her late father, World War II pilot Bob Reynolds, Valor Tours had been conducting tours to European and Pacific battlefields for more than three decades, including the 2003 tour of Tarawa I considered joining. By now, I qualified as an old Betio hand, and following my working trip in April, Vicky hired me to lead a ten-person group for the seventieth anniversary of the battle in November.

I was ecstatic when my aunt Alix Prejean and her daughter Andra decided to join two American couples, an Ohio businessman, a Dutch World War II history enthusiast, and an Australian Vietnam veteran and his wife for the trip. Unlike on my previous visits, our accommodations were not great. The Otintaai Hotel, once the go-to spot for visiting government and non-governmental officials, was now falling down—in fact, half condemned. Worse, it was an uncomfortable forty-five minute ride on bumpy roads to Betio.

When we arrived in late November, I was impressed by the Kiribati government's efforts to spiff up the island in advance of the anniversary. There was considerably less garbage in the vacant lots and gutters and evidence of Betio's sanitation problems had mercifully declined. And though I was busy working, it was old-home week for me on the island—Kristen Baker and Jeremy Shiok were there, as was navy veteran Kurt Hiete, who had helped pay for my first trip to Tarawa. I also got to meet JPAC anthropologist Jay Silverstein and geospatial analysis expert Anthony Hewitt.

And despite three and a half years' worth of emails and phone conversations, it also would be the first time I met Mark Noah in person. Mark had always been immensely helpful and supportive, and I was looking forward to shaking his hand.

At the same time, I felt a little nervous. I'd learned from experience that he fiercely protected his proprietorship over History Flight's work—understandable, given the various attempts at co-option he'd endured. Paradoxically, he was also curiously trusting, preferring handshakes to signed contracts, and the tension between those two instincts could result in misunderstanding and, on occasion, the abrupt reclassification of an erstwhile ally into a foe.

Mark had high expectations of his team, and many who'd worked with him had been on the receiving end of a snappish late-night email or a semi-public takedown at one time or another. A brave few—marine veteran Katie Rasdorf comes to mind—learned that defending their arguments actually seemed to earn Mark's respect.

Tenacious as a bulldog, disinclined to suffer fools, gladly or otherwise, and prone to speaking his mind, Mark hadn't developed the seamless, deferential relationship with JPAC that had served Pat Scannon and his recovery organization BentProp for decades.

But maybe none of that mattered. Spending time with him, I found him cheerful, funny, opinionated, and generous to a fault. Before the week was out I'd had an epiphany: Mark Noah was exactly the right man, at the right time, to tackle a difficult, dirty, thankless job on Tarawa, far from the comforts of home—just like Sandy Bonnyman, seven decades earlier.

Thanks to our local guide, Toka Rakobu (mother of Kantaake, whom I'd met in April), we were treated as VIPs and even invited to President Anote Tong's home for a dinner reception. On our third day, we boarded a noisy Air Kiribati puddle jumper for the forty-five-minute flight to the island of Butaritari in Makin Atoll.

Today a population of 4,400 lives amid pristine jungle and clean, sugary beaches constantly caressed by fresh breezes off the open sea. There are fewer reminders of the war than on Betio, but the people of Butaritari celebrate their 1943 liberation every year on November 20, and the only flag that flies over the village of Ukiangong is the Stars and Stripes.

Arriving one day before the actual anniversary, our group was feted with dancing, singing, speeches, and lunch featuring fish, lobster, squash, rice, and fruit. At the end of the ceremony, a village elder bowed low before the three Bonnymans present.

"We thank you for your father and your grandfather," he said through a translator. "It is because of him that we are free."

On November 20, the anniversary commemoration was held before dawn, the usual time for outdoor gatherings on Betio, where the temperature quickly soars to ninety degrees as soon as the sun boils up over the horizon. The expatriate community, mostly Aussies and Kiwis, showed up in force, many with well-dressed children in tow. President Tong and First Lady Bernadette Meme Tong invited our group to sit with them for the short ceremony in the hardscrabble yard around the national sports complex (not as impressive as it sounds), where a simple granite spike remains the only official American monument to the battle. Citing a drain of resources from the embassy in Fiji due to Typhoon Haiyan two weeks earlier, the US government did not send an official delegation, though members of the JPAC team did arrive in dress uniforms.

Beneath fluttering Kiribati and American flags, members of the Kiribati marines stood at attention while dignitaries spoke a few words and my aunt laid a wreath. Following refreshments, the president and first lady led attendees on a short walk to Red Beach 2, where a New Zealand aid program had recently built a wide concrete plaza with basketball hoops and a plaque expressing gratitude for the American liberation of the islands in 1943.

As I talked to the president about his nation's future, he said he was most concerned the by the threat of rising sea levels from global warming.

"Our landmass will be reduced, based on the scenarios projected. And our underground (fresh) water will be contaminated with the rising seas," said Tong, a graduate of the London School of Economics who was elected in 2003. "Unfortunately, that means Kiribati's ability to sustain its population of around 100,000 also will be reduced."[14]

He applauded the efforts of Americans like Kurt Hiete to raise money for sewer, trash disposal, and other infrastructure, and noted that a World Bank-funded project to repave the main road and lay fiber-optic conduits was about to begin. But he cautioned that change on the islands would be incremental, at best.

"We are making progress, but we have many difficult problems to overcome," he told me. "We appreciate what the Americans are doing here, but they must have realistic expectations."[15]

Following the ceremony, Mark Noah invited us to walk a couple hundred yards to look in on an active History Flight dig site in a cluster of cinder-block houses built by the Taiwanese in "downtown" Betio. When we arrived, Kristen Baker was down in the hole, carefully brushing sand from three sets of skeletal remains, one of which she believed to be American—right where that older archaeologist had told her she was just a "kid" who didn't know what she was doing.

"From the (ground-penetrating radar) and cadaver-dog survey of the area it was clear there was something in that spot. The remains of two other US Marines had been recovered from approximately this area as well," she said.

At the end of the trip, the *New York Times Magazine* published a long piece by Wil S. Hylton, author of *Vanished: The Sixty Year Search for the Missing Men of World War II*, detailing History Flight's long, unwavering efforts to recover the Tarawa missing and the oscillating relationship between Mark Noah and JPAC. The story ended on an optimistic note, with JPAC civilian administrator Johnie Webb forecasting a future in which the agency would work closely with private groups while maintaining the highest professional standards. The bottom line, Webb said, was that "there's more work to do than we can get done."[16]

After I got home, I received an email from JPAC geographic-information systems expert Anthony Hewitt, whom I had met on Betio.

"We wanted to show you our latest theory on where we thought Cemetery 27 might be located, but the time ran out and we were not able to meet with you," he wrote. He attached a document showing an area of subsurface anomaly running underneath the traffic circle just south of the copra mill. "We hope to test this theory on the next mission by having the recovery team put some test pits in the north end of the traffic circle."[17]

It was encouraging news, and I asked for more details. But our email exchange was abruptly terminated days later when, in a horse-already-out-of-the-barn effort to douse its mounting PR brushfires, JPAC put its entire staff under a gag order.

SEVENTEEN
LEFT BEHIND
JANUARY-MAY 1944

Having admired, even idolized, my grandfather my whole life, it was immensely satisfying to know that I was gradually becoming my family's, even the world's, foremost expert on Sandy Bonnyman. But my research also was forcing me, for the first time, to confront the sobering impact of his heroic death on his family, for my grandfather's story did not end with his death on Tarawa.

Unlike most Americans killed in World War II, Sandy came from a prominent, wealthy, connected family, and his death was noted on the front pages of newspapers in Knoxville, Santa Fe, San Antonio, and Atlanta, as well as in the *National Catholic Register* and the *New York Times, Tribune*, and *Sun*. There was even a story on the front page the *Glasgow Herald* (Scotland) about the sacrifice of "Kinsman of Glasgow Priest," Father Peter Bonnyman.

Within days after Jo finally received the telegram informing her of her husband's death on December 29, 1943, the first of more than five hundred letters of sympathy began pouring into Bonniefield from friends, religious and political leaders, and most notably, marines who wanted to pay their respects to the Bonnymans.[1]

"We fought at Guadalcanal and Tarawa together and believe me Mr. Bonnyman you should be the proudest man in the world," Capt. Joseph R. Clerou, commanding officer of my grandfather's

Fox Company, wrote to Alex. "Sandy may be gone; but he has given us new life and inspiration through his leadership, devotion and courage. If any of us can do one fourth the job he has done, we will be true men."[2]

Photographer Obie Newcomb carried on an extended exchange with Blue Diamond Coal Company secretary Edna Schneider before summoning the courage to write directly to the Bonnymans: "He will go down in history as one of the heros [*sic*] of this war. . . . I sincerely hope he receives the Congressional Medal of Honor."[3]

The family received letters of condolence from the governors of Tennessee, Georgia, and New Mexico, titans of the mining and railroad industries and Alex Bonnyman's many high-profile friends, including US Attorney General Francis Biddle and Archbishop (later Cardinal) Francis Spellman of New York, who said a special Mass for Sandy in early January.[4]

Even Jimmie Russell, who had carried on an affair with my grandmother, wrote to the Bonnymans to express his condolences.

"I have loved Sandy as a younger brother and never met or hope to meet a finer, cleaner, all man. . . . All of us only wish we had the stuff to emulate him," he wrote.[5]

Alex Bonnyman replied graciously to every missive and asked marines for any detail of his son's life and death overseas. Haunted by the thought that he would not be able to bury his son, he also struck up extended correspondences with reporters, marines, and chaplains, hoping to learn where Sandy was buried.

In February, Clerou wrote the Bonnymans that they would be able get a final glimpse of their son if they could get ahold of a new Paramount newsreel.

"Sandy is shown in action in several scenes. . . . One scene shows three (3) Marines going up the side of the pill box. The man in the middle has a flame thrower, the man on his right is Sandy. His back is toward you, but you can pick him out by his stature, also he has no camoflage [*sic*[cover on his helmet whereas all the other Marines do," he wrote.[6]

In late March, the manager of the stately Tennessee Theatre in downtown Knoxville arranged a private showing of the newsreel for Alex, Frances, Gordon's wife Isabel (whose husband was off fighting with Merrill's Marauders in the jungles of Burma), and a number of her Ashe relatives. The local papers reported that the family was pleased to see the footage, but Isabel would later declare that "watching that film in the empty theatre was one of the saddest experiences" of her life.[7]

Sandy's shocking death was the beginning of a long, painful period for his young family. Almost immediately, Jo decided to break it apart, sending nine-year-old Fran off to stay with her Sanford relatives at the ranch in Rosita Coahuila, Mexico and once more leaving seven-year-old Tina with the Bonnymans before she returned to Santa Fe with baby Alix, her nurse, and Jimmie Russell. If my grandmother felt any grief, she wasn't letting it show.

"When you arrived [in Knoxville] that day early in January 1944, it was as if the bride of another had arrived," my Granny Great wrote to Jo. "You seemed so far away from us in our sorrow, so aloof in spirit, so preoccupied with things other than our Common grief. . . . In that dark hour, it seemed almost as if God had answered your prayer, not ours. Living, we could not have shielded [Sandy]. Leave us to sit alone with our beloved dead in the shadow of that white cross far away on Tarawa."[8]

Yet Jo did find time to write the Marine Corps three days after receiving the news to request that, "government insurance proceeds . . . be made immediately available to me as it is needed for current expenses."[9]

Nobody was talking to nine-year-old Fran about her father, but being sent to the child's paradise of the ranch was a great relief. Living with her beloved Aunty Blanche and Uncle Henry meant she could play with her cousin Ann every day after school, ride horses and bikes along dusty roads, and celebrate birthdays with piñatas. But she would never escape her loss, and remembered that Ann and a friend would prod her with questions—"How many people are in *your* family?"—intended to get her to talk about her dead father, out of curiosity, childish cruelty, or probably a bit of both. She never took the bait.

On leap day 1944, two months after receiving news of her husband's death, Josephine Bell Bonnyman and James Hobart Russell were married by District Judge William Barber in Santa Fe—"in haste, like Hamlet's mother," as one relative noted.[10] The couple then went to the Arizona Biltmore in Phoenix for a brief honeymoon.

In a long letter to my great-grandmother, whom she called Aunt Frances, Jo insisted she'd had to marry to stop tongues wagging in Santa Fe. She declared her abiding love for Sandy "and all the fine things he stood for," and claimed he'd told her "he'd rather see me marry Jimmie than anyone he'd ever known." She promised that the girls would "be raised as Catholics and *Bonnymans* and will be taught always to love and revere their father who was such a beautiful person and such a hero."[11] (Emphasis in original.)

Jo insisted that Russell was a positive influence on her girls. "Conservative" and "a very temperate drinker," he would provide "a very quiet and peaceful life with a beautiful home. . . . This will be better for me and Sandy's children in the long run."[12]

In reality, it was the beginning of twenty years of cruelty, neglect, and abuse for both Jo and the girls. Both Jo's parents in Texas and the Bonnymans had spent enough time with Tina and Fran during the tumult of the past year to know that the girls hated Jimmie

Russell, and why. Blanche Bell wrote Frances Bonnyman that her daughter had become "a perfect fool in the hands of a knave," and noted with concerned circumspection that Russell had arranged the house in Santa Fe "with [the children] seeming to the fore and gives a show of more than expected interest."[13]

The grandparents all knew that Jo had married a sexual predator—though they wouldn't have used that modern term—who was committing "indecencies" with their beloved granddaughters, but they were at a loss about what to do. It was, as they say, a different time.

"Maybe they should have taken the children away from Jo," said Robert McKeon, Sandy's oldest nephew, at age eighty-one. "That was discussed between Granny and Grandfather Bonnyman."[14]

My grandfather's beloved younger sister Anne Atkinson, whom he playfully called "Rooney" after a popular actress who shared her name, was so appalled by the situation that she came to believe his tragic death in battle was better than the "unhappy homecoming" he would have experienced if he'd returned.[15]

As Catholics, Alexander and Frances Bonnyman believed in the resurrection of the body, and bringing their son's remains home for burial in Knoxville's Calvary Cemetery was their highest priority. Jo, having detached herself from her former life, surrendered her rights as next of kin to Alex, who immediately informed the marines that he wanted his son's remains "brought . . . back to Knoxville when it is possible to do so."[16]

Thus began a relentless campaign by Sandy's father—ably assisted by three Blue Diamond secretaries, Helen O'Rourke, Clara Hood, and Edna Schneider—to discover his son's whereabouts and lay him to rest in consecrated ground.

As I put together a paper trail of inquiry and response, I was baffled and appalled by the number of different explanations received

by my great-grandfather and his employees over the next several
years. I could understand how the grave locations had been "lost,"
but not why authorities would not come clean to my family and, no
doubt, hundreds of others.

Given all the subsequent dissembling, it was more than ironic
that the *first* information provided to the family about my grandfather's burial place was absolutely correct: "Grave #17, 8th Marines
Cemetery No. 2, Central Division Cemetery, Betio," which would
later be known as Cemetery 27.[17] Weeks later, Alex was informed
that he had been temporarily interred in Grave #17 of the 2nd Battalion, *18th Marines* cemetery, which never existed.[18] A year and a
half later he was told that none of the previously reported burial
sites for Sandy was accurate, including a memorial grave featuring
a cross with his name misspelled as "A. Bonneyman."[19] But, he was
assured, his son was somewhere on the island, and "everything
humanly possible to care for the remains has been done by the military authorities."[20]

But in June 1946, my great-grandfather received a letter from
the Marine Corps Commandant's office explaining that, "While
some of the dead were quickly buried in temporary graves ashore,
the majority of the bodies were of necessity buried at sea."[21] (Author
emphasis.) Alex took that to mean Sandy now slept in Davy Jones's
locker.

In fact, fewer than two hundred of the more than 1,100 Americans killed at Tarawa were given marine burial,[22] and ships' logs
indicated that the number might be less than one hundred.[23] The
reason was simple: most bodies were already in a state of advanced
decomposition by the time they were buried; ferrying such remains
out to ships to consign them to the deeps would have been not just
ghastly, but absurd.

A few months later, the War Department wrote Alex Bonnyman to say that it had not been able to locate his son's grave,

"which apparently was not well marked in the confusion of the disaster at Tarawa," he wrote a friend. The cacophony of conflicting information was taking its toll on my seventy-seven-year-old great-grandfather: "I have almost given up hope of having him sent here for interment in our cemetery."[24]

US Army Maj. G. Gordon Bonnyman, Sandy's younger brother, did not come home from the war unscathed. Gravely wounded and suffering from severe malaria, he'd spent months in a hospital in Calcutta, India, before was well enough to be sent to recuperate in Nashville. But he was suffering from what would now be called post-traumatic stress disorder, and when it became clear he wasn't ready to assume his duties as a husband, father, and Blue Diamond heir apparent, his father arranged for him to spend a couple of months recuperating at the Sanford ranch in Mexico, where he and Sandy had used to go bird hunting.

Once recovered, Gordon returned to Knoxville, where he began a long, sometimes frustrating, apprenticeship to his father, and took command of the quest to find his brother's remains. He would leave no stone unturned, continuing to track down the thinnest of leads over the next two decades. And where Alex Bonnyman's persistent inquiries regarding Sandy's remains were polite to a fault, Gordon was familiar with military bureaucracy—and less inclined to deference.

In July 1947 a friend sent Gordon a page torn from *Life* magazine with a letter to the editor from former marine Bob McGuire, who wrote that he had seen Sandy's grave on Betio on December 10, 1943, "surrounded by his fallen Marine comrades and the simple wooden marker over him read 'Good Luck Bonny.'"[25] But when Blue Diamond secretary Clara Hood wrote to McGuire for details, he was no help. "I can't give you any further information," he wrote;[26] he pointed her to a *Time* magazine photo from "two or three years ago," but it did not show what he had reported.

Later that year, after hearing from a Graves Registration officer that all remains had been exhumed from Tarawa and were now stored at Schofield Barracks in Honolulu, Gordon wrote to officials offering to send his brother's dental records, which included X-rays of extensive, highly distinctive gold dental work, to help with identification.[27] He received the following reply: "Until you receive word from the Office of the Quartermaster General, I can only assure you that the American Graves Registration Service is sparing no effort or expense in the tremendous task of identifying unknown war dead."[28] In other words, don't call us, we'll call you.

For all his tenacity, Gordon wasn't getting anywhere, either.

In 1946 the 604th Quartermaster Graves Registration Company had spent two and a half months on Betio for the purpose of locating, disinterring, identifying, and "reinterring the remains located in a master cemetery." Among those involved in the search were two navy chaplains who had overseen some of the burials in the immediate aftermath of the fighting, my grandfather's friend Father William O'Neill and Father Francis "Foxhole" Kelly, as well as dental experts, a bulldozer operator, and a licensed undertaker. From March 4 to May 20, the team recovered bodies from eight named or numbered cemeteries and numerous isolated graves on the island, as well as from burial sites on Buariki at the northern end of the atoll, Abemama to the south, and a C-47 transport plane that had crashed in the lagoon.

In the end, they located forty-nine percent of the bodies believed interred on Tarawa; of those, just fifty-eight percent were identified, less than a third of the total number of those killed. No remains were found beneath hundreds of markers in both large cemeteries and isolated graves and the survey noted that hundreds of others probably were not marked at all.[29] In March 2015, the Defense POW/MIA Accounting Agency—successor to JPAC—found that

that of 1,049 Marines and Navy servicemen killed on Tarawa from November 20–23, 1943, 510 "are not accounted for."[30]

In the end, AGRS recovered at least some remains from every named or numbered burial locations in 1946–47—except one. They failed to locate Cemetery 27, despite an apparent clue in the form of an elaborate 1944 monument with a plaque listing twenty-four men and sixteen unknowns buried "near this spot," near the boat basin and a Quonset hut that served as a theater.

The team confidently removed the monument and dug the surrounding area to a depth of seven feet. Finding nothing, they began digging exploratory trenches in every direction, "but all this work was in vain." Kelly and O'Neill even climbed an old Japanese watchtower in an effort to pinpoint the location of the trench, but after three weeks "it was felt that this was only a memorial site and there was no value in continuing the search in that area."[31]

Shortly thereafter, authorities declared that "All original burial sites on Tarawa Atoll were disinterred in 1946 and concentrated in the Lone Palm Cemetery, Betio Island, Tarawa."

The construction of gleaming white cemeteries neatly studded with crosses bearing the names of some 680 Tarawa dead (including some 400 known to be buried elsewhere, 122 purportedly buried at sea, and 88 missing and presumed dead) didn't fool those in the know.

"Existing cemeteries on Tarawa . . . are fictitious," Col. David Shoup wrote to Gen. Julian Smith in 1946. "Although they may appear neat and properly cared for, the markers may not identify the remains buried under them, if there are any remains buried there at all. . . . There were other instances where bodies were disinterred completely during the process of construction with no attempt to move them to proper burial spots so the remains of many may have been entirely lost. . . . It's a disgraceful mess but I am damned if I can see any measures we can take to remedy it at this late date."[32]

Smith thought the answer was to turn the entire island into a marine memorial.

"It seems to me that Betio is such a small piece of real estate that an agreement could be made with the British Government whereby it would remain as a shrine to the Marines who fell recapturing a piece of British territory," the general mused, noting that it might also "go a long way toward improving the relationship between the United States and England."[33] I've found no further documents indicating whether Smith or Shoup broached the idea with higher-ups.

But by 1949, the government was ready to end its search, despite having reclaimed only around half of the missing remains.

"In view of the fact that two separate operations have already been conducted to recover all remains on Tarawa; that further attempts would be difficult and costly; that in the event identifiable remains were recovered, it is quite possible they might not actually prove to be those of persons whose remains have supposedly been delivered to their next of kin; it is recommended that the findings of non-recoverability approved on 20 and 21 October 1949 be confirmed," advised the Quartermaster's Memorial Branch.[34]

Unidentified remains brought back from Tarawa were buried individually in the Courts of the Missing at the National Cemetery of the Pacific on Oahu beneath engraved letters reading, "The names of Americans who gave their lives in the service of their country and whose earthly resting place is known only to God."

According to a review of Sandy Bonnyman's case, "Dental and physical characteristics of the above-named individual were compared with all unknowns from Tarawa with negative results."[35] In 1949, his remains were determined to be "non-recoverable."[36]

That year, Alex Bonnyman ordered a ten-foot-long marble headstone from Italy. He had "BONNYMAN" carved on the front, and on the back, these words:

FIRST LT. ALEXANDER BONNYMAN, JR.

UNITED STATES MARINE CORPS RESERVE

BORN ATLANTA, GEORGIA

MAY 2, 1910

KILLED IN ACTION

TARAWA, GILBERT ISLANDS

NOVEMBER 22, 1943

BURIED AT SEA

He had the monument placed atop the highest hill in what is now Knoxville's Berry Highland Memorial Cemetery, just a couple miles from Bonniefield, and purchased seventeen plots for his family and succeeding generations of Bonnymans. Alex would be the first to be buried there, in 1953, followed by Frances and their daughter Margot in 1968, daughter Anne in 1990, son Gordon in 2004, and Gordon's wife Isabel in 2007. All went to their graves believing that Sandy had been lost forever.

As momentous as it had been in late 1943, the Battle of Tarawa receded quickly in the American imagination, replaced on front pages by ever-bigger battles and brutal fighting in the grim competition for bloodiest battle in Marine Corps history.

"It is strange the way life goes," photographer Obie Newcomb wrote Alex Bonnyman in July 1945. "Tarawa is so far away. Iwo Jima has sort of replaced it with its terrible memories."[37]

But for my family, Tarawa would always be painfully close. In hopes of easing his parents' grief, my great-uncle Gordon continued to pull at the most tenuous of threads in his dwindling campaign to bring his brother home. More than two decades after Sandy's death, a former navy Seabee named LeRoy J. Kain from Raton, New Mexico, gave some black-and-white photos he had taken in 1943 of a memorial cross marked "1st LT A. Bonneyman" (*sic*) to one of his bank customers, Gertrude Bonnyman, a cousin by marriage to Alex Bonnyman. Gordon immediately contacted Kain after his parents received the photos.

"The advice that the family received after Sandy's death was that he had been buried at sea. We had heard conflicting stories indicating that he had been buried on the island, but all efforts to substantiate this through the Marine Corps were fruitless, and I tried writing to the Graves Registration Officer in Hawaii in 1947 and again hit a dead end. The snapshots that you sent are the only conclusive (*sic*) proof that we have obtained indicating that he was buried on land,"[38] he wrote.

Kain dashed his hopes, saying he believed the cross was strictly memorial and closing with, "I can assure you the cemetery is well kept."[39]

Eventually, even Gordon gave up the search. Perhaps embittered, he told some of his children that Tarawa's dead had simply been "bulldozed into the sea."[40]

Amid all the heartache and disappointment in the winter and spring of 1944, my grieving family was able to hang on to one bit of solace. In the weeks following news of Sandy's death, the Bonnymans began receiving letters from marines who had fought at Tarawa, as well as one from an official in the Roosevelt administration, reporting that my grandfather's actions were so extraordinary that he had been recommended for the nation's highest military honor.[41] In March the *Princeton Alumni Weekly* and the Knoxville papers published stories about rumors of a pending Medal of Honor, making it seem all but certain.

In my research, I found accounts of several marines who reported recommending Sandy for the medal: Harry Niehoff, John

Borich, Joseph Clerou, Marvin Sheppard (who said "the other kid" who helped him remove the body from the bunker did likewise), and Col. David Shoup, who described Sandy as "one of the officers whose supreme valor won the battle of Tarawa for us."[42] Sadly, their recommendations either were not written down (Niehoff recalled that he and Borich made spoken recommendations), no longer exist, or remain hidden from even the most-skilled researchers in the deepest recesses of some Washington archive.

Maj. William Chamberlin, attesting that that he had personally witnessed Sandy's actions, made the official recommendation for the award in a December 27, 1943, memo to Maj. Henry P. "Jim" Crowe. Gen. Julian Smith, commander of the Second Marine Division, approved it on December 29, followed by Gen. Holland M. "Howlin' Mad" Smith, Commanding General of the Fifth Amphibious Corps, on January 19, 1944. On February 8, Admiral Chester Nimitz, commander of the US Pacific Fleet, signed off on recommendations not just for Alexander Bonnyman, Jr., but also William Bordelon and William Deane Hawkins. Marine Corps Commandant A.A. "Archie" Vandegrift added his signature on March 1 and forwarded the paperwork to the Navy Department Board of Decorations and Medals. The board considered all three cases, as well as a separate Medal of Honor recommendation for Shoup, on March 9.[43]

In early May, the families of Hawkins and Bordelon received notification that the two men had been posthumously awarded the Medal of Honor; Shoup's nomination was delayed for further consideration. And Jo Russell received a letter in Santa Fe informing her that "There is being forwarded to you this date the Navy Cross with Citation posthumously awarded your husband."[44]

Without explanation, and despite the exact same endorsements, the board had not deemed my grandfather's actions worthy of the medal given to Hawkins and Bordelon. I was shocked when I first read that letter; nobody had ever mentioned this to me.

Still, the Navy Cross was nothing to sneeze at, and news that Sandy had received the nation's *second*-highest honor was reported from New York to New Mexico, Texas to Tennessee; letters of congratulation poured into Bonniefield. The Bonnymans were as always gracious, and grateful that their son's sacrifice had been so recognized.

But after five months of assurances that he would receive the Medal of Honor, they were privately disappointed.[45]

Even before Jo married Jimmie Russell, her relationship with the Bonnymans had been fraught with tension. She continued to send the girls to Knoxville each summer, but began accusing their grandparents of letting them regress into filthy, rebellious, wild animals. Fran, who one summer broke her elbow in a tumble down a waterfall, looked "horrible . . . pale . . . her finger nails have been chewed down to the quick. . . . I don't see how any living creature could have experienced what Fran did and not forever have scars on more than her body," Jo sniped. The girls' stepfather, she wrote, "detested every minute (they) spent with you and they have returned home each time spoiled and difficult for me to manage."[46] She continually threatened to curtail their visits to Knoxville.

But the feuding came to a screeching, if temporary, halt in October 1946 when Jo received a letter in Santa Fe from Marine Corps Commandant Gen. A.A. Vandegrift, requesting that she return the Navy Cross and contact his office to discuss arrangements for a formal presentation of the Medal of Honor "to your eldest daughter, Miss Frances B. Bonnyman," Sandy's next of kin.[47]

Again, no explanation was given.

"While I knew Sandy had been recommended by his Colonel (Shoup) for the Medal, it had been about three years, and when it did come it came unexpectedly," Alex told a friend.[48]

After so much difficulty and heartbreak, the Bonnymans were overjoyed that their son would now ascend to the loftiest ranks of American military honor. Even my grandmother, who had so quickly put her previous life behind her, was elated. Jo informed Vandegrift that she would take her daughter to Washington to receive the medal, rather than attend a ceremony in Albuquerque or Santa Fe.

The presentation was scheduled for noon on January 22, 1947. The Bonnymans' guest list included family and friends, priests, bishops, and cardinals, railroad and mining barons, and Alex's friend, Attorney General Biddle, who said he would lobby the man who had signed the citation, President Harry S. Truman, to make the presentation in person. Jo's list included friends and business associates from New Mexico.

On a cold, cloudy day in the nation's capital, twelve-year-old Fran, wearing matching wool coat and hat, loafers, and white gloves, received the medal from acting Navy Secretary James Forrestal. Photos of my mother, flanked by her mother, grandfather, uncle, and Forrestal, went out over the wires and appeared in newspapers around the nation, from the *Washington Post* to the *Duluth News-Tribune* and *Santa Fe New Mexican*. The autographed photo of young Fran standing between two living Medal of Honor recipients, Shoup and Vandegrift, would remain her private treasure.

The semantic differences between the Navy Cross and Medal of Honor are subtle. The Navy Cross is awarded to those who have shown "extraordinary heroism and intrepidity" in battle, while the Medal of Honor for "conspicuous gallantry and intrepidity above and beyond the call of duty." But the numbers tell a different story: Fewer than 1,100 Medals of Honor have been awarded, compared to about 20,000 service crosses since 1918, when the latter were first awarded.

Thus, the moment my grandfather, 1st Lt. Alexander Bonnyman, Jr., received the nation's highest military honor, he was instantly elevated from a man honored among family and friends to one who would be revered by generations. Finding him was truly no more important than locating any of Tarawa's hundreds of missing. But he was the only one of the battle's Medal of Honor recipients to remain unaccounted for, and it was all but inevitable that his grave would become the "Holy Grail" of Betio's many mysteries.

EIGHTEEN
STRIKING GOLD
2014–2015

For seven years, Mark Noah had endured sabotage, slander, shunning, and scheming by everyone from a US military agency to the Kiribati government. But with every slight, he only grew more determined to bring Tarawa's MIAs home.

By 2014 History Flight had recovered more than thirteen thousand American bones and countless artifacts. But Mark's ardor puzzled even the *New York Times,* which reported that he "couldn't fully explain" why a private citizen with no connection to the military would be willing to endure so much frustration and financial drain to pursue long-forgotten bones.[1] I, too wondered, but Mark had always waved off the question when I asked about his motivations. So I was equally surprised and intrigued when he contacted me in February 2015 to say he was ready to talk.

He told me his earliest interest in World War II was spurred by an uncle who served in the First Marine Division and showed him artifacts brought back from Peleliu and Okinawa, sites of two of the most gut-churning Pacific battles to follow Tarawa.

Though he never served in the military himself, he'd been deeply affected by violence. While living in the People's Republic of China during the 1980s (his father worked for the US Department of State), some of his young friends in the pro-democracy movement disappeared during the government's brutal 1989 crackdown. Some later turned up dead, but Mark was even more haunted by those who had simply vanished, their fates unknown.

His own initiation into violence came during his years of running with a "punk-rock" street gang, when he learned to be a street fighter and enforcer of a violent code of ethics.

"I saw a tremendous amount of street violence and bloodshed in Atlanta and LA," he told me. "I saw friends screaming out to God to save them when they knew they were going to die, and they knew there was no salvation."[2]

Memories of those dead and disappeared friends, which he told me he'd never even shared with his wife, would later inform a kind of spiritual motivation for finding Tarawa's MIAs.

"A lot of these beard-stroking academics and PhD anthropologists approach this work as if they are more interested in themselves than helping other people. They act very nonchalant and cavalier around deceased people, with not even a semblance of dignity," he said. "But I have something they don't have: They've never been there when a 'forensic event' happened, they've never been violently injured themselves."[3]

Mark outgrew his violent youthful diversions to become a responsible husband and father of two, and his punkish pugnacity evolved into a marine-like tenacity in the face of adversity.

"One of my strongest points is that I'm hard as nails, and I've never taken shit from them [JPAC]. They tried to undermine me every way they could. They started their big slander campaign, and it blew up in their faces," he said. "But they didn't know me very well, and every time they pulled anything, we doubled down and made our efforts even more successful."[4]

So here's Mark Noah: an adventurous, driven, stubborn, sometimes impetuous son of privilege, ever ready—even eager—for a fight.

Now who did that remind me of?

In 2014 Mark Noah added a new member to the History Flight team, former Army Special Forces medic John Frye, whom Kristen had met while both were working on JPAC missions in Korea and Vietnam. John's expertise in field medicine would prove a valuable asset to History Flight's work on Betio.

"At JPAC they couldn't care less about my experience. They wouldn't listen to me if I'd tried to stand on somebody's desk and shout, because I wasn't a forensic anthropologist," he said. "But I've seen a few people blown up and shot, so I know a little about what those injuries do to the body."[5]

On Memorial Day that year, History Flight announced the repatriation of partial remains of "at least forty individuals" recovered between January and May, mostly from the Cemetery 26 and 33 areas, and invited six Tarawa veterans—Wendell Perkins, C.J. Daigle, A.J. Bowden, Jim Morrows, Dean Woodward, and Dean Ladd—on a tour of Betio and Wellington, New Zealand, where they had been stationed before and after the Second Marine Division's time on Guadalcanal.

Finally, after four years of sporadic effort, JPAC recovered its first set of Tarawa remains without any input from History Flight in October 2014. Following up on a tip from a Betio resident, a team led by anthropologist Jay Silverstein zeroed in on the grave by overlaying a historic photo on a modern aerial image of the island. A dog tag bearing the letters "RED" was the first clue in the eventual identification of Pvt. Jack Redman, who was killed on the last day of the battle.[6]

JPAC also had officially identified the American remains unearthed at the Taiwanese housing development by Kristen Baker her first weeks on the job. Pfc. Randolph Allen of Watseka, Illinois, was one of just nine marines killed on the final day of fighting on Betio. (The other remains recovered at the site were Japanese.)

Both discoveries, along with their subsequent funerals, drew attention from the media, and casual observers might well have concluded that the score was JPAC 1, History Flight 1. But things were about to change in a big way for the agency and the nonprofit alike.

On March 31, 2015, US Secretary of Defense Chuck Hagel announced a major reorganization of the nation's efforts to identify and recover the estimated 83,000 missing American war dead around the world. Three agencies tasked with those duties, JPAC, DPMO, and the Central Identification Laboratory, would be merged into the new Defense POW/MIA Accounting Agency, or DPAA, "a single accountable organization that has complete oversight of personnel accounting resources, research and operations" under the oversight of a director in the Pentagon.[7]

Meanwhile on Betio, Kristen Baker was poised to make the discovery of a lifetime. Kristen, like Mark, had never lost her interest in thoroughly exploring the crushed-coral yard at Kiribati Shipping Services Ltd., believing that CIL deputy director Bill Belcher had ignored JPAC's own protocols by failing to further excavate the site after finding small bones and American artifacts in 2012.

But numerous hurdles, both logistical and political, had prevented History Flight from conducting a more systematic search of the area. The cramped yard was hemmed in by two hulking post-World War II Quonset huts, a dilapidated two-story office building, a twenty-foot high tin-sided warehouse, and the boat basin, rendering it all but impossible for the company to conduct regular business around a large hole in the ground.

But in late November 2014, Kristen noticed that the company had begun tearing down the Quonset huts. If they weren't replaced, there might enough room for both commerce and archaeology. But when History Flight fixer Kautebiri Kobuti made inquiries, the manager declined to grant permission to dig in the yard.

After spending the holidays in Hawaii, Kristen and John Frye returned to Tarawa in January. But a destructive "king tide"— a perigean spring tide, the precise opposite of the weak high tide that doomed so many marines during the battle—battered the island, smashing one of Betio's myriad hulking reef wrecks through the seawall on Red Beach 2 and waterlogging the island, making it impossible to work at their current site, Cemetery 26.

Kristen used the delay to press for access to the shipping yard. By then, the shipping company had a new general manager, Tamana Natanaera, who green-lighted the project, provided the team stopped working when the company's fifty-six-foot inter-island transport *Butimari* was in port.

"I'm amazed to this day at the way everything suddenly came together so perfectly," Kristen said.[8]

On March 15 Kristen, John, and volunteer Rick Snow, founder of Knoxville-based Forensic Anthropology Consulting Services, Inc., opened up an exploratory trench east of the lamp pole where Pfc. Herman Sturmer had been found in 2002. Within hours, the team encountered American remains some three to four feet beneath the surface (later identified as belonging to Cpl. Roger K. Nielsen of Denver, killed on D-day).

"That was all the confirmation we needed," Kristen said.

The excavation process was slow and painstaking. Once the local laborers— Aman, Titang, Eru, and Katerak—had broken through the layer of crushed coral, the team gently "shovel shaved" a half inch of soil at a time and dumped it into five-gallon plastic buckets for sifting. As soon as a shovel struck anything solid, Kristen called a halt to the digging to examine the find. Once they hit human remains or artifacts, she, John, and experienced volunteers would use spades, brushes, and small wooden tools to fully expose the remains. Each individual would take up three days to expose, document, and remove.

Though painstaking, this kind of archaeology absolutely *was* a spectator sport, as the team discovered four nearly intact, and two partial, sets of American remains as well as a torso on a stretcher. Through dental comparisons and artifacts, Kristen was able to provisionally identify three of the six marines as Nielsen, Sgt. James J. Hubert, and Pvt. Robert Carter Jr., all of whose casualty cards listed only memorial graves at Cemetery 33.

Carter's hand was literally a couple of inches from the telltale remains of JPAC's exploratory trench—"almost like he was reaching out to Bill Belcher," Kristen said.[9] But none of three identified marines seemed to be associated with Cemetery 27. Had the team stumbled onto a completely different site? Kristen numbered the remains as "individuals" 1–6, tentatively labeled the trench "Row B" of Cemetery 27, and began digging exploratory trenches in search of the mother lode.

"If you are looking for something that is running east-west, you dig north-south," she said. "Otherwise you can dig all day long and miss what you are looking for."[10]

When they found only "sterile soil" to the south, they began digging to the north, toward an anomaly identified through ground-penetrating radar in 2012. Once beneath the hard upper layer, the first shovel cuts revealed the distinctive soil profile Kristen now recognized as a bulldozer trench. She laid out a grid for a large unit and in short order the team had unearthed an intact set of remains.

Back at the lab—a tile-floored, three-room suite at the Betio Lodge II—a dog tag and dental comparisons led Kristen to make a strong provisional identification of Pfc. Charles E. Oetjen. Killed on D-day, Oetjen was recorded as having been buried in "Grave #6,

8th Marines #2, Central Division Cemetery"—Cemetery 27. It was a tantalizing clue, but Kristen wanted more data before making any sweeping conclusions.

Digging west, the team recovered five more sets of remains over the next couple of weeks: Pvt. Frank Penna, an unknown later identified as Cpl. Walter Critchley, Pvt. Palmer Sherman Haraldson, and Pvt. Fred Evert Freet, whose casualty cards indicated that they were buried in grave numbers 6 to 2, respectively, and an unknown later identified as Cpl. James D. Otto, whose arm was partially exposed in the western wall of the unit and recorded as occupying grave #1.

Now there could be no doubt.

"We knew we'd found Cemetery 27," Kristen said.

(It's worth noting that the location was about fifty yards southeast of the coordinates "at or very close" to where Bill Niven originally predicted the trench containing my grandfather's remains would be found.[11] Close, but definitely no cigar; I had learned that in archaeology, missing by an inch is the same as missing by a mile.)

After carefully exhuming twelve sets of remains in under six weeks, Kristen flew back to Hawaii on May 1 for a scheduled ten-day break. But she couldn't wait to get back to Betio to solve the puzzle of Cemetery 27.

"When we came back," Mark Noah said, "we began to dig east and the burial feature began to yield an eerie similarity to the historical record that we had recreated."[12]

And according to that record, my grandfather would be found in "grave" #17, less than six meters to the east.

Mark first called me in mid-March to say that his team may have finally located Cemetery 27. I forced myself to tamp down expectations. How many times, after all, had we agreed that finding Sandy Bonnyman was comparable to searching for the proverbial the needle in a haystack? And by now I knew the vagaries of Betio all too well. Who knew if locals had backhoed through the part of the trench where my grandfather should have been, or dug up his remains while digging a trash pit, or if his grave was otherwise disturbed, even removed? Still, knowing that Kristen had identified marines whose names appeared on that monument next to my grandfather's went far beyond any previous tantalizing hints.

Over the next few weeks, Mark continually updated me on the good news. Finally, in May, I got the call I'd been waiting for: "You need to get down there. And bring a video camera."

To my surprise, conditions on Betio and South Tarawa in general had not fully relapsed into pre-seventieth-anniversary squalor. Whether due to seasonal conditions or some human effort, the air seemed less infused with the corpse-like odor of the reef and residents were now making use of green plastic garbage bags emblazoned with *Kiribati te Boboto* or "Keep Kiribati Clean." For the first time ever I saw dogs wearing collars and sporting shiny coats, even one running happily alongside a boy on a bicycle.

Or maybe I was just seeing the place through Sandy-tinted glasses.

Responding in part to a cultural-resources management proposal drawn up by History Flight, the Kiribati Board of Tourism had scraped away the junk and overgrowth around Admiral Shibasaki's bunker and strategically placed wrecked cars and rusty sheet metal around Bonnyman's Bunker in an effort to discourage residents from using the top as a latrine. There also was profusion of new "restraunts" and curious offerings of consumer goods for sale, from blow-up Santas to Mylar balloons and shiny new bicycles.

All those changes were due, in part, to a bevy of internationally funded projects that had brought an influx of Australian and Kiwi workers. These included various initiatives funded by the European Union, the United Nations, Australia, New Zealand, and the United States, including a major road-improvement project funded by the World Bank and managed by New Zealand's McDowell Construction, which also had put up razor-wire fencing around the airport for the first time.

By the time I walked over to the dig site that first day, the sun was high and hot. Kristen and John had fully exposed the remains in grave #8, carefully removing and wrapping every bone, fragment, and piece of material evidence—the rubber soles of boondockers, the standard-issue marine combat boots; shreds of sock; ammunition clips; and more—in aluminum foil before placing it into large plastic evidence bags.

Like three-quarters of the remains that eventually would be recovered from "Row A"—which was, in fact, Cemetery 27—those in #8 were wrapped in a green, rubberized canvas poncho. Like all but three of the marines buried in Cemetery 27, Pfc. James Mansfield was killed on the first day of fighting but wasn't buried until several days later. Given the advanced state of decomposition, burial details simply wrapped remains in ponchos, apparently making little or no effort to remove gear or personal items.

Exhuming poncho-covered remains day after day, Kristen Baker was seeing the fascinating effects of the moisture-retaining microenvironment, which had preserved a host of typically biodegradable materials, including leather, hair, even a pack of Camel cigarettes. But the moisture inside the ponchos also made many bones porous and fragile.

"Things fall apart," Kristen murmured down in the hole, quoting Yeats.

I had seen bits and pieces of human remains in my previous work with History Flight, as well as the skeletons of Randolph Allen and four Japanese at Cemetery 26, but that was the first time I was able to get in for a closer look. The soles of Mansfield's boots seemed so human; they awoke me to the reality of what lay before me.

"Jesus, I don't want to die alone," Johnny Cash sang mournfully from Kristen's boom box on the edge of the hole.

Kristen worked assiduously to follow and even surpass the standard operating procedures she learned at JPAC. When a JPAC team recovered three sets of remains from Cemetery 25 in 2012, they didn't bother collecting every tiny toe or finger bone or fragment of rib, but Kristen was intent on preserving even the smallest grain of evidence, right down to sock threads that fit on the tip of her little finger.

"They have good standards, but I tend to go above and beyond," she said. "It's a matter of respect, too. These guys deserve the best treatment we can give them."[13]

Based on solid provisional identifications of remains whose grave locations neatly corresponded with casualty cards, Kristen was confident that we were on track to find Sandy Bonnyman in grave #17. When we did—if we did—his teeth would provide virtually instant confirmation of his identity: Kristen had practically memorized my grandfather's dental chart, which revealed extensive work and multiple gold restorations. Upon examining each successive set of remains, Kristen took to pronouncing, "No gold."

"Gold was very expensive and unusual at the time, and there weren't very many people, particularly in the marines, who had gold bridges and fillings," Kristen said. "In the forty people buried here, only maybe three or four had any gold fillings at all."[14]

After all these years of anticipation, my mind refused to share her confidence, and in my jittery state, I constantly imagined nightmare scenarios: "Unfortunately, it looks like there's been extensive disturbance after #15 . . . " or "There's a trash pit where your grandfather should be . . . " To combat the constant fluttering of butterfly wings in my gut, I kept myself busy shooting video and photos, chipping in with screening or digging, walking to the store to buy cans of Pringles for the crew. I was indescribably grateful that I happened to share most of Kristen's musical tastes—Creedence Clearwater Revival, Johnny Cash, Metallica, Rise Against, the Black Keys, Lynyrd Skynrd. It would have driven me around the bend to have my butterflies flapping to bad country or disco.

When I first arrived, each set of remains was taking three to four days to expose, document, and remove, including time for Kristen to make highly detailed *in situ* sketches of all remains. My wife Jody and I had agreed that I would stay on Betio as long as needed to either find Sandy, or confirm that he was not buried here, but I was feeling antsy. After a couple of days, I got up the nerve to ask Kristen if it would save time to make the drawings later, based on photographs. Had she told me that would violate best practices, I would have understood; after all, where I was focused on one particular grave, it was her job to give her utmost professional attention to every set of remains. But after giving it some thought, Kristen thanked me for suggesting the idea. After she made the change, it generally took between one and two days to fully process each set of remains.

Mindful that the shipping company's inter-island cargo ship *Butimari* was due to dock within a couple of weeks, the crew also stepped up their already grueling work schedule, working straight through rain squalls and staying "in the hole" from seven or eight o'clock in the morning until six in the evening. Kristen drove herself so hard that she suffered a relapse of chikungunya, a debilitating, mosquito-borne viral disease recently arrived from Africa. Though sore and exhausted, she refused to take a day off, even when John suggested it.

With the team now processing a new set of remains nearly every day, a huge backlog of lab work began to mount. Once removed from the ground, all remains had to be carefully cleaned, dried, cataloged, and photographed, and a full report (typically ten or more pages) had to be written for each individual set. All that work had literally ground to a halt upon the departure of forensic anthropologist Rick Snow (one of Kristen Baker's early mentors) before I arrived. On Snow's recommendation, Mark hired a PhD candidate from the University of Tennessee—home to one of the country's top forensic anthropology programs—to pick up the slack.

Hillary Parsons had completed her coursework and was now living in her hometown, Bozeman, Montana, working at a whiskey distillery and completing her dissertation. To speed things up in the lab, I began assisting Hillary after visiting the dig site and capturing video and photos each morning. I had ulterior motives for helping out: The lab was air conditioned and scrubbing bones—not to mention lots of banter—kept me blessedly distracted and my mind (mostly) free from its usual doom-and-gloom chatter.

Little did I know that working in the lab would come to resemble a mini-seminar in forensics—call it bones for boneheads—courtesy of Professor Parsons. As I carefully brushed and washed away grains of sand, she answered all my questions, gave me the name of even the tiniest bones, pointed out clues to determine age, sex, ancestry, and cause of death.

Hillary also let me play Watson to her Sherlock Holmes. After cleaning up a brass watch found with the remains in grave #3, I noticed that "PSH" and "C-1-6" had been scratched into the cover. Guessing that these were the marine's initials and unit number, I flipped through History Flight's research on the missing and discovered that a Pvt. Palmer Sherman Haraldson, with C Company, 1st Battalion, 6th Marines, had been killed on D+3. After a dental comparison, Hillary was able to confirm that provisional identification with a high degree of confidence.

"You need to be there now. All the time," Paul Schwimmer advised me one night after dinner at the Betio Lodge II. Paul, a US Army Special Forces veteran, had been doing *pro bono* survey work for History Flight for years. "This is *Raiders of the Lost Ark*, and I'm telling you, we are coming closer and closer to the ark."

The next morning I woke at five o'clock and ran to Bairiki. As the sun rose I found myself staring up at the clouds, remembering my first trip to Tarawa, and CNN reporter Ted Rowland's fruitless attempts to wring some tears from me.

Back then, the idea that we would actually *find* my grandfather had seemed little more than a fantasy. Now, the team had exposed grave #15, less than a meter from where my grandfather might lay. There had been no glitches so far, just one set of intact remains after another, day after day, and no reason to think that would change.

Jogging along the causeway, I felt myself . . . untethered. I no longer feared that we *wouldn't* find my grandfather, but that we *would*—or rather, what I would feel in that moment. I once told CNN cameraman John Torigoe that going to Tarawa had divided my life into before and after. But the after had really been a kind of limbo, a liminal state that I never really expected to end. Now, as I tried to imagine the once unimaginable, I saw myself collapsing, going mad, drifting away.

Suddenly I was overcome with sadness—for my grandfather, my mother and aunt, my great-grandparents, for all Tarawa's dead and all their families, too. I stopped atop a culvert on the causeway; stripped off my shirt, socks, and shoes. Plunging into the blue current rushing below, I rode it seaward, my tears swallowed up by the mighty Pacific.

When I got to the dig site at eight o'clock, the team had shovel-shaved down to a bench about two feet deep, exposing the butt of a green,

World War II-era Japanese beer bottle in the south facing wall. At mid-morning, sand began to trickle into a small, oval void below the beer bottle. Kristen, sporting one of her trademark skull bandanas, pulled on blue latex surgical gloves and gently palpated the hole.

"It's the edge of a helmet," she said. "There is a cranium inside."

Over the next few minutes, she carefully brushed away sand, keeping it level and smooth. As I looked over her shoulder, something else came into view: a small, smooth patch of brown just a few inches from the helmet. My heart began to thud faster.

"Another cranium," Kristen said evenly.

She continued to expose the area, singing along with Shinedown's rendition of Lynyrd Skynyrd's "Simple Man": "Boy, don't you worry, you'll find yourself/Follow your heart and nothing else . . . And be a simple kind of man/Oh, be something you love and understand . . ."

I'd always seen a little of myself in the song, but now I thought of my grandfather: "Take your time, don't live too fast/Troubles will come and they will pass."

Goosebumps prickled my skin in the tropical heat and I raised the camera to my eye, focusing on Kristen's hands. I held my breath, trying to steady my own. From behind me, I heard John say, "Yup."

"Gold," Kristen said a split second later.

Then I dropped the camera.

It was 10:49 in the morning, May 28, 2015—seventy-one years, six months, five days and perhaps twenty hours since 1st Lt. Alexander Bonnyman, Jr., Sandy, Bonny, *my grandfather*, had taken his last breath.

NINETEEN
RIPPLES
1946-PRESENT

Even as the memories of World War II began to fade into the past, the world never stopped remembering and honoring my grandfather for his singular courage, self-sacrifice, and indomitable spirit in battle.

On November 21, 1948, combat correspondent Robert Sherrod, who accompanied the marines at Tarawa, sent Alex Bonnyman a telegram to say that "A few of us gathered tonight and drank a toast to a thousand brave men who died five years ago. We especially remembered Alexander Bonnyman, Jr."[1]

A gold star bearing my grandfather's name adorns the window of his former dorm in Blair Hall at Princeton University; I've had active-duty marines from Camp Lejeune, NC, approach me to say they enjoy drinking a beer or two at the Bonnyman Bowling Center; you can drive across the First Lt. Alexander "Sandy" Bonnyman Bridge on the Pellissippi Parkway west of Knoxville; and the Maersk Line's *1st Lt. Alex Bonnyman* plied the high seas as a marine pre-positioning ship until it was decommissioned in 2009. Marines born thirty, forty, even fifty years after Sandy's death know his story; people who recognize the Bonnyman name sometimes approach his descendants, right down to his twenty-something grand-niece, to ask for an autograph or handshake.

But before he left for the marines in July 1942, my grandfather was a black sheep in his prominent Southern family. Stubborn and rebellious, he had a habit of drinking too much and picking fights, and proved less than reliable when it came to other people's money. And as romantically appealing as his story has been to those crafting the legend, Sandy's appetite for adventure and danger led him to make choices that were not always in the best interests of his young family. Gordon Bonnyman dearly loved, admired, and missed his older brother, but he always said leading men into battle suited him better than leading the life of a husband, father, and businessman.[2]

A legend is a story that grows over time with embellishments, exaggerations, and, just as often, strategic editing. In my grandfather's case, irresistibly dramatic details were being offered within weeks of his death through second- or third-hand accounts—the flamethrower, the hand-to-hand combat, that final, stoic smile.

A more-subtle shift also began to take place, as his rougher edges were smoothed away and his life was gradually reduced—and that is the right word for it—to only those truths that seemed to suit a hero. Embalmed in legend, my grandfather was enclosed in a suit of silver armor, set upon a white charger, and placed behind glass, forever frozen within a spotless diorama.

"He became the great mythic hero of the family," said his nephew Robert McKeon, a Catholic deacon. "But when we idealize people, we overlook the reality that all human beings are very complex."[3]

Bonnyman family members, spanning generations, have described Sandy as everything from "spoiled" and "impetuous" to "fearless" and a "rock star." He was all that, and more. But where the historians, authors of legend, and propagandists have always had the luxury of ignorance, only those who most loved Sandy Bonnyman—his children, wife, parents, and siblings—had to live with the shattering consequences of the valor for which he is so justly admired.

"The nation glorifies World War II; it was called the Great Crusade, and we now idolize the men of the Greatest Generation and immortalize the dwindling legions of these heroes constantly in film and in literature," writes historian David P. Colley. "In so doing we have lost touch with the immense pain and suffering caused by the war and the ripples of sorrow that still flow across America from that devastating conflict. We know little of the men who gave their lives and nothing about the struggles of their families."[4]

Encouraged by politicians and generals, many Americans—certainly a great majority of those with no close connection to the mere *half-percent* of the population that serves in the all-volunteer armed forces—today view all things military with sentimentality and uncritical admiration, unburdened by the harsh realities of war borne not just by those who fight, but also their families.

I met US Army Capt. Don Gomez Jr. not long after I returned from my first trip to Tarawa. He served two tours of duty in Iraq with the 82nd Airborne Division before stepping out to earn a degree from the London School of Economics and get married. He re-upped in 2011 and redeployed to the Middle East in 2014.

"Sometimes I think my decision to go back into the military is very selfish. I'm doing it, frankly, because I like the lifestyle. I think it's exciting and fun," he said. "But I'm married now. What happens if you get hurt? How heroic are you then? What if I'm permanently injured and my wife has to take care of me?"[5]

Col. Bill Bower, one of the pilots who bombed Tokyo with Jimmy Doolittle's Raiders in April 1942, was a surrogate grandfather to the kids in the neighborhood where I grew up in Boulder, Colorado. He helped us build and launch Estes model rockets, fixed our bicycles, and always had a Jolly Rancher candy if you stopped by. We all knew "the colonel" had done something in the war, but Bill wasn't one to push his stories, and we didn't ask.

I saw him last in August 2010, right after my return from Tarawa. I had hoped to hear his thoughts about heroes and heroism, but by then he was suffering from advanced dementia and offered only a wrinkled brow whenever I spoke. Later, however, as he dozed in a wheelchair in the shade of a ponderosa pine, Bill suddenly opened his eyes and spoke to me as lucidly as when I'd been six years old.

"I didn't do anything heroic," he whispered, blue eyes bright and watery. "The real heroes are the guys who raise a family. The men who stick by their families."

Bill never spoke another word to me. He died a few months later at ninety-three. When I told his son Jim about his last words at the funeral, he told me something I never knew: Bill's father had abandoned his family.

Sandy Bonnyman did not abandon his family; he is not responsible for the terrible tragedies that befell his daughters. But in coming to know my grandfather, I've come to believe that we must never allow tales of "perfect" heroes, legends, or bright, shining lies distract us from the brutal realities and consequences of war. As Hemingway wrote, "Never think that war, no matter how necessary, nor how justified, is not a crime."[6]

"Your grandfather deserves to be honored for his extraordinary deeds, as do a lot of other people," US Army Special Forces and Vietnam combat veteran William T. Hathaway told me in 2011. "But that should always be coupled with the thought, 'What about his family? What about the little girls who had to grow up without a daddy?' You grew up admiring that mythical hero on the wall and there is nothing wrong with that. But there are costs. There is a downside when the hero story is told in isolation, used to whip up emotions. We should remember that."[7]

Whether, like Nabokov's Humbert Humbert, Jimmie Russell took up with my grandmother to gain access to her young daughters, will never be known. But I will not judge family members who knew he was abusing Sandy's little girls, yet did nothing. My great-grandmother Blanche Bell felt such terrible shame about the situation that it prevented her "from looking even into the face of God and praying."[8]

But it was a different time.

As they grew older, my mother, Fran Bonnyman, and her younger sister Alix, showed some of their father's pugnacity, going so far as to confront their abuser at the dinner table one time. Russell did not deny the accusations, but my grandmother, alcoholic and suffering from neglect and emotional abuse in her marriage, refused to believe them.[9] She was, sadly, not equipped to protect her children.

Fran, the oldest of Sandy's three blondes, had a stubborn streak a mile wide that her stepfather did not appreciate. Surely that's one reason she was packed off to St. Mary's Hall, a girls' school in San Antonio, at age fourteen. She felt bad leaving her sisters, but, possessed of a childlike acceptance of things she could not change, she made up her mind to "just have fun in life."

Courtesy of her father's careful planning, Fran lived well, traveling to Europe and being toasted on social pages from Knoxville to San Antonio. Kicked out of Connecticut College for Women for "partying too much"—she was, after all, her father's daughter—she eventually graduated from the University of New Mexico, where she met and married my father, Clayton Anthony Evans. He later graduated from the University of Colorado School of Medicine and they raised my sister, brother, and me in Boulder.

Sandy's youngest daughter, Alix, attended Santa Fe High School before also being sent to St. Mary's Hall, and graduated from the University of Arizona. She, too, traveled, but also spent much of her young adulthood caring for my grandmother and my aunt Tina, whose addictions she attributed to neglect and abuse by Russell.

"Jimmie stifled my mother. He had such a terrible reign over her. He wouldn't let her do the things she always loved to do, ride or go skiing. He made her perform like a circus pony in front of their friends," Alix said. "She became alcoholic after she married him."[10]

My aunt met her late husband, Carroll Prejean, a true-blue Cajun and marine veteran from Lafayette, Louisiana, in the jungles of Ecuador, where she was teaching and he was working as an oil rough-neck. They bought a ranch in Hackett, Arkansas, where they raised Peruvian Paso Fino horses, Beefmaster cattle, and their daughter Alexandra. In the 1990s, they moved to the remote paradise of Hana, Maui. Tough, irrepressibly social, and insistently affectionate—she takes special delight in doling out hugs to presidents, generals, and marines—Alix is, like her older sister, a survivor.

Sandy's middle daughter Josephine, my Aunt Tina, was not. Mocked by her mother for her neediness as a child, she was to become "Jimmie's favorite,"[11] and—not coincidentally—seemed destined for alcoholism from the moment she took her first drink as a teenager. She graduated from the University of Texas at Austin, and was a ski bum in Taos before she married and had a daughter. But drinking led her into dangerous situations and away from motherhood. She was also a lot of fun; as a boy, I loved watching *Outer Limits* with her and visiting her mountain A-frame cabin.

Eventually, she was placed in a mental institution in Galveston, Texas. There, in a gambit for freedom, she married a male nurse, an abusive former Nazi paratrooper. Sandy's shy "curly blonde" was just forty when she died. Her husband, who once shouted, "I'll kill you just like I killed those Jews!"[12] while choking her, had my aunt cremated immediately. Her daughter is not the only family member who considers her death suspicious.

My grandmother Jo also drank too much, and suffered years of cruelty and neglect as the wife of Jimmie Russell. They finally divorced in 1964, and Russell married a former high school classmate of Alix, then 24. Russell managed to win the lion's share of the assets. While he continued to live in their spacious home in Santa Fe with his new wife, Jo lived the rest of her life in a small apartment across town.

Jo got sober late in life, but for my sister and me, it was too little, too late; we told my mother we didn't want to see "Mimi" again after she refused to allow our three-year-old brother to enter her home. She died during abdominal surgery in 1976 and is buried in Santa Fe. More than any other person, except perhaps my Uncle Gordon, I wish I'd had the opportunity to talk to her about my grandfather. Whatever their difficulties, and despite her weaknesses, I believe she knew him better than anyone and loved him fiercely. Given her propensities and deep insecurity, I suspect she, too, may have experienced abuse as a child.

James Hobart "Jimmie" Russell lived a charmed life. His 1999 obituary omitted his age, date, and city of birth (ninety-seven; September 9, 1902; Fairland, Oklahoma) but described his many accomplishments, including his role in the formation of the Santa Fe Opera, the fact that he had "almost" been drafted by the Republican Party to run for governor, and his role in creating the New Mexico Film Commission. "He was," according to the tribute, "a good friend and advisor to many people for the seven decades that he resided in Northern New Mexico and a generous contributor to variety of community organizations and charities that in turn have recognized and applauded his warmth and generosity."[13]

The obituary did not mention his two-decade marriage to my grandmother, his friendship with local hero Sandy Bonnyman, whom he had "loved . . . as a younger brother," the three blonde girls who grew up under his roof, or his involvement with the Guadalupe Mining Company.

Perhaps that tragic history is the real reason for the curious silence about my grandfather I encountered while growing up. My sister and I spent time with our Granny Great at Bonniefield each summer until her death in 1968, swimming in the same pool where Sandy had made his daring dives, eating homemade blackberry ice cream and grits under the watchful eye of a British nanny. We loved roaming the estate's remaining ten acres, catching lightning bugs, and exploring the woods, just as our grandfather had. Granny continued to tell stories about her beloved son, but never to my sister or me; perhaps we were just too young to understand.

We also spent time around our great-uncle Gordon, who was stern, but kindly; we were fascinated that he'd trained his hunting dogs to ride in the trunk of his car. The simple fact is, Gordon Bonnyman succeeded in every way that his famous older brother had failed, graduating from Princeton, enduring his father's difficult tutelage before taking Blue Diamond to new heights (annual revenues soared to $12.5 million dollars during his tenure, well beyond $100 million in inflation-adjusted terms), and marrying a beautiful girl from a prominent, respectable Knoxville family. Gordon's military career was no less outstanding: He earned a Silver Star and Bronze Star and in 2020, shared in a Congressional Gold Medal awarded to his unit, known as Merrill's Marauders. He retired from the US Army as a major.

Given that, I was surprised and saddened to find many letters in which his father compared him unfavorably to Sandy and bluntly described him as lacking in imagination and unexceptional. My great-grandfather even (wrongly) judged that his younger son's "work was not spectacular" during his time overseas.[14]

Yet family members never heard Gordon utter a bitter or resentful word about standing in his brother's shadow. In his final years, Sandy was much on his mind.

When interviewers from the University of Tennessee Veterans' Oral History Project asked him to talk about Sandy, he spoke just a few sentences, ending with "and then he got killed at Tarawa." The interviewers then turned off the recorder to give him time to compose himself. There was no more talk of Sandy after they restarted the interview.[15]

And in the days leading up to his own death in 2004, George Gordon Bonnyman experienced visions of only one person: the beloved older brother he'd tried so hard to bring home.[16]

TWENTY
TENDER HANDS
MAY 28-JUNE 1, 2015

Even as Kristen Baker pronounced the word we'd been waiting to hear, we all saw the telltale glint in that burnished jaw beneath her brush.

I should have steadied my hand and kept the video camera rolling. Instead, my body yielded involuntarily to a sudden, powerful yearning to freeze everything around me so I could experience that instant fully, for as long as I desired. I found myself thinking—as I often do—about Tolkien's great quest story, *The Lord of the Rings*, thinking that this was how Frodo and Sam must have felt at the end of their own seemingly impossible quest, the world collapsing around them.

But time didn't stop. Keenly aware of all those eyes upon me, I instinctively donned the inquisitive armor that had served me so well in my long career as a journalist: I turned to Kristen and asked what *she* was feeling.

"I really don't know what to say in a situation like this," she said haltingly.

I knew exactly how she felt.

A couple minutes later John Frye called the two of us out of the hole. He handed cold bottles of New Zealand Tui beer to Kristen and me, as well as Paul and Aman, Titang, Eru, and Katerak, our incredibly hard-working local crew. John toasted Sandy Bonnyman, Mark Noah, Kristen, and everyone else who had made this possible.

And then Kristen got back to work. Per protocol, she turned her attention to the remains in grave #16. The skeleton (eventually identified as Pvt. Emmet L. Kines) lay on its back, shrouded in poncho, face to face with my grandfather, his left arm beneath my grandfather's shoulders, a bony embrace that had lasted seventy-one years.

Meanwhile, Paul turned the tables—and camera—on me. I rambled for eleven minutes, struggling to keep my emotions in check.

"I'm sorry that I didn't make more effort twenty-five years ago, when a lot more of the Tarawa veterans were alive," I said. "But this alone is a five-year odyssey and it's thanks to Mark Noah."

Yet the man responsible would miss this astonishing moment by just one hour. In continual contact with him by satellite phone, Kristen had advised him that team was fast approaching grave #17. He arrived at the site shortly before noon, having driven straight from the airport.

"There's number 21," John said, pointing to grave #16 (Kristen began numbering individuals with first row, not the main trench), "and right there next to him is Alexander Bonnyman."

Mark laughed.

"No. I'm not kidding," John said. "That's him."

"Super. Super nice," Mark said. "Wow."

Instead of returning to duty at the lab, where I would have been far more productive, I remained at the site for the rest of the day. Having found my grandfather, I was now reluctant to leave his side; I even mused out loud about camping out in the unit that night, but came to my senses when I remembered the shipping company always kept a guard on duty. By late afternoon, the remains of Pvt. Kines had been safely delivered into Hillary's hands. Tomorrow was going to be quite a day.

Later that night at the Betio Lodge, Paul said he was surprised that I hadn't shown more emotion.

"I felt it; you saw me choking up on the video. But I had to shut it down," I said. "I wasn't about to start blubbering in front of two special-forces guys."

"Believe me," Paul said, "when guys lose a friend from their outfit, they show their emotions."

"Of course," I said. "But that's different; I didn't risk myself like my grandfather did and I just couldn't . . . I don't know. I just had to keep a lid on it."

"Well, just remember," he said, shaking his head, "that's on *you*."

The next day the crew began removing sand from around my grand-father's skeleton, meticulously brushing away a few grains at a time, as if his bones were made of delicate crystal. His were just the third set of remains in the main trench not to be wrapped in a poncho, and where other graves had yielded everything from grenades and hel-mets to watches and a pack of cigarettes, Sandy had been buried with almost nothing by his side. But the hard rubber soles of his boots were still pressed to the bones of his big feet and we recovered numerous corroded metal buttons and the shards of his metal belt buckle.

More intriguing, I found a lump of sand-crusted metal in the area that would have been his left front pants pocket, which turned out to be an astonishingly well preserved Zippo lighter on which Sandy had scratched the initial "B," fused to a heavily corroded medallion I hoped was a dog tag. Mark would go so far as to send the tag to specialists at the Getty Museum in Los Angeles, but it was beyond restoration and we never knew for sure what it was. (My mother said he might have been wearing a St. Christopher medal which, it's worth noting, did not show up a list of personal property returned to Jo after his death.)

The fact that there was so little material evidence with my grandfather's remains made sense. Buried less than twenty-four hours after his death, my grandfather's remains were likely fairly intact, allowing his burial detail to remove anything useful and place him in the trench without a poncho.

Late in the afternoon, as the team began removing rib bones, they found two tiny, unused morphine syrettes (mini-syringes), their small wire caps still in place, in the area of his right breast pocket, and a third, *uncapped* syrette, adhered to a rib, its tip slightly bent. The syrettes would provide an interesting clue in the mystery of how he died.

Like most of the men in Cemetery 27, Sandy was face down. His left cheek resting on the sand, his arms were crossed beneath his chest, and his right ankle crossed over his left leg just below the knee. His bones were as solid and sturdy as any History Flight had found on the island, except for a small portion of his upper right thoracic area that had been in contact with poncho material in grave #18.

Even without the rock-solid evidence of his gold dental work, my grandfather was pretty easy to identify. His bones were long and strong; the hands and feet his daughter remembered so well led Kristen to pronounce, "He was a big man."

As the afternoon wore on and the team placed his remains into evidence bags, Kristen and John saw no immediate sign of skull trauma. There was, however, abundant evidence of apparent shrapnel wounds on the right side of his torso and right hand.

Until that moment, I had never considered that my grandfather's remains could shed light on the mystery of what really happened atop the bunker. I suddenly realized that here was hard physical evidence to set against all the words ever spoken and ink spilled about his death over the last seven decades. No more hearsay: We had the goods.

Sandy's remains were in Hillary Parsons's hands by four o'clock. Mark Noah felt strongly that, as a family member, I shouldn't take part in the processing of the remains, so I just lurked around the edges of the examination table as Hillary and Kristen went into full forensic-geek mode.

They huddled together over the remarkably well-preserved maxilla and mandible bones, matching all the gleaming gold to dental records. Hillary carefully cleaned the mandible and Kristen gently brushed sand from the cranium as evening fell, and they refused to be distracted even by offers of beer and wine from Paul. I'm sure they would have worked until midnight, or through the night, but once it got dark, John insisted they knock off.

"Don't worry," Hillary said, finally accepting a glass of white wine. "I know you're leaving Monday, but we have this on the fast track."

Upon careful examination the next day, Sandy Bonnyman's remains provided indisputable testimony that he had *not* been shot in the head or spine. It remained conceivable that he died from "gunshot wounds"[1] to soft tissues that left no trace on his bones—say, in the neck. But it was clear that Harry Niehoff's memory of him being shot in the head and dying instantly were not accurate.

What's more, the trauma to his torso and hand intriguingly pointed to a grenade or mortar shell as the proximate cause of death.

"Perimortem trauma [occurring at the time of death] is present in the form of a series of skeletal lesions consistent with damage from bomb fragments on the anterior and inferior surfaces of right ribs #3-#8, the anterior surface of the right scapula, the anterior surface of the left and right ilia, and the anterior surface of the sacrum," Hillary wrote in her report, an opinion endorsed by Kristen and by John, who had seen his share of such injuries in the field. The affected areas revealed "thermal alteration"—burning—that surrounded a series of "depressed fractures and nicks. That the trauma occurred perimortem is indicated by the consistency of coloration along fractures with surrounding bones."[2]

Hillary had been initially confused about what appeared to be burn marks on many of the osseous materials discovered in Cemetery 27. However, as the data piled up, she and Kristen realized that those dark marks were an anomalous decomposition pattern seen only in remains affected by the rubberized-canvas ponchos. Although Sandy's remains had incidental contact with poncho material from adjacent graves, the shrapnel-damaged areas of his scapula, ribs, pelvic, and hand bones were not affected.

History Flight essentially was pioneering a new micro-study in the effects of being wrapped in a poncho in tropical sand for seven decades.

"This appears to be due to microclimates inside the ponchos. That's not something that DPAA has really looked at," Hillary said, "so it's new territory."[3]

I was caught off guard two months later when DPAA forensic anthropologist Laurel Freas, who conducted the agency's examination of my grandfather's remains, concluded that "no perimortem trauma was observed."[4]

Kristen wasn't surprised in the least.

"The management is very strict and risk-adverse there. They also are very limited in the types of analysis and judgments they can make. For instance, they are only allowed to use the references listed in their SOP (standard operating procedures), so they don't have or use the reference we used to help ID that type of trauma," she told me. "Basically, sometimes they can't call a spade a spade because someone thinks that might be going out on a limb."[5]

Where Freas had made her determination in a lab thousands of miles from the recovery site, Kristen and Hillary had made theirs based on a large and growing body of evidence from remains found in the same, distinctive environment. That critical context was completely unavailable to Freas.

Puzzled, I asked Capt. Edward A. Reedy, science director and medical examiner for DPAA, about the discrepancy. For starters, he confirmed Kristen's assessment of the agency's caution.

"Our forensic anthropologists are conservative when assigning damage as perimortem trauma," he said.[6]

Reedy said the DPAA analyst concluded that the discolored and damaged ribs, pelvic bones, scapula, and hand were probably due to the age and fragility of my grandfather's remains, despite the fact that the damage occurred in an isolated pattern, not generally. But, he told me, "This is not to say that no perimortem trauma was present."[7] In other words, the agency didn't dispute History Flight's findings.

Hillary and Kristen found DPAA's caution absurd. They'd seen plenty of brittle, crumbling bones in poncho-covered remains uncovered at Cemetery 27, and the damage to Sandy's remains was of an entirely different character. What's more, the distinctive trauma was restricted to his right ventral torso and hand, which had lain on sand and was otherwise well preserved. Consistent with every other set of remains recovered from the trench so far, the only portions of his skeleton in a notably fragile condition were those on his *left* ventral side, which had been in contact with the rubberized poncho material from grave #18. DPAA's remote assessment of the trauma contradicted everything History Flight's experts had observed regarding the highly anomalous environments created by ponchos at Cemetery 27.

The agency's timidity opened my eyes to the critical importance of context, and the absolutely irreplaceable value of observation in the field, when it comes to forensic anthropology.

I knew now that there was no evidence that my grandfather had been struck in the head by gunfire, but that there was extremely compelling evidence that he'd suffered perimortem shrapnel wounds to his right side.

The forensic evidence was conclusive: Sandy Bonnyman had not been shot in the head. And damage extending from his right shoulder to his right hip compellingly suggested that he was not prone, as Niehoff claimed, but had been standing or, at the least, kneeling, when he received mortal wounds from grenade or mortar shrapnel that penetrated one or more vital organs, perhaps in combination with gunshot wounds to soft tissues.

And while more speculative, there was also the intriguing evidence of the morphine syrettes. The uncapped, bent syrette found stuck to one of my grandfather's ribs suggests the possibility that he, or perhaps someone else, had administered morphine as he lay dying atop the bunker.

Physical evidence is the gold standard, and my grandfather's remains bore mute testimony to vindicate my long suspicion that the account of his death published in Joseph Alexander's 1995 book *Utmost Savagery* was not accurate. I didn't blame Harry Niehoff, on whose memories Alexander had based his version (and something about his highly specific recollection that he had used my grandfather's lifeless body as a shield has always rung true to me).

But I did fault Alexander, who should have known better, for accepting one man's fifty-year-old memories as definitive proof that all other previous accounts were incorrect, thereby diminishing my grandfather's achievement.

I raised the issue with Alexander in 2014. He told me he found "the essence of (Niehoff's) comments to be plausible and positive." He noted, however, that he had chosen not to publish Niehoff's claim that he and John Borich had planned the assault on the bunker, finding it implausible.

I asked the author whether it would have made more sense for Niehoff to receive the Medal of Honor, rather than my grandfather.

After all, in his account, he had stood alone—or rather, lain alone—firing on the Japanese counterassault. I reminded the author of the citation for Niehoff's Silver Star, which made no mention of such a stand, and the fact that he had put my grandfather's name forward for the Medal of Honor.

"Did he inject a more significant role for himself?" Alexander answered. "Likely so. We all do."[8]

Sadly, Alexander died of cancer in September 2014. He never received the good news about finding Sandy Bonnyman and I was never able to present him with the compelling physical evidence of Cemetery 27. I still think highly of *Utmost Savagery*, but Alexander's counterfactual rewrite of my grandfather's history led later historians to repeat his errors; one author even contacted men who had fought beside my grandfather and questioned whether he deserved the Medal of Honor.

"You go ahead and write whatever you want but all those guys who were there said he deserved it," Sandy's former commanding officer Joseph Clerou told the man, according to his son, George. "I'm sure as hell not going to let some author tell me what happened."[9]

Nor was I.

In the end, the skeptical author's book did not even mention my grandfather, except to note his Medal of Honor and print the citation.[10]

Thanks to History Flight, 1st Lt. Alexander Bonnyman, Jr. has spoken from the grave, and I hope the indisputable evidence of his bones will forever banish Joseph Alexander's revisionist history of what happened atop that bunker on Betio on November 22, 1943.

The Saturday after Sandy was recovered, the History Flight team met four guys from an Australian road crew who used an excavator to strip away the layer of crushed coral to extend the unit another meter to the west. But everyone had been working nonstop for weeks, and that was it for the day (except for Hillary, who was busily processing and documenting my grandfather's remains).

That night, Kristen made dinner at her small rented beach house on Betio's tail. As we ate shrimp, rice, and baked pumpkin (the Kiribati name for squash), she and Hillary engaged in forensic anthropologist banter about the various odors of decomposing bodies (everything from barbecue to kalamata olives), while John put forth the theory that the Tarawa marines had been sacrificed to aid Admiral Chester Nimitz's aspirations for higher office and Hobbes, Kristen's sleek, orange adopted tomcat, entertained us with acrobatics. We drained a bottle of Hillary's Roughstock whiskey and started in on some (much-inferior) Jack Daniel's.

Sunday morning, John and Paul approached me for a confidential conversation. Like me, they were uneasy about how this might now play out with DPAA. All remains would be surrendered to the agency and flown to Hawaii, where scientists and technicians at the Central Identification Laboratory would simply repeat all the testing and reporting done by History Flight before issuing any legal identification.

I had seen a couple of the agency's reports and found the level of detail unnecessary for the job at hand, which was identifying remains. For example, the report on Pfc. Manley Forest Winkley (recovered from Cemetery 25 in 2013) expended fifty words to explain why the image of Mercury on the back of a dime is sometimes mistaken for Lady Liberty. (Weirdly, given that taxpayers foot the bill, DPAA reports include a note that, "This document contains information EXEMPT FROM MANDATORY DISCLOSURE under the FREEDOM OF INFORMATION ACT"; in other words, the agency claims the right keep its reports secret.)

I also knew that one of the most damning findings in the 2013 Government Accountability Office report was that JPAC had let remains languish on its shelves, sometimes for years, before identifying them. That was the case with Pvt. Herman Sturmer, the clue that led Mark Noah to Cemetery 27, who was found in 2002 but not identified until 2011.

Under US law, DPAA is the only entity that can officially identify battlefield remains. Now, despite the slam-dunk identification of my grandfather's bones—soon to be confirmed by a team of top odontologists flown by History Flight to Betio in June—I worried that someone at the agency might delay the process, perhaps even deliberately, as a slap at a pesky "avocational." I'd seen that kind of behavior before, after all.

John and Paul, former Green Berets, didn't trust DPAA, either, and had come up with a plan: Hillary and Kristen would finish up their report on my grandfather, then pack up his remains and material evidence in a Pelican case. When I boarded the plane for Fiji the next day, I would simply check the case as baggage.

"You can't trust these people," John said, explaining that I would only be doing what any next of kin (I had been designated my mother's legal power of attorney) had a right to do. Think of it this way, John said: Were I to keel over on Tarawa, my wife would have every right to retrieve my body. "This is the same thing," he said.

I loved the idea; it was exactly the kind of thing Sandy Bonnyman might do. And there was even a recent precedent for a family claiming remains without DPAA involvement: the case of Army Pfc. Lawrence Gordon, the World War II pilot who had to be identified by German and French labs when JPAC had declined to get involved.[11]

But I also knew that Mark Noah had signed agreements with both the DPAA and the government of Kiribati regarding repatriation of all remains found. For me to try to force the issue might not just land me in jail, but could theoretically spark a minor international incident. More important, attempting to spirit away my grandfather's remains might well jeopardize History Flight's ability to continue working on Tarawa. As much as I distrusted DPAA, based on past experience, I just couldn't agree to the plan.

Mark had not yet informed DPAA about the discovery of Cemetery 27, fearing interference. But the agency was scheduled to send a team out in July to review History Flight's work and conduct its own research, so our cat was wriggling in the bag already (I had to hold my tongue when DPAA archaeologist Jay Silverstein sent me a friendly note in May to let me know his team would be looking for Cemetery 27). Mark expected that the agency would take all the remains back to Hawaii in late July.

"So," I said flatly as we stood in the shade of a coconut palm on Black Beach, "we will hand my grandfather over to them and they will have custody. I will no longer have any say in anything."

It was true, Mark said. But he promised to do everything in his power to make sure they didn't unnecessarily delay my mother and aunt from burying their father.

I didn't like it one bit. But I had a few cards up my sleeve, too.

The day after we removed Sandy Bonnyman's remains from his grave in Cemetery 27, I ran across the causeway just as the sun was rising. Toad the Wet Sprocket was playing on my iPhone—"Would he fly from Heaven/To this world again?"

Before returning to the hotel, I took a detour on the rutted, dusty road that passed Admiral Shibasaki's bunker, Bonnyman's Bunker, and the pier. When I arrived at Kiribati Shipping Services, Ltd., the guard smiled and waved me through the gate.

Peeling back a tattered blue tarp, I climbed down in the hole and sat on the flat sand where my grandfather had rested for so long. One by one, I thought of all those who had been shattered by his death: the little girl left to mourn by herself; Sandy's "curly blonde," doomed to a life of addiction and mental illness; Aunty

Alix, yearning to know everything she could about her missing father; Granny Great sitting quietly in the sun room at Bonniefield, heart forever broken; Alex Bonnyman, burdened by memories of clashes with his beloved son; my aging Uncle Gordon, painfully stooped with progressive supranuclear palsy, weeping at visions of his beloved older brother; and even myself, missing a man I never knew but needed so much, more like me than I had ever imagined but whose courage I feared I lacked.

I felt a sense of deep gratitude toward much-maligned Betio, whose sepulchral sands had, after all, preserved my grandfather's bones for all those years. And remembering the day before, I knew I'd missed an opportunity to show real courage.

"When you are afraid of something, you know that you are alive," Faulkner wrote. "But when you are afraid to do what you are afraid of, you are dead."

I sat there, silent, for half an hour. And by the time I rose from my grandfather's empty grave, I understood for the first time that my grandfather had never been fearless. He had just had the courage to choose life.

TWENTY-ONE
CONSPICUOUS
GALLANTRY
2014–2015

The discovery of Cemetery 27 had solved the mystery of grandfather's death.

But even after five years of investigation, tens of thousands of miles traveled, countless hours of interviews, and the best efforts of the top researchers I could find, I still didn't have answers to some vexing questions: Why was my grandfather denied the Medal of Honor in 1944, only to receive it two and a half years later?

"All medals," Rich Boylan told me, "are political to some extent. And the Medal of Honor is the most political award of all."[1]

He would know. In his thirty-six years with the National Archives and Records Administration, Boylan served as an expert witness in the cases of fifty-five eventual Medal of Honor recipients who were overlooked in World War I and World War II because of anti-black or anti-Asian racism or anti-Semitism.

Although the Medal of Honor is supposed to be awarded to individuals for discrete acts of "conspicuous gallantry" at the clear risk of one's life above and beyond the call of duty, you need look no further than one of the medal's most famous recipients to understand that those criteria are sometimes overlooked for reasons of politics, public relations, or even propaganda.

On the night of March 11, 1942, under orders from President

Franklin D. Roosevelt, Gen. Douglas A. MacArthur, his wife, his son, a nanny, and fourteen staff officers boarded a PT boat and fled the Philippine island of Corregidor for Australia. The general had been a powerful symbol of resistance and strength to Americans, and even the Japanese enemy, who would soon claim America's far western Pacific outpost and initiate the brutal Bataan Death March.

Not long after, Gen. George C. Marshall gave the order to award MacArthur the Medal of Honor, "to offset any propaganda by the enemy directed at his leaving his command." Gen. Dwight D. Eisenhower, who had served under MacArthur from 1932 to 1939, strenuously objected, pointing out that his former boss hadn't actually engaged in the kind of singular action required for the medal.

Whatever MacArthur's qualities, his Medal of Honor was not so much to recognize actions, but rather to soothe anxious American *reactions* and, ostensibly, undermine Japanese *overreaction*.

But simply knowing that medals can be political didn't tell me anything about what had happened in the case of my grandfather. At the beginning of my search, I was absolutely certain that somewhere, perhaps at the bottom of a dusty box in the deep recesses of the National Archives—à la *Indiana Jones*—yellowing pieces of paper would explain, at last, why Sandy Bonnyman was awarded the Medal of Honor after first being denied. To my great frustration, no such evidence materialized.

"I've searched as hard for this as anything I've ever looked for, and it's just not there," said researcher Katie Rasdorf.[2]

Experts cautioned me not to expect answers to my questions.

"There is a slim-to-none chance that such documents as you are looking for exist," said Laura S. Jowdy, archivist for the Congressional Medal of Honor Society. Award recommendation packets from World War II, she said, consist mostly of "a lot of 'rubber stamps' that say in essence whether the award is approved to go further up the ladder."[3]

With no new information to guide me, I repeatedly pored over every page of my grandfather's military records, as well as every letter that mentioned the medal, searching for the tiniest clue. Finally, a detail so mundane I had never noticed it before caught my attention: Every page in my grandfather's case that had been examined by the awards board on March 8, 1944, bore a stamp reading, "FILE–SELECTION BOARD CASE" (some pages also bore the scribbled initials, "ngw" and "JM"). That stamp appears on just four pages of my grandfather's military records, all pertaining to his arrest for "rendering yourself unfit for duty by excessive use of intoxicants" in Wellington, New Zealand on July 27, 1943.

Lt. Col. Chester Salazar, commander of 2/18 at Tarawa, acknowledged the incident in his October 1, 1943, fitness report supporting Sandy's promotion to first lieutenant, but made clear that it should not "materially affect" the promotion of an officer whose "value to the service" he rated "excellent."[4]

But the awards board may have had other considerations. There was already some concern that too many high awards were being given out, and given the public attention paid to the Medal of Honor, recognizing a marine of questionable character might—in their eyes—result in a public relations snafu. If the board was going to make someone a hero, perhaps he needed to be, or at least appear to be, squeaky clean. Had Sandy Bonnyman's case been judged differently than those of William J. Bordelon and William Deane Hawkins, who had received the exact same endorsements, because of concerns about character?

"It's very plausible," Rich Boylan told me. "But they probably would not have documented that. Nothing was kept."[5]

Indeed, the secretary for a post-war navy board created to review all high medals given during the war noted, "The Senior Member cautioned the Board that conversations or votes taken in session were not to be revealed for obvious reasons."[6]

The evidence is circumstantial, but concern over my grandfather's arrest makes for a logical, believable solution to the mystery. There was, after all, no doubt among those who were with Sandy during his final hours that his actions (the *only* factor that was supposed to matter) warranted the Medal of Honor, and many of his fellow marines and superior officers were deeply distressed that he did not receive the medal.

But someone, somewhere, must have continued to fight on Sandy's behalf.

"Getting an upgrade usually requires a rabbi [senior officer] with both a staff and the political will to go to bat. I'll bet an irate field-grade officer who was there went to work on the upgrade as soon as he found out about the downgrade," said Tarawa historian Eric Hammel. "But in your grandfather's case, I have no idea who that would be."[7]

Finding the identity of my grandfather's "rabbi" became my new mission.

First, I obtained hundreds of pages of minutes from the Horne Board, a committee convened by Adm. Frederick J. Horne, Vice Chief of Naval Operations, in January 1946. The board was tasked with reviewing the twelve percent of cases in which the navy awards board had not approved recommended medals, as well as all Medals of Honor, posthumous and in-absentia awards, and considering "cases not previously recommended."[8]

Notes from the first meeting reported that, "The idea started back in October in the Naval Affairs Committees. . . . The committee felt that . . . many deserving persons were not getting or had not received awards."[9]

The Horne board systematically considered cases in chronological order, declining in virtually every case to upgrade Navy Cross awards to the Medal of Honor. The most notable exception was Capt. Jefferson J. DeBlanc, a marine pilot who risked his life to attack

Japanese planes and destroyers, shooting down five enemy aircraft before being forced to crash-land in the sea off the Solomon Islands on January 31, 1943. Although the senior naval officer "strongly recommended" DeBlanc for the Medal of Honor, the awards board approved him for the Navy Cross on May 27, 1944, confirming its decision on August 11. The Horne board overruled both decisions, but the minutes, to my frustration, offered no detailed explanation, noting only that DeBlanc's "acts of heroism . . . are sufficient to justify the award of the Medal of Honor" *and* the Navy Cross.[10]

I was even more frustrated to discover that the Horne board minutes made no mention of my grandfather's case at all. And James E. Nierle, president of the US Navy Board of Decorations and Medals, told me that I'd seen every Horne board document his researchers had found in the National Archives or Bureau of Naval Personnel or post-war papers of the chief of naval operations and secretary of the navy.[11] And even if there were notes on my grandfather's case, it's unlikely they would have been any more detailed than those for DeBlanc.

"Even if the minutes existed somewhere," Nierle said, "there really isn't much discussion of why in the minutes. . . . I doubt you would get a satisfactory answer."[12]

No rabbi, no minutes, no nothing. It was hard to accept, but perhaps too much time had passed and I would simply never get an answer.

Then one hot August day, I dropped my mother off at Denver International Airport for a trip to meet my aunt Alix for opera and chile in Santa Fe.

"Oh, I remember what I wanted to tell you," my mother said as the porter put her luggage on the conveyor belt: She had hired a professional organizer who had found a few things about her father scattered in boxes, trunks, and files in her basement. "They're all in one box somewhere, but you'll have to find them."

I broke my personal best time for driving from the airport to her house and was lucky not to break my neck when I bounded down into the dark, cluttered confines of her Old Curiosity Basement. It took me a while, and when I found the hoard, it was not the shoebox and "few" items I'd expected, but two cubic feet of letters, photos, clippings, and other oddments I'd never seen before, including my grandfather's Second Marine Division patch. I spent every hour I was not working, sleeping, or running going through thousands of pages, eagerly copying down fascinating, if obscure, details about my grandfather's life, before picking up the crinkly, brown-edged letter written by one of his old friends that finally put me on the scent of the missing rabbi.

Many of my grandfather's friends had mentioned Tarawa Medal of Honor recipient Col. David M. Shoup in letters to the Bonnymans, prompting my great-grandfather to write him in 1944 to inquire about the whereabouts of his son's remains. He never received a reply.

But in 1946, Navy Cmdr. J. Gordon Reid, an old Knoxville friend of Sandy's, wrote Alex Bonnyman to say that he'd spoken with Shoup at the navy hospital in Bethesda, Maryland, where the colonel was recovering from an emergency appendectomy. At Reid's mention of Sandy, Shoup "loudly sang his praises."[13] He also told Reid that he had formally requested that the US Navy Board of Review, Decorations and Awards reconsider Sandy's recommendation for the Medal of Honor in 1944 and after the war.

"In fact, he was of the impression that it had already been awarded," Reid wrote. "Perhaps I should keep my big mouth shut and wait for you to hear something in the normal course of events— but on the other hand, I knew you would like to know that the matter is under consideration."[14]

Shoup had endorsed Sandy's case from the beginning, but may have found additional motivation in his own circuitous path to the

Medal of Honor. After planning the assault and leading the marines to victory on Tarawa, he was named chief of staff for the Second Marine Division in December 1943. At division, he schemed out battle plans for and later fought on Saipan and Tinian in the summer of 1944, for which he received the Legion of Merit with a combat "V."

Even as Shoup was putting his name on recommendations for Bonnyman, Bordelon, and Hawkins, someone put his name forth for the Medal of Honor for leadership on Tarawa. But not even Shoup's two biographers reported that, despite the enthusiastic recommendation of Gen. Julian C. Smith and endorsements up the line, he, like Sandy, was initially denied the highest honor and awarded the Navy Cross instead, also in May 1944. But at the urging of Shoup's superiors, the awards board reconsidered his case and in August 1944 substituted the Medal of Honor in lieu of his Navy Cross.[15]

Shoup would go on to reach the pinnacle of Marine Corps achievement, becoming commandant under President John F. Kennedy. After his retirement in 1963, he bluntly spoke out about "the limits of US power and our capabilities to police the world," the nation's growing militarism, and the dangerous intrusion of "business interests" into foreign policy and war making. Beginning in 1966, he vocally opposed American involvement in Vietnam. Above all, he was angry that marines were being put in harm's way for an unwinnable war driven by politics rather than sound military strategy.[16]

"Civilians can scarcely understand or even believe that many ambitious military professionals truly yearn for wars," Shoup wrote in an *Atlantic* article in April 1969. In a personal copy of the issue, he wrote, "I believe responsible protest is the most sincere kind of patriotism," in the margin on the same page.[17]

What followed Shoup's bold candor and prescience is a cynical example of the use and misuse of heroes by politicians, generals, and media who may not always have the best interests of the troops, or the American public, at heart. Rightly celebrated for two decades as a hero for his actions at Tarawa, Shoup was suddenly subjected to savage attacks by members of Congress and the military establishment, vilified as a traitor, a coward, and a mental defective by editorialists, and monitored by the FBI on the orders of President Lyndon B. Johnson. The message was loud and clear: "Real" heroes do not question war.

"The whole 'heroic' trope answers questions before they get asked," retired Air Force Lt. Col. William Astore told me. "Heroes follow orders without question, just like ordinary Americans should. . . . The rhetoric of universal heroes enables war and silences dissent. That's why it's so dangerous. And so universally pronounced by our so-called leaders."[18]

With that tantalizing clue about Shoup to guide me, I flew to California and spent a day in the archives of the Hoover Institution at Stanford University, which houses thirty-five boxes of papers donated by Shoup's estate. It was a long shot, but I was hoping to find evidence to tie the late general to my grandfather's Medal of Honor. After several hours, I had just begun to think I'd wasted a good deal of time and money when I came across a small, elegant envelope written in a now-familiar hand.

"My Dear Colonel Shoup," began my great-grandmother. "I am giving myself the pleasure of thanking you for the kind words you have spoken for my son, Alexander Bonnyman, Jr. to Commander Reid, and also the pleasure of writing to my son's commanding officer in the Battle of Tarawa."

Frances Bonnyman described her son's pride in being a marine, and offered her own praise: "The Second Division fought and won against such odds, it seems to us that it was made up of heroes all."[19]

The letter is short, mournful, and painfully personal: "We never saw our son in uniform. When he came to say good-bye and to announce his enlistment in the Marines, we were shocked. He had every exemption. When we mentioned this, his reply was that after Pearl Harbor, every red-blooded American should act on the feeling in his heart—what was more natural than he should join the Marines!" She closed with the heart-rending words, "I would visit Tarawa if I could."[20]

Next I came across a typewritten letter from my great-grandfather, dated January 24, 1947, explaining why he had pressed so hard for Shoup's attendance at Sandy's January 22, 1947, Medal of Honor ceremony in Washington: "I am certain that it was your persistent effort that secured for Sandy this recognition."[21]

And finally, there was Shoup's belated reply to my great-grandmother, dated March 24, 1947, in which he expressed regret that he hadn't been able to meet her at the ceremony in Washington, D.C. Mysteriously ill, my Granny Great was recuperating in Oklahoma at the time; some diagnosed her condition as heartbreak.

"As I told both your husband and your granddaughter, your son, Alexander Bonnyman, Jr., by the very actions which brought on his death had made certain that he would never die but instead would live forever in the annals of our history," Shoup wrote.[22]

He offered an explanation for why he had not previously responded to her letter: "I felt that my best reply would be to continue pushing for a reconsideration of the recommendation for (the) award for your son which was submitted as a result of his gallant action during the struggle for possession of the island, Betio, Tarawa Atoll."[23]

David Shoup was the missing rabbi. He had lobbied his old friend Gen. A.A. Vandegrift to rectify what he had always seen as an injustice, the denial of the Medal of Honor to 1st Lt. Alexander Bonnyman, Jr.

The last of the mysteries that had haunted me since I'd set out to reclaim my grandfather, in every way imaginable, had been solved.

TWENTY-TWO
TO HOME SOIL WAITING
JUNE-SEPTEMBER 2015

When I returned from Tarawa in early June 2015, I was steeled for battle. I had reluctantly left my grandfather behind, and now it was my job to make sure his daughters would see him buried with honor—and soon.

I also dived into my next assignment for History Flight: contacting family members of marines whose remains we had recovered from Cemetery 27 to request DNA samples. Although I wasn't in a position to confirm we'd found their relative (information that by law must come from DPAA), most enthusiastically agreed to help.

"I, along with my family, hope that we can have my uncle, John Frederick Prince, identified and brought home to the US for burial," responded Patricia Donigian of New York state. (The remains in grave #20 were later confirmed as Prince's.)

There were a few, however, who said they'd already been asked to send samples and didn't understand why they should do it again. Over time, DPAA had contacted many families, as had a former Dallas police detective and one-time JPAC staff member Rick Stone, who had taken it upon himself to issue official-looking reports that included confident assertions of the whereabouts of each of Tarawa's missing. (According to Stone, Sandy Bonnyman's remains were "most likely" those interred at the Schofield Barracks Mausoleum as unknown number X-198.[1] The Rick Stone Foundation changed the information on its website following publication of this book, claiming it had known all along that my grandfather was buried on Betio.) I did my best to persuade doubters by noting that of the three organizations, *only* History Flight had actually recovered remains from Cemetery 27.

There also were a couple of older family members who were not interested. One cousin said, "Leave the guy alone, let him rest! There's nobody left but me. I'm ninety-three years old and I'll be going soon." Another said her parents had been very clear that they did not want their son's remains disturbed.

"I just think it would be disrespectful to their memory," she told me.

On June 17, 2015, I received a copy of History Flight's odontology report for my grandfather, written by Dr. David R. Senn, director of the Center for Education and Research in Forensics at the University of Texas Health Science Center at San Antonio. Senn had arrived just as I left and began working with forensic dentists Corinne D'Anjou of Montreal and James Goodrich of New Zealand to identify Cemetery 27 remains.

It may come as a surprise to a *CSI*-loving public, but the science of odontology—dental matching—remains the primary method of identifying military remains, presuming teeth are present; DNA is just a cherry on top. After x-raying the teeth found in grave #17 and making a visual comparison with my grandfather's 1942 dental records, the team ran its data through OdontoSearch, a vast online database containing tens of thousands of dental x-rays, to assess "the frequency of occurrence of specific dental patterns and (provide) objective means to quantify the relative frequency . . . in the general population."[2]

Calling the evidence "exceptional and extraordinary . . . striking," Senn concluded that the teeth recovered from grave #17 were "distinctive and concordant and not found in the Odonto Search combined civilian and military databases . . . indicating a very distinctive dental pattern."[3]

For all practical purposes, those gold fillings could belong to no one else but Alexander Bonnyman, Jr.

Armed with new confidence, I wrote a long letter to retired Army Lt. Gen. Michael S. Linnington, whom US Secretary of Defense Ashton Carter had named DPAA's first permanent director on June 19, to formally request that the agency accept History Flight's findings and not unnecessarily delay the return of my grandfather's remains, explaining that we planned to hold a funeral in September. I cc'd the commandant of the Marine Corps and Carter's office, as well as US senators from Colorado, Hawaii, and Tennessee, and the head of the armed services committees in the US House and Senate. I included a detailed description of my concerns and history with the agency and offered an honest assessment of the public relations choice facing the agency.

"What a shame it would be if the DPAA chooses to delay two aging women from seeing their World War II hero father properly buried after more than seventy years, for no more reason than to duplicate the excellent work of History Flight professionals at taxpayer expense," I wrote. "Surely that's not the kind of story the agency wants the public to hear as it emerges from a tumultuous period under new leadership and oversight."

Mark Noah asked me to hold off on sending the letter until he notified DPAA about the discovery of Cemetery 27, which he had kept under wraps for fear that the agency would try to swoop in and usurp the excavation. Finally, on June 24, he gave me the go-ahead, and I sent the letter via certified mail.

Two days later, I was on a conference call with Linnington, a deputy commandant for the Marine Corps, and Hattie Y. Johnson, head of repatriation for the Marine Corps Casualty Section.

"I've gotten a look at the odontology on your grandfather's remains, and I'm very impressed with the quality of the work as well as the very uniqueness of your grandfather's dental work," Linnington said. "That makes it easy to make the identification by dental alone. Just to be completely open and transparent, we are not going to do our own DNA testing in this case. Dental will be sufficient."

He requested time for DPAA to conduct "the necessary and important step" of a peer review of History Flight's work, but promised that "we will be able to meet your September time frame, based on the dental."[4]

Halfway around the world, Kristen, Hillary, John, and Paul remained skeptical, but it was clear from our conversation that Linnington had been hired to take DPAA in a new direction, and he had no interest in starting his tenure with another public relations snafu. He was already negotiating with History Flight and other nongovernmental organizations to create public-private partnerships, which he described as "the exact future of this agency." That new spirit of cooperation would soon translate into History Flight's first contracts with DPAA, to recover remains from cemeteries 27 and 33.

"The fact the we found and identified Alexander Bonnyman is going to open up the possibility of finding many more—not hundreds, but thousands—of MIAs simply because his history is so spectacular," History Flight archaeologist Chet Walker said at the 2016 meeting of the American Society of Forensic Odontology. "He shows that this is possible—and that it is deeply personal."[5]

After more than seventy years, the marines of Tarawa had won a battle of a different kind, and once again, my grandfather had played a crucial role.

I told Mark I'd handle media about the Cemetery 27 recovery, which would without question attract attention from around the globe. But as the end of June approached, we'd still made no public announcement and I was starting to feel impatient.

Long before going to Tarawa in May, I had decided to "thru-hike" the 486-mile-long Colorado Trail from Denver to Durango. I had initially planned to depart in mid- to late June, but thanks to weeks of heavy late-spring precipitation, the higher sections of the trail—which averages more than ten thousand feet in elevation—remained impassable. Now the snow was melting and I was eager to head down the trail.

Mark had granted me permission to put the word out on the Bonnyman telegraph in advance of an annual family get-together at a mountain lodge in North Carolina. Inevitably, word was beginning to get out beyond the family, and one cousin in the military reported that he'd heard about the find from friends in the Marine Corps. I urged Mark to pull the trigger, and I finally sent our press release on June 29, a month after my grandfather's exhumation.

For the next seventy-two hours, Mark and I juggled interviews, sat in front of cameras, and Skyped with journalists around the world, talking about the remarkable discovery of Cemetery 27. Stories aired on ABC, CBS, NBC, and local affiliates in Tennessee, Hawaii, Colorado, New Mexico, California, and beyond. News organizations from the *Honolulu Star-Advertiser* to the *Washington Post*, *Santa Fe New Mexican*, and *Agence France Presse* ran stories. The story was broadcast on National Public Radio and the Canadian Broadcasting Corporation, as well as radio stations in New Zealand, Australia, and Japan.

Soon, I began receiving congratulations from around the world. Some people expressed disappointment that Sandy would not be buried at Arlington National Cemetery, but there had never been any doubt that he should come back to Knoxville.

"God knows after all these years he may never be found. But if he is, I would love nothing better than anything in the world than to have his remains back in Knoxville; he is the only one (of his family) not there," my aunt Alix had said in 2010. "If he's buried on Tarawa forever, that's okay. But if he's found, he belongs in Knoxville."[6]

We decided as a family that he would be laid to rest, at long last, on September 27, next to his parents, sisters, and brother.

"They all died without knowing the truth," I told the *Washington Post*. "I'm not a woo person. I don't believe in ghosts or whatever. But I still feel like I've been able to play a little part in closing the circle for the family. And I feel great about that."[7]

More than one reporter asked if we planned to have the words "BURIED AT SEA" removed from beneath my grandfather's name on the back of the Bonnyman monument.

"Absolutely not," I said. "It's a beautiful irony. It's part of the story."

On July 2, head swirling with everything that had happened in the last three months, I abandoned the world for the trail. For the next three and a half weeks my life was reduced to its most basic elements—walking, finding water, making sure I had enough to eat, making and breaking camp, and walking again, interrupted only by brief trips into town for resupply (and the occasional media interview).

Like many other first-time thru-hikers—the name for people who hike the world's long trails from end to end—I wondered how I would fare in body, mind, and spirit while walking mostly alone through the wilderness. Every day on the trail brings some kind of physical discomfort, a new blister or swelling, painful chafe, stiff muscles. Successful hikers just keep walking.

Though I often walked for eight or ten hours without seeing anyone, I was never alone. Watching the last few sparks of a dying campfire rise into a perfectly still, moonless night, or gazing in awe over some vast mountain valley, I recalled my grandfather's passion for the outdoors and tried to imagine the trials he'd experienced on

Guadalcanal and Tarawa, so far removed from anything I might face in the wilderness. At times, thinking about him woke me from mindless rage at rain, stinging chafe, a swollen ankle—*If you're never uncomfortable,* I imagined him saying with a grin, *how much of an adventure can it really be?*

Walking the trail step by step with my grandfather's memory, I considered the life I'd led. Like him, I'd always sought adventure, loved the outdoors. Like him, I'd been impetuous, thoughtless, and sometimes reckless. I'd even abandoned my own Ivy League education and run off to work as a cowboy, just as Sandy had gone to the mountains of Virginia to, well, learn to blow stuff up.

Like Sandy, I'd always had a hard time sitting still. I was ever on the hunt for that next great adrenaline rush or endorphin high—riding bucking horses, skydiving, running ultramarathons, mountain climbing, surfing, night diving with sharks, hiking five hundred miles, dangling from the roof of a twenty-two-story dormitory just to prove to myself I wasn't afraid. Indignant at the thought that there were any limits on how I chose to live my life, I made personal choices that shivered some branches of the Bonnyman family tree. Yet I can honestly say that I did it not to rebel, but out of an almost irresistible compulsion to seize every opportunity for love and every thrilling thrilling moment of life, which, I knew, could be taken in an instant.

Of my grandfather at twenty-two, I remembered, a family friend had written, "There will always be much of the boy and a sheer joy of living in him."[8]

Walking for hundreds of miles through bristlecone pines and flickering aspen groves, along windblown rocky ridges, shielding my face from torrents and tempests, or blissfully ambling across high mesas through bright asylums of mountain flowers, I reveled in every part of myself. I *was* strong, resourceful, determined, stoic, flexible, friendly, compassionate, generous, and creative—but also petty, angry, judgmental, self-centered, and prideful.

When my grandfather died, a friend wrote, "I don't mean that he wasn't intensely human, but I've always thought of him as 'good'—in the best sense of the word."[9]

Having spent all those years searching for my grandfather, I came to the conclusion at last that while I was no hero, maybe we weren't so different after all.

Lost in the wilderness, I missed Mark Noah's ultimate vindication: On July 26, he received the title of Honorary Marine from the US Marine Corps, joining fewer than 100 figures—including such notables as Gary Sinise, Chuck Norris, and former US senators Max Cleland and Daniel Inouye, not to mention Bugs Bunny and Jim Nabors—for his contributions to the corps. I sent a letter in support of his nomination a year before, describing a man who, though he had not served, perfectly represented the determination and grit that has for so long characterized the US Marine Corps.

"He is so damn smart and determined," said retired Marine Col. Michael Brown at the ceremony. "He doesn't want accolades. He just looks at it as mission accomplishment, and there is nothing more marine than that."[10]

Five years had shown me that anything could happen in the recovery business, and it wasn't until my grandfather's flag-draped casket rolled off Delta Airline Flight 1292 into the waiting arms of six marines on the rain-soaked tarmac at Knoxville's McGhee-Tyson Airport that I could finally exhale: Home at last. It was four months since we'd seen that first glint of gold.

More than a hundred members of the Patriot Guard Riders led the way and countless well-wishers braved a three-hour delay along rain-washed Alcoa Highway and Kingston Pike as the procession wound from the airport to Berry Highland Memorial funeral home, less than three miles from where Sandy had grown up. There was not a dry eye among the usually stoic Bonnymans in that limousine as we watched children waving flags and veterans saluting our passing cortege. At the funeral home, the fire department had hoisted a twenty-foot-high American flag from the end of a hook and ladder.

By the time bagpiper Kay Irwin began to play "The Marine Corps Hymn" the following afternoon, the rain had passed. Smoky autumn sunlight infused the East Tennessee Veteran's Memorial plaza in downtown Knoxville, where my grandfather's casket had been brought to lie in honor. Hundreds of people turned out for the ceremony, including Lt. Col. James Michael "Mike" Sprayberry, a Vietnam-era Medal of Honor recipient who had driven 200 miles from Alabama.

"If a guy can wait seventy years to be back on native soil," he declared, "it's the least I can do."

I spoke briefly, reading from my great-grandparents' letters.

"This is where he belongs," I said. "I'm glad he's home, and I'm glad Tennessee's glad he's home."

I reserved the pub-like top floor at Armada Craft Cocktails in downtown Knoxville for that night, inviting anyone and everyone to come and toast Sandy Bonnyman and History Flight. It was exactly what I'd hoped for: a free-wheeling, boisterous celebration of a hundred or more, including two Tarawa veterans, C.J. Daigle and Elwin Hart, DPAA chief Mike Linnington, Mark Noah, Kristen Baker, Hillary Parsons, John Frye, and a dozen other people from History Flight who had worked on Cemetery 27, along with assorted Bonnymans, friends, members of the Alexander Bonnyman Detachment of the Marine Corps League, active-duty marines, and even a framed photo of Buster the cadaver-detecting canine, who, though invited, wasn't able to attend.

It was a hell of a party. Sandy would have loved it.

Marine Barracks Washington, better known as 8th & I, is the oldest Marine Corps unit in the nation. Founded in 1801 by President Thomas Jefferson and Lt. Col. William Ward Burrows, third commandant of the corps, it is home to the famous Marine Corps Silent Drill Platoon, Marine Corps Drum and Bugle Corps, Marine Band, the official Marine Corps Color Guard, and the Marine Corps Body Bearers. The unit's official duties are to support "ceremonial and security missions in the Capital."

But early in the morning of September 27, 2015, for the first time in recent memory, members of 8th & I left Washington to honor the burial of a marine five hundred miles away in Knoxville, Tennessee. At noon, led by Maj. Gen. Burke W. Whitman and Col. Robert A. Couser, who had escorted Sandy Bonnyman's remains from Hawaii, some eighty-five marines in full ceremonial dress—red for members of the band and drum and bugle corps, blue for the drill team, bearers, and color guard—followed the casket on a custom-made, horse-drawn caisson (built by a local nonprofit reenactors' group, Burroughs' Battery) for a solemn, half-mile journey to the highest point at Berry Highland Memorial Cemetery, where the ten-foot-long marble Bonnyman monument has stood since 1949. A remarkable end to a very long journey.

Hundreds of citizens, including retired Army Col. Walter Joseph Marm, Jr., awarded the Medal of Honor for his actions in Vietnam, gathered atop the hill as four Marine Corps Cobra helicopters thudded overhead, one peeling off in the famous, heart-rending "missing man" formation. Rev. Dr. Robert McKeon and Rev. Anne Bonnyman, nephew and niece of the deceased, led a brief service, followed by a twenty-one-gun salute and "Taps."

Just as three pairs of white-gloved hands removed the flag from the casket and began to fold it, a cool breeze rolled across the hilltop, breaking the heat of that perfectly clear, blue, autumn afternoon. A few golden leaves twirled down from high branches, one settling into the folds of the flag. Gen. Whitman—tall, blond, and blue-eyed, he bore a resemblance to my grandfather—solemnly received the flag from the bearers, walked over and knelt before Fran Bonnyman Evans, now eighty-one.

"On behalf of the president of the United States, the United States Marine Corps, and a grateful nation, please accept this flag as a symbol of our appreciation for your father's honorable and faithful service," he said quietly, eyes glistening.

He laid the flag on my mother's lap, clasped her spotted hands in his, and leaned in to whisper words I could not hear.

At long last, someone had come to console the little girl with a broken heart.

AFTERWORD

All told, History Flight, Inc. teams recovered thirty-six sets of intact remains and seven sets of partial remains, including one skull, from the Cemetery 27 site on Betio, making provisional identifications on twenty-eight. Since then, History Flight has turned over scores more sets of remains found on Tarawa to the DPAA.

History Flight teams continue the search for America's World War II MIAs, not only on Tarawa, but also in Europe, the Philippines, and other locations. As of 2017, the organization had recovered intact remains of some seventy Tarawa MIAs and partial remains of scores more. To learn more, go to historyflight.org.

As of May 2020, DPAA's Central Identification Laboratory in Hawaii had identified the following men recovered from Cemetery 27 (listed by rank, name, and hometown; all are marines, unless otherwise noted):

1st Lt. Alexander Bonnyman, Santa Fe, New Mexico

2nd Lt. George S. Bussa, F Van Nuys, California

Navy Pharmacist's Mate 3rd Class Howard P. Brisbane, Birmingham, Alabama

Navy Pharmacist's Mate 3 Howard P. Brisbane, Birmingham, Alabama

Pfc. Anthony N. Brozyna, Hartford, Connecticut

Pvt. Robert Carter, Jr., Corvallis, Oregon

GySgt. Sidney A. Cook, Hemlock Grove, Ohio

Cpl. Walter G. Critchley, East Norwich, New York

Pfc. Maurice Drucker, New York

Pvt. Fred E. Freet, Gary, Indiana

Pvt. Dale R. Geddes, Grand Island, Nebraska

Pfc. Paul Gilman, Belen, New Mexico

Pfc. Ben H. Gore, Hopkinsville, Kentucky

Pvt. Palmer S. Haraldson, Los Angeles

Sgt. James J. Hubert, Duluth, Minnesota

Pfc. James B. Johnson, Poughkeepsie, New York

Pvt. Emmett L. Kines, Grafton, West Virginia

Pvt. John F. Lally, Holyoke, Massachusetts

Pfc. Wilbur C. Mattern, Oelwein, Iowa

Pfc. John W. MacDonald, Boston

Pfc. James F. Mansfield, Plymouth, Massachusetts

Pfc. Elmer L. Mathies, Hereford, Texas.

2nd Lt. Ernest Matthews, Dallas

Sgt. Fae V. Moore, Pine Ridge, South Dakota

Pfc. Edward Nalazek, Chicago

Cpl. Roger K. Nielson, Denver, Colorado

USN Pharmacist's Mate 1st Class Warren G. Nelson, Lakota, North Dakota

Pfc. Charles E. Oetjen, Blue Island, Illinois

Cpl. James D. Otto, A 3/8 [Los] Angeles

Pvt. Frank Penna, Canastota, New York

Pfc. John F. Prince, New York

Pvt. William Rambo, LaPorte, Indiana

Pfc. James P. Reilly, New York

Pfc. Larry R. Roberts, Damascus, Arkansas

Pfc. John N. Saini, Healdsburg, California

Pfc. Roland Schaede, Maywood, Illinois

Pfc. James S. Smith, Liberty, Mississippi

Pvt. Donald S. Spayd, Los Angeles

Pfc. George H. Traver, Chatham, New York

Pvt. Harry K. Tye, Gallagher,   Pfc. James O. Whitehurst,
   West Virginia   Ashford, Alabama
Pfc. Ronald Vosmer, Denver,   Pfc. Louis Wisehan, Richmond,
   Colorado   Indiana
Pfc. Raymond Warren,
   Silverdale, Kansas

In addition, the DPAA has exhumed and identified dozens of Tarawa MIAs previously buried as "unknown" at the Punchbowl outside Honolulu.

Buster, the friendly black Labrador retriever who played a key part of History Flight's success on Tarawa, died in February 2015 at the age of twelve.

On September 2, 2017, my aunt Alix Bonnyman Prejean, her daughter Andra Prejean, and I buried a few small pieces of material evidence collected from Sandy's grave—the soles of his boondockers, buttons, a broken belt buckle—and a small piece of bone in an unmarked grave on the property where he operated his copper mine near Santa Rosa, New Mexico.

My mother, aunt, and I always agreed that Sandy should be buried in Knoxville alongside his parents and brother, who had tried so hard to bring his remains home. But like my grandfather, we all love New Mexico, and wanted to commit a small part of him to the Land of Enchantment, his final home on earth.

ACKNOWLEDGMENTS

Many people helped make this book a reality. The manuscript has changed radically over the years, and their contributions may not be explicit in this published version, but I am grateful to them all for their kind assistance.

History Flight: Eric Albertson, Kristen Baker, Drew Buchner, Corinne D'Anjou, Paul Dostie and Buster, John Frye, Harlan Glenn, James Goodrich, Ed Huffine, Reid Joyce, Kautebiri Kobuti, Marc Miller, Hillary Parsons, Glenn Prentice, Katherine Rasdorf, David Senn, Paul Schwimmer, Rick Snow. Above all, Mark Noah.

Tarawa veterans: Ed Bale, Max Clampitt, Leon Cooper, C.J. Daigle, Roy Elrod, Ed Gazel, Elwin Hart, Norman Hatch, Allen E. Heminger, Dean Ladd, Victor Ornelas, Robert Sheeks, Marvin Sheppard, Karol Szwet.

Other World War II veterans: Bill Bower, Edward Wood, Jr.

Tarawa MIA and veteran family members: Carol Bryant, George Clerou, Jim Crue, Patricia Donigian, Rick Gilliland, Paul Govedare, Jr., Michelle Guy, Pat Hallin, Lulane Harrison, Ron Harrison, Michael Heminger, Michael Hibner, Leroy Kisling, Jr., Robert Kossow, Ken Lally, Cory Maupin, Katherine Moore, Alan Leslie, John Murphy, Kenneth Oetjen, Frederick F. Penna, John

Ratomski, John Saini, Theresa Schaede, Jennifer Sheppard, Jane L. Shumate, David Silliman, Kirk David Stewart, Ellen Stoll, Jennifer Torgerson, Rick Voorhees, Garret Vreeland, Robert Zalesky.

Family: Margot Atkinson, Alexander "Al" Bonnyman, Anne Bonnyman, Brian Bonnyman, Gordon Bonnyman, Jr., Jean Webb Bonnyman, Isabel Ashe Bonnyman, 1st Lt. Norman Bonnyman (Army National Guard, First Troop, Philadelphia City Cavalry), Frances Bonnyman Evans, Catherine Evans Lambert, Margot McAllister, Hugh Nystrom, Alexandra Bonnyman "Alix" Prejean, Alexandra "Andra" Prejean, Alexander "Sandy" McKeon, Robert McKeon, Brooke Stanley, Jr., Isabel Bonnyman Stanley.

Researchers: Katherine Rasdorf, Tim Frank, James E. Nierle, Rich Boylan, Daniel Flores, Hana Y. Masters, Danielle J. Miera, Bill Niven, Dennis M. Spragg.

Archives and libraries: Hoover Institution (Stanford University), Santa Rosa (NM) Public Library, National Archives and Records Administration, National Personnel Records Center, United States Marine Corps Museum, National World War II Museum, Norlin Library (University of Colorado Boulder).

Joint POW/MIA Accounting Command/Defense POW/MIA Accounting Agency: Bill Belcher, Gregory Fox, Tyler Green, Anthony Hewitt, Michael S. Linnington, Ernest Nordman, Ramon Osorio, Wayne Perry, Rachel Phillips, Stephen Tom, Jay Silverstein, Lee Tucker, Johnie E. Webb. Armed Services Network: Navy Petty Officer First Class Justin Whiteman.

Veterans, active-duty military, and veterans' organizations: Marine Corps League, Bonnyman Detachment (Knoxville), Marine Corps League, Jake Puryear Detachment (Rome, Georgia), Hubert Caloud, Brant Clark, Thomas McKelvey Cleaver, Dave Collins, Dennis Covert, Chris Diplock (Australian Royal Navy), East Tennessee Veterans Memorial, Jack Garber, Don Gomez Jr., Travis Haan, William T. Hathaway, Matthew Hoh, Kurt Hiete, Gerald A.

Meehl, Patriot Guard Riders, Melinda Plett, Carroll Prejean, Roland Sharette, Dan Sidles, Ted Somes, Durk Steed, Walt Stewart, Wes Stowers, Gary Stump, David L. Vickers, Edward W. Wood, Jr., Michael Wizotsky, Virgil Young.

Authors and historians: Joseph Alexander, Don K. Allen, William Astore, Mike Campbell, James Carroll, Eric Hammel, Chris Hedges, Howard Jablon, Karl Marlantes, Peter McQuarrie, Douglas Pricer, David Smallwood, Frank Wallace, John Wukovits,

Tarawa residents, past, present, and part-time: Susan Barrie, Zahra Boluri, Kantaake Kerry Corbett, Toka Rakobu, Scott Dawson, Kim T. Harrison, Mareta Hinokua, Kautebiri Kobuti, Lisa Leidig, David Little, Chris Mahoney, Tamana Natanaera, Bill Newton, Kelle Rivers, Sister Margaret Sullivan, Petis Tentoa, Reire Timon, President Anote Tong, J.J. Williams, Tekinaa Taboaki, Temoana Tabokai.

Journalists, videographers, and webmasters: John Becker (WBIR), Fred Brown (*Knoxville News-Sentinel*), Matthew M. Burke (*Stars and Stripes*), Mark Emmons (*San Jose Mercury News*), Paul Freedman, Michael Goldstein (*Princeton Alumni Weekly*), Jim Hildebrand (Tarawa on the Web), Marc Miller, John Reitzammer, Ted Rowlands (*CNN*), M.E. Sprengelmyer (*Guadalupe County Communicator*), Jeremy Edward Shiok, Steve Terrell (*Santa Fe New Mexican*), John Torigoe (*CNN*).

Santa Rosa: Mayor Joseph Campos, Davy Delgado, Daniel Flores, the family of Jerry and Patricia Gallegos, George Gonzalez, Joe Martinez.

Knoxville: Jayme Rich Beeler and all the staff at Berry Highland Memorial, Patrice Collins, Joleen Dewald, Tim Eichhorn, Mary Tate, Ann Young.

Editors, readers, and advisers: William Astore, Robert Castellino, Margaret Coel, Jody Frank Evans, Tom Irwin, Jennifer Knerr, Bruce Leaf, Jerry Meehl, John Reitzammer, Elizabeth

Scarboro, James Scott, John Shors, Brooke Stanley, Jr., Daniel Zantzinger.

Many thanks to my agent, Maryann Karinch. And my deepest gratitude to my editors, Michael Campbell and Hector Carosso, who helped me make this the best book possible.

WORKS CONSULTED

This book was many years in the making, and underwent numerous changes. Although it may not be directly reflected in this final version, each of the works below influenced its writing in some way.

Alexander, Col. Joseph, USMC (ret.) *Utmost Savagery: The Three Days of Tarawa*. Annapolis: Naval Institute Press, 1995.

Across the Reef: The Marine Assault of Tarawa. Washington, D.C.: History and Museums Division, USMC, 1993.

"Tarawa: The Ultimate Opposed Landing." Marine Corps Gazette, November 1993.

Allen, Donald K. *Tarawa—the Aftermath*. Self-published, 2001.

The Atlanta Journal, "Lieut. Bonnyman Killed in Pacific," January 6, 1944.

Barber, Steven C. *Return to Tarawa: The Leon Cooper Story*, DVD. Directed by Steven C. Barber. Los Angeles: Vanilla Fire Productions, 2009. .

Until They Are Home. DVD. Directed by Steven C. Barber. Los Angeles: Vanilla Fire Productions. 2012.

Blakely, Tom. *Tarawa: The Dramatic Story of One of the Most Devastating Battles in Marine History*. Connecticut: Monarch Books, 1963.

Brown, Dave. "Tarawa: Seeking a Conclusion." *Follow Me*, October-November- December 2010.

Burke, Matthew M. "Internal memo alleges JPAC ethics violations." *Stars and Stripes*, January 28, 2014.

Campbell, Joseph. *The Hero With a Thousand Faces,* Commemorative Edition. Princeton, N.J.: Princeton Univ. Press, 2004.

Catsoulis, Jeannette. "The Fallen in 1943 Get an Audience in 2012." *The New York Times*, August 30, 2012.

Center for the Study of War and Society. "Kyle Campbell Moore: Hometown Hero." Knoxville, Tennessee: University of Tennessee, Knoxville, 2010.

Colley, David P. *Safely Rest*. New York: Berkley Caliber, 2004.

Cooper, Leon. *The War in the Pacific: A Retrospective*. Los Angeles: 90 Day Wonder Publishing, 2007.

Costello, John. *The Pacific War: 1941–1945*. New York: Atlantic, 1981.

Crane, David. *Empires of the Dead: How One Man's Vision Led to the Creation of WWI's War Graves*. New York: William Collins, 2013.

Dao, James. "Medal of Honor Nominee Picks Up Supporter." At War, nytimes.com, September 23, 2011.

Dedman, Bill. "Pentagon recognizes efforts to ID MIAs after NBC News series." nbcnews.com, March 31, 2014.

"Pentagon unit held 'phony' ceremonies for MIAs." nbcnews.com, October 10, 2013.

Delgado, Davy. "Navy ship named after Santa Rosa war hero." *Santa Rosa News*, June 7, 1984.

The Denver Post, "Ship named for Marine hero killed in '43," August 25, 1985.

De Wind, Dorian. "Why U.S. troops deserve to be called heroes." *Los Angeles Times*, July 27, 2010.

Doolittle, Gen. James H. *I Could Never Be So Lucky Again*. New York: Bantam Books, 1991.

Edey, Maitland. "The Class of '32: Fifteen years later 273 Princeton men answer some personal questions." *LIFE*, June 16, 1947.

Emmons, Mark. "Search for World War II hero's remains hinges on South Bay man's research." *San Jose Mercury News*, August 14, 2013.

Faulkner, William. *Requiem for a Nun*. Vintage, 1975. New York: Random House, 1950.

The Sound and the Fury. Vintage, 1991. New York: Jonathan Cape and Harrison Smith, 1929.

Fenwick, Robert W. "Coloradans and the Medal of Honor." *The Denver Post*, February 3, 1963.

Fitzpatrick, George. "The Medal of Honor." *New Mexico Magazine*, April 1968.

Flores, Daniel B. *Military Heroes of Guadalupe County*. Santa Rosa: Self-published, 2014.

Cuentos de la Pastura: Tales of a Guadalupe County Railroad Town. Santa Rosa: Self-published. 2015.

Friend, Craig Thompson. *Southern Masculinity: Perspectives on Manhood in the South Since Reconstruction*. Athens, Georgia: University of Georgia Press, 2009.

Gantter, Raymond. *Roll Me Over: An Infantryman's World War II*. New York: Presidio Press, 1997.

Garth, John. *Tolkien and the Great War: The Threshold of Middle-earth*. New York: Houghton Mifflin, 2003.

Glasgow Herald, "Kinsman of Glasgow Priest, U.S. Officer, Killed in Action Against Japs," January 15, 1944.

Goldstein, Michael. "Issue in Doubt: After 65 years, a Princeton family has guarded hopes that a loved one's remains might come home." *Princeton Alumni Weekly*, May 13, 2009.

Graham, Michael B. *Mantle of Heroism: Tarawa and the Struggle for the Gilberts, November 1943*. Novato, California: Presidio, 1993.

Hammel, Eric and John E. Lane. *Bloody Tarawa: A Narrative History with 250 Photographs.* Pacifica, California: Pacifica Military History, 1998.

Hannah, S.Sgt. Dick. *Tarawa: The Toughest Battle in Marine Corps History.* New York: U.S. Camera/Folmer Graflex, 1944.

Hayward, Louis and Richard Brooks. *With the Marines at Tarawa,* DVD. United States Marine Corps Photographic Unit: 1944.

Hemingway, Ernest and Sean Hemingway (editor), *Hemingway on War.* New York: Scribner, 2004.

Herndon, Booton. "Bloody Tarawa." *Saga: Adventure Stories for Men,* March 1959.

Hiete, Kurt. "A Plan for an Environmental Living Memorial to Honor the Veterans of the Battle of Tarawa." Self-published, 2011.

Hitchens, Christopher. "Poor Old Willie." *The Atlantic,* May 2004.

Homer. *The Iliad and the Odyssey.* New York: Barnes & Noble, 1995.

Hurwitz, Staff Sgt. Hy. "Marine Correspondent Writes of Bonnyman's Death in Gilbert Islands." *The Santa Fe New Mexican,* April 3, 1944.

Hylton, Wil S. "The Long Road Back." *The New York Times Magazine,* November 24, 2013.

Vanished: The Sixty-Year Search for the Missing Men of World War II. New York: Riverhead Books, 2013.

Jablon, Howard. *David M. Shoup: A Warrior Against War.* Lanham, Maryland: Rowman & Littlefield, 2005.

Jacobs, Bruce. "The Island Hoppers: The Story of the 2nd Marine Division." *Saga: Adventure Stories for Men.* November 1955.

Johnston, Richard W. *Follow Me! The Story of the Second Marine Division in World War II.* New York: Random House, 1948.

Joint POW/MIA Accounting Command Public Affairs. *Joint POW/MIA Accounting Command,* DVD. Honolulu, 2007.

Jones, James. *From Here to Eternity.* New York: Charles Scribner's Sons, 1951.

The Thin Red Line. New York: Charles Scribner's Sons, 1962.

Kane, Harnett K. *Miracle in the Mountains: The Inspiring Story of Martha Berry's Crusade for the Mountain People of the South.* Garden City, New York: Doubleday, 1956.

Secretariat of the Pacific and Government of Kiribati, "North Tarawa Socioeconomic Report 2008."

The Knoxville Journal, "Bonnyman is cited for high medal," March 29, 1944.

"Bonnyman's Pacific death is reported." December 31, 1943.

"Film shows Lt. 'Sandy' Bonnyman in Last Battle Against Jap Pillbox." April 1, 1944.

"Navy Cross goes to Lt. Bonnyman." May 14, 1944.

The Knoxville News-Sentinel, "Bonnyman was sure of Tarawa ere the end," April 1, 1944.

Kyodo News International, "Kiribati president says climate change is shrinking his country," September 4, 2013.

Ladd, Dean. "Tarawa: Repatriation Mission." *Follow Me,* January-February-March 2011.

Manchester, William. *American Caesar: Douglas MacArthur, 1880–1964.* New York: Little, Brown, 1978.

Goodbye, Darkness: A Memoir of the Pacific War. New York: Little, Brown, 1979.

Manning, Robert, ed. *Above and Beyond: A History of the Medal of Honor from the Civil War to Vietnam.* Boston: Boston Publishing, 1985.

Marlantes, Karl. *What It Is Like to Go to War.* New York: Grove Press, 2011.

McAvoy, Audrey. "U.S. military finds two sets of remains in Tarawa." Associated Press, September 22, 2010.

McCullough, David G., ed. *The American Heritage Picture History of World War II.* New York: McGraw-Hill, 1966.

McQuarrie, Peter. *Gilbert Islands in WWII*. Oakland, California: Masalai Press. 2012.

Meehl, Gerald A. *One Marine's War: A Combat Interpreter's Quest for Humanity in the Pacific*. Annapolis: Naval Institute Press, 2012.

Pacific Legacy: Image and Memory from World War II in the Pacific. New York: Abbeville Press, 2002.

Melville, Herman. *Moby-Dick*. Oxford Univ. Press, 2008. New York: Harper & Brothers, 1851.

Milford, Humphrey and R.M. Leonard, eds. *The Pageant of English Poetry: Being 1150 Poems and Extracts by 300 Authors*. London: Oxford University Press, 1919.

Moisie, Norman. "Unconquerable Ground Reclaimed." *Leatherneck*, June 1993.

Morison, Samuel Eliot. "The Gilberts & and The Marshalls." *LIFE*, May 22, 1944.

Naval History, "'What War Was Like': An Interview with Major Norman Hatch, U.S. Marine Corps (Retired)," December 2008.

Nelson, Kristi L. "War hero's childhood home: Bonnyman family, staff resided in Kingston Pike mansion." *Knoxville News-Sentinel*, May 20, 2012.

Newcomb, Obie. Jr. "Combat Photog on Tarawa." *Liberty*, March 18, 1944.

The New York Sun, "Lieut. Bonnyman Killed in Action in Pacific," January 4, 1944.

The New York Times, "Marine Officer Killed: Alexander Bonnyman, Mining Man, a Casualty in Pacific," January 4, 1944.

The New York Tribune, "Lt. Alexander Bonnyman, Jr.: Marine Office, Former Football Man, Princeton, Killed in Combat," January 4, 1944.

Niven, Capt. William L., USMC (ret.) *Tarawa's Gravediggers*. Morgan Hill, Calif.: Self- published, 2007.

Noah, Mark. *The Lost Graves of Tarawa*. Marathon, Florida: History Flight, Inc., 2009.

Owens, Darryl E. "Taps for man's lost WWII cousin brings closure." *Sun-Sentinel*, May 27, 2013.

Perry, Tony. "Hagel refuses to reopen Medal of Honor bid for Sgt. Rafael Peralta." *Los Angeles Times*, February 21, 2014.

Personnel, Bureau of Naval, ed. *Medal of Honor 1861–1949*. Annapolis: Navy Department United States of America, 1949.

Pfaff, William. *The Bullet's Song: Romantic Violence and Utopia*. New York: Simon & Schuster, 2004.

Philpott, William. *War of Attrition: Fighting World War I*. New York: Overlook Press, 2014.

Piehler, Kurt and Tim Bracken. "An Interview with G. Gordon Bonnyman." Knoxville, Tennessee: University of Tennessee Veteran's Oral History Project, 2000.

Poole, Robert M. *On Hallowed Ground: The Story of Arlington National Cemetery*. New York: Walker & Company, 2010.

Press-Telegram (Long Beach), "Remembering Tarawa: A Special Section," June 26, 1988.

The Register (Tennessee Edition), "Knoxville Pair Hear Marine-Son Dies in Action," January 16, 1944.

"Alexander Bonnyman, Hero of Knoxville, To Receive Medal of Honor Posthumously." November 17, 1946.

Remarque, Erich Maria. *All Quiet on the Western Front*. New York: Little, Brown, 1928.

Rome (Georgia) *Journal*, "Lt. Bonnyman is Killed in Action," January 4, 1944.

Rooney, Andrew A. *The Fortunes of War: Four Great Battles of World War II*. New York: Little, Brown, 1962.

Santa Fe New Mexican, "Bonneyman Reported Slain," December 21, 1943.

Scheck, Frank. "Until They Are Home: Film Review." *The Hollywood Reporter*, August 30, 2012.

Shaw, Henry I., Jr. *Tarawa: A Legend is Born*. New York: Ballantine Books, 1968.

Sherrod, Robert. "The 76 Frightful Hours of Tarawa." *Saturday Evening Post*, November 28, 1953.

Tarawa: The Story of a Battle. New York: Duell, Sloan and Pearce, 1944.

Shiner, J.S. *Fulois and the U.S. Army Air Corps: 1931–1935*. Washington, D.C.: Office of Air Force History. 2012.

Shiok, Jeremy Edward. "JPAC Mission to Tarawa—August 2010." Anchorage: Self- published. 2014.

Shoup, David M. and James A. Donovan. "The New American Militarism." *Atlantic Monthly*. April 1969.

Sledge, E.B. *With the Old Breed: At Peleiliu and Okinawa*. New York: Random House, 1981.

Smith, Holland M. *Coral and Brass*. New York: Scribner's, 1949.

Stanley, Isabel Bonnyman. *I Was a War Baby*. Johnson City, Tennessee: Self-published, 2010.

Stanton, Doug. *In Harm's Way: The Sinking of the USS Indianapolis and the Extraordinary Story of Its Survivors*. New York: Henry Holt, 2001.

Steed, Rev. Durk. *Tarawa 1943: Red Beach 3*. Richmond, Virginia: Self-published, 2011.

Stockman, Capt. James R. *The Battle for Tarawa*. Washington, D.C.: U.S. Marine Corps Historical Division, 1947.

Svoboda, Elizabeth. *What Makes a Hero? The Surprising Science of Selflessness*. New York: Penguin, 2013.

Tait, Don, and Leon Cooper. *90-Day Wonder: Darkness Remembered*. Los Angeles: Self-published, 2003.

Thompson, Mark. "Combat Deployments: Unbalanced Burden," *TIME*, March 16, 2012.

Tolkien, J.R.R. *The Letters of J.R.R. Tolkien.* Edited Humphrey Carpenter. New York: Houghton Mifflin, 2000.

The Lord of the Rings. One-volume edition. New York: Houghton Mifflin, 1954–55.

Troost, J. Maarten. *The Sex Lives of Cannibals.* New York: Broadway Books, 2004.

United States Department of Defense. "Report to the Senate and House Armed Service Committees on the Medal of Honor Award Process." Washington, D.C. 2011.

United States General Accounting Office. "DOD's POW/MIA Mission: Top-Level Leadership Attention Needed to Resolve Longstanding Challenges in Accounting for Missing Persons from Past Conflicts." Washington, D.C. 2013.

United States Marine Corps. "Second Marine Division Report on Gilbert Islands Operation." Quantico, Virginia: Department of the Navy. December 23, 1943.

Wallace, Frank. *Kennedy's General: The Remarkable Life of David M. Shoup.* Berkeley: Self-published, 2013.

Wright, Derrick. *Tarawa, 20–23 November, 1943: A Hell of a Way to Die.* London: Windrow & Greene, Ltd., 1996.

Wukovits, John. *One Square Mile of Hell: The Battle for Tarawa.* New York: New American Library, 2006

ENDNOTES

Prologue

1. Bonnyman, Frances Berry, letter to Alexander Bonnyman, Jr., June 9, 1943.
2. Horne, George. F, "We Win Gilberts in 76-Hour Battle," *New York Times*, November 25, 1943.
3. Horne, "We Win Gilberts in 76-Hour Battle."
4. Sherrod, Robert, *Tarawa: The Story of a Battle*. (New York: Duell, Sloan and Pierce 1944), 150.
5. Keys, Henry, "Vast U.S. Forces Used at Gilberts," *New York Times*, November 26, 1943.
6. Johnson, Richard W., "Gilberts Battle Is Called Fiercest Fought in the Pacific," *New York Times*, November 27, 1943.
7. *New York Times*, "The Lesson of Tarawa," December 6, 1943.
8. *New York Times*, "Battle of Tarawa in Newsreels Today," December 7, 1943.
9. Sherrod, Robert, "Report on Tarawa: Marines' Show," *Time*, December 6, 1943.
10. "Dock" (no other name given), letter to Mary Ramey, December 20, 1943.
11. Alexander Bonnyman, Sr., letter to Ralph DuPress, December 28, 1943.
12. *Santa Fe New Mexican*, "Bonneyman Reported Slain," December 21, 1943.
13. Bonnyman, Josephine B., letter to Capt. Earl Wilson, March 7, 1944.
14. Holcomb, Lt. Gen. Thomas, telegram to Josephine Bonnyman, December 28, 1943.

15. Evans, Frances Bonnyman, interview with the author, November 13, 2016.
16. Russell, Josephine, letter to Frances Bonnyman, April 11, 1951.

One

1. Prejean, Alix, interview with the author, June 4, 2011.
2. Alexander, Joseph, letter to Fran Bonnyman Evans, April 5, 1994.
3. Alexander, Joseph, letter to Alexandra Bonnyman Prejean, August 6, 1994.
4. *Denver Post*, "Veteran remembers," November 24, 1985.
5. Alexander, Joseph, letter to Alexandra Bonnyman Prejean, August 6, 1994.
6. Alexander, Col. Joseph, USMC (Ret.). *Utmost Savagery: The Three Days of Tarawa,* (Annapolis, 1995), 240.
7. Evans, Frances Bonnyman, letter to Jones, Gallegos, Snead & Wertheim, P.A. November 3, 1976.
8. Edison, Maj. A.E., letter to Frances Bonnyman Evans, May 21, 1990.
9. Prejean interview, June 4, 2011.
10. Stevens, Jonathan, "Introduction," tarawaontheweb.org, June 15, 2003.
11. Lipinski, US Rep. Daniel, office of, "Lipinski presses Defense Department to Locate Remains of U.S. Service Members in Battle of Tarawa," June 26, 2009.
12. Stevens, Jonathan, "Lipinski Presses for DOD to find Tarawa Dead." tarawaontheweb.org, June 26, 2009.
13. Hiete, Kurt, email to multiple recipients, December 19, 2009.
14. Shane, Leo, III, "Remains found on Pacific island likely to be those of 139 WWII Marines," *Stars and Stripes*, November 28, 2008.

Two

1. Marshall, J. F.; Jacobson, G., "Holocene growth of a mid-Pacific atoll: Tarawa, Kiribati," *Coral Reefs*, April 1985.
2. Allen, Donald K., *Tarawa: The Aftermath*, (self-published, 2001), 2.
3. Secretariat of the Pacific and Government of Kiribati, "North Tarawa Socioeconomic Report 2008," climate.gov.ki.
4. Morison, "The Gilberts & Marshalls."
5. Morison, "The Gilberts & Marshalls."
6. McQuarrie, Peter. *Gilbert Islands in WWII* (Oakland, Calif.: NAL Caliber, 2012), 4.
7. Allen, *Tarawa—the Aftermath*, 5.

8. Sacred Heart of Mary convent, private collection, Bairiki, Tarawa.

9. Alexander, *Utmost Savagery*, 28.

10. Russ, Martin, *Line of Departure: Tarawa* (New York, 1975), 6.

11. Wukovits, John, *One Square Mile of Hell: The Battle for Tarawa* (New York, 2006), 17.

12. Bonnyman, Alexander, Jr., letter to Frances Berry Bonnyman, October 2, 1943.

13. Hammel, Eric, and John E. Lane, *Bloody Tarawa: A Narrative History with 250 Photographs* (Pacifica: Pacifica Military History, 1998), 6.

14. Hammel and Lane, *Bloody Tarawa*, 6.

15. Ellis, Maj. Earl H., "U.S. Marine Corps 712H Operation Plan: Advanced Base Operations in Micronesia," July 23, 1921.

16. Hammel and Lane, *Bloody Tarawa*, 7.

Three

1. Troost, J. Maarten, *The Sex Lives of Cannibals,* new title edition (New York: Broadway Books 2004), 255.

2. Shiok, Jeremy Edward, email to the author, May 21, 2011.

3. Osorio, Maj. Ramon, email to Steven Barber, July 1, 2010.

4. Barber, Steven C., email to the author, August 4, 2010.

5. Noah, Mark, email to the author, July 8, 2010.

6. Noah email, July 8, 2010.

7. Hylton, Wil S., *Vanished: The Sixty-Year Search for the Missing Men of World War II* (New York, 2013), 16.

8. Defense POW/MIA Accounting Command, "Tarawa Summary," March 11, 2015.

9. Noah, Mark, *The Lost Graves of Tarawa* (self-published, 2009), 16.

10. Noah, Mark, interview with the author, June 1, 2015.

11. Niven, Capt. William L. USMC (ret.), *Tarawa's Gravediggers* (Morgan Hill, California: self-published, 2007), 16.

12. Noah, *The Lost Graves of Tarawa*, 94.

13. Noah, *The Lost Graves of Tarawa*, iii.

14. Noah, Mark, interview with the author, February 17, 2015.

15. Noah, *The Lost Graves of Tarawa*, 4.

16. DPAA, "Tarawa Summary," March 11, 2015.

17. Niven, Capt. William L. USMC (ret.), interview with the author, December 11, 2011.

18. Niven, Capt. William L. USMC (ret.), *Tarawa's Gravediggers*, 4.

19. Niven, Tarawa's Gravediggers, 320–321.

20. Niven interview, December 11, 2011.
21. Akaka, US Sen. Daniel, letter to Alexandra Bonnyman Prejean, September 9, 2009.
22. Joint POW/Accounting Command (JPAC) 2010 Annual Report.
23. Niven interview, December 11, 2011.
24. Noah, Mark, interview with the author, October 29, 2011.
25. JPAC (source redacted), email (recipient redacted) July 15, 2010.
26. Tarawa Talk forum, tarawaontheweb.org, July 29, 2010.
27. Covert, Dennis, email to the author, August 3, 2010
28. Asian Development Bank, "Economic Costs of Inadequate Water and Sanitation, South Tarawa, Kiribati," 2014
29. Rivers, Kelle, letter to the author, January 1, 1995

Four

1. McKeon, Robert, interview with the author, September 6, 2010.
2. Bonnyman, George Gordon, interview with G. Kurt Piehler and Tim Bracken, University of Tennessee Veteran's Oral History Project, April 20, 2000.
3. *Knoxville Journal*, "University Of Kentucky To Honor Bonnyman," May 23, 1950.
4. *Knoxville Journal*, "University Of Kentucky To Honor Bonnyman," May 23, 1950.
5. Nelson, Kristi L. "War hero's childhood home: Bonnyman family, staff resided in Kingston Pike mansion," *Knoxville News-Sentinel*, May 20, 2012.
6. Leonard, R.M., editor, *The Pageant of English Poetry: Being 1150 Poems and Extracts by 300 Authors,* (Oxford: Oxford University Press, 1911).
7. Headman, Mary, letter to Frances Bonnyman, August 26, 1932
8. McKeon interview, September 6, 2010.
9. Bonnyman, George Gordon, Jr., interview with the author, June 20, 2014.
10. Tate, Mary, interview with the author, August 11, 2015.
11. Friend, Craig Thompson, editor, *Southern Masculinity: Perspectives on Manhood in the South Since Reconstruction,* (Athens, Georgia, 2009).
12. *New York Times*, "Non-Flopping Student Trousers Evoke Praise from Coolidge," November 24, 1927.
13. Almond, Steve. *Against Football* (Brooklyn, New York: Melville House, 2014), 19.
14. Gore, Frank, letter to Alexander Bonnyman, Sr., (undated) 1928
15. Van Schiack, A.G., letter to Alexander Bonnyman, Sr., May 20, 1947

16. Bonnyman, George Gordon, Piehler and Bracken interview.
17. US Marine Corps, memorandum recommending Alexander Bonnyman, Jr. for Officers' Candidate School, October 5, 1942,
18. Bonnyman, Alexander, Sr., letter to Charles Scarlett, Jr., January 29, 1944

Five

1. Bale, Ed, interview with the author, July 13, 2011.
2. Bale interview.
3. Bale interview.
4. Moore, Katherine, interview with the author, June 4, 2011.
5. Kossow, Robert, interview with the author, June 28, 2015.
6. Evans, Frances Bonnyman, interview with the author, August 3, 2013.
7. Silliman, David, interview with the author, June 28, 2015.
8. Bonnyman, Alexander, Sr., letter to Lt. Gen. A.A. Vandegrift, January 17, 1944.
9. Faust, Drew Gilpin, *This Republic of Suffering: Death and the American Civil War* (New York: Alfred A. Knopf, 2009), 100.
10. Poole, *On Hallowed Ground*, 145.
11. Colley, *Safely Rest*, 220.
12. Crane, David. *Empires of the Dead: How One Man's Vision Led to the Creation of WWI's War Graves* (New York: William Collins, 2013), passim.
13. Poole, *On Hallowed Ground*, 143.
14. Poole, *On Hallowed Ground*, 145.
15. Poole, *On Hallowed Ground*, 145.
16. Poole, *On Hallowed Ground*, 189.
17. Fussell, Paul. *The Boys' Crusade: The American Infantry in Northwestern Europe, 1944–1945.* (New York: Modern Library, 2004.)
18. Trotter, Mildred. "Operations at Central Identification Laboratory," US Army Graves Registration Service (AGRS), 1949.
19. Hylton, *Vanished*, 97.
20. Appy, Christian. *American Reckoning: The Vietnam War and Our National Identity,* (New York: Penguin Books, 2015.)
21. Title 32, Part 371, Defense Prisoner of War/Missing in Action Office, Code of Federal Regulations, September 5, 1993.
22. US Government Accounting Office, "DOD'S POW/MIA MISSION: Top-Level Leadership Attention Needed to Resolve Longstanding Challenges in Accounting for Missing Persons from Past Conflicts," July 17, 2013.

Six

1. Perry, Lt. Col. Wayne, email to superior (name redacted), August 6, 2010.
2. Miller, Marc, interview with the author, January 24, 2011.
3. Miller interview, January 24, 2011.
4. Osorio, Maj. Ramon, audio recording by the author, August 11, 2010.
5. Osorio, Maj. Ramon, audio recording by the author, August 11, 2010.
6. Fujioka, Nobukatsu, *Atarashii Rekishi Kyo kasho: Shihanbon* (Tokyo, Fusosha, 2006). (Translated by Hana Y. Masters, July 29, 2011.)
7. Noah, *The Lost Graves of Tarawa*, 53.
8. Defense POW/MIA Accounting Agency, "Tarawa Summary," March 11, 2015.
9. Noah, Mark, email to the author, July 26, 2013.
10. *New York Times*, "Tarawa Foe Accused in Massacre of 22," March 24, 1945.
11. Fox, Dr. Gregory, interview with the author, August 14, 2010.
12. Fox interview, August 14, 2010.
13. Fox interview, August 14, 2010.
14. Fox interview, August 14, 2010.
15. Shiok, Jeremy Edward. "JPAC Mission to Tarawa—August 2010," self-published report, 2014.
16. Shiok report.
17. Joint POW/MIA Accounting Command (JPAC) public-affairs office (sender and recipient names redacted), August 31, 2010.

Seven

1. Noah, Mark, interview with the author, October 29, 2011.
2. Tabokai, Temoana, interview with the author, August 12, 2010 (translated by Kautebiri Kobuti).
3. Talu, Alaima, letter to Margaret Sullivan, June 24, 1999.
4. Tabokai interview, August 12, 2010.
5. Tabokai interview, August 12, 2010.
6. Shiok, Jeremy, interview with the author, August 13, 2010.
7. Sullivan, Margaret, interview with the author, August 16, 2010.
8. Niven, Bill, interview with the author, December 11, 2011.
9. Noah, Mark, email to JPAC, July 23, 2010.
10. Noah interview, March 11, 2011.
11. Noah email, May 13, 2011.
12. Noah, Mark, interview with the author, March 13, 2011.

13. Kiribati Ministry of Foreign Affairs, email to JPAC (recipient redacted), July 21, 2010.

14. JPAC official (name redacted), email to Mark Noah, August 4, 2010.

15. Belcher, Dr. Bill, interview with the author, September 6, 2015.

16. McAvoy, Audrey, "U.S. military finds 2 sets of remains in Tarawa," Associated Press, September 22, 2010.

17. Rowlands, Ted, interview with the author, February 11, 2011.

18. Rowlands interview, February 11, 2011.

19. DPAA, "Tarawa Summary," March 11, 2015. 152

Eight

1. Shiner, J.S. *Foulois and the U.S. Army Air Corps: 1931–1935* (Office of Air Force History, 1983), 109.

2. Headman letter, August 26, 1932.

3. Bonnyman, Sandy, letter to Frances Berry Bonnyman, October 2, 1943.

4. Alexander, *Utmost Savagery,* 187.

5. USMC general pay data record, November 25, 1942.

6. Young, Virgil L., Jr., USMC (ret.), interview with the author, August 25, 2015.

7. Prejean, Alix, interview with the author, August 16, 2015.

8. Prejean interview, August 16, 2015.

9. McKeon interview, September 6, 2010.

10. Russell, Josephine Bell, letter to Frances Bonnyman, April 1951 (no day specified).

11. Evans, Frances Bonnyman, interviews with the author, passim.

12. Evans interviews.

13. Russell letter, April 1951

14. *Albuquerque Morning Journal,* "Copper mine is operating near town of Pastura," June 6, 1925.

15. Bonnyman, Alexander, Sr., letter to Josephine Bonnyman, December 8, 1942

16. Prejean interview, August 16, 2015.

17. Campos, Joseph, interview with the author, July 27, 2015.

18. US Marine Corps, "Report of physical examination," November 23, 1942.

19. *Santa Rosa News,* "'Sandy' Bonnyman Wounded Saturday Following Argument," March 14, 1941.

20. *Santa Rosa News,* "Damages Are Awarded in Santa Rosa Affair," March 20, 1942.

21. *Santa Rosa News*, "'Not Guilty' is Verdict of Jury," April 17, 1942.
22. Bonnyman, George Gordon, Piehler and Bracken interview.
23. Flores, Daniel, interview with author, July 27, 2015.
24. Evans, Fran Bonnyman, interview with the author, November 13, 2016.
25. Kisling, Leroy Jr., interview with the author, September 20, 2010.
26. Hitchens, Christopher, "Poor Old Willie," *The Atlantic*, May 2004.

Nine

1. Clerou, George, email to the author, September 14, 2010.
2. Sheppard interview, August 18, 2010.
3. JPAC public-affairs officer (name redacted), email to JPAC official (name redacted), September 3, 2010.
4. JPAC public-affairs officer (name redacted), email (recipient name redacted), August 31, 2010.
5. Barber, Steven C., email to Cortland D. Joyce, February 6, 2012.
6. Barber, Steven C., email to Ken Moore, May 19, 2010.
7. Barber, Steven C., email to JPAC public-affairs office, October 27, 2010.
8. Miller, Marc, email to the author et al, May 29, 2012.
9. Scheck, Frank, "Until They Are Home: Film Review," *Hollywood Reporter*, August 30, 2012.
10. Catsoulis, Jeannette, "The Fallen in 1943 Get an Audience in 2012," *New York Times*, August 30, 2012.
11. Noah, Mark, *History Flight 2011 Tarawa Trip Summary*, 2.
12. Dostie, Paul, interview with the author, March 24, 2012.
13. Dostie, Paul, interview with the author, February 20, 2011.
14. Noah, Mark, interview with the author, April 10, 2011.
15. Noah, Mark, interview with the author, October 29, 2011.
16. Sears, David, "Bring the Fallen Home," *Air & Space*, September 2015.
17. Noah, Mark, interview with the author, September 30, 2012.
18. Belcher interview, September 6, 2015.
19. Noah, Mark, interview with the author, February 7, 2015.
20. Belcher interview, September 6, 2015.

Ten

1. Bonnyman, Alexander, Sr., letter to Robert Sherrod, November 30, 1948.
2. Russell letter, April 1951.
3. Russell, James H., and Bonnyman, Alexander Jr., "Limited Partnership Agreement,' June 29, 1942

4. Bonnyman, Alexander, Sr., letter to Josephine Bonnyman, December 8, 1942.

5. Bonnyman, Sandy, letter to Frances Berry Bonnyman, May 10, 1943.

6. Jackson, Col. Gilder D., Jr., letter to Alexander Bonnyman, Sr., May 30, 1944.

7. Bonnyman, Josephine, letter to Alexander Bonnyman, Sr., July 22, 1942.

8. Bonnyman, Sandy, letter to France Berry Bonnyman Sept. 22, 1942.

9. Headquarters US Marine Corps, Circular Letter No. 602, August 31, 1942.

10. Bonnyman, Alexander, Sr., letter to Sandy Bonnyman, October 6, 1942.

11. Jackson letter, May 30, 1944.

12. Johnston, Richard W., *Follow Me! The Story of the Second Marine Division in World War II,* (New York: Random House, 1948.), 84.

13. Jackson letter, May 30, 1944.

14. Bonnyman, Sandy, V-Mail to Alexander, Sr. and Frances Berry Bonnyman, November 26, 1942.

15. *New York Times,* "The Engineers," Sept. 17, 1943.

16. Bonnyman, Sandy, letter to Frances Berry Bonnyman, March 9, 1943.

17. Jackson letter, May 30, 1944.

18. Jackson letter, May 30, 1944.

19. Marston, Capt. John, letter to Hugh Matthews, February 12, 1943.

20. Bonnyman, Sandy, letter to Josephine Bonnyman, September 22, 1943.

21. Boos letter, April 20, 1944.

22. Bonnyman, Sandy, letter to Anne Atkinson, May 12, 1943.

23. *An Encyclopedia of New Zealand,* Auckland 1966.

24. Bonnyman, Sandy, V-Mail to Frances Bonnyman, February 14, 1943.

25. Bonnyman, Sandy, letter to Anne Atkinson, May 12, 1943.

26. Bonnyman letter to Atkinson, May 12, 1943.

27. Kisling interview, March 26, 2011.

28. Griswold, Capt. Tracy, letter to Frances Berry Bonnyman, July 31, 1952.

29. Bonnyman, Sandy, letter to Frances Berry Bonnyman, March 9, 1943.

30. Ornelas interview, May 13, 2015.

31. Bonnyman, Sandy, letter to Frances Berry Bonnyman, April 25, 1943.

32. Bonnyman letter, April 25, 1943.

33. Graham, Michael B. *Mantle of Heroism: Tarawa and the Struggle for the Gilberts, November 1943.* (Novato, California: Presidio, 1993). 111.

34. Johnston, Richard W., letter to Alexander Bonnyman, Sr., January 12, 1949.

Eleven

1. Johnston, *Follow Me!*, 93.
2. Hammel and Lane, *Bloody Tarawa*, 6.
3. Johnston, *Follow Me!*, 98.
4. Bonnyman, Sandy, letter to Josephine Bonnyman, September 22, 1943.
5. Bonnyman letter, September 22, 1943.
6. Evans, Frances Bonnyman, interview with the author, June 18, 2014.
7. Bonnyman, Sandy, letter to Frances Bonnyman (daughter), April 25, 1943.
8. Bonnyman letter, October 2, 1943.
9. Bonnyman letter, October 2, 1943.
10. Bonnyman, Frances Berry, letter to James H. Russell, November 3, 1943.
11. Evans interview, August 23, 2013.
12. Bonnyman, Josephine, letter to Alexander Bonnyman, Sr., December 5, 1942.
13. Bonnyman, Sandy, letter to Clara Hood, October 4, 1943.
14. Bonnyman, Alexander, Sr., letter to Josephine Bonnyman, December 8, 1942.
15. Bonnyman letter, March 9, 1943.
16. Brown, Monte E., letter to HQ, Second Marine Division, July 27, 1943.
17. Bonnyman letter, September 22, 1943.
18. Hammel and Lane, *Bloody Tarawa*, 16.
19. Alexander, *Utmost Savagery*, 93.
20. Johnston, *Follow Me!*, 102.
21. Russell, Josephine Bell, letter to Frances Berry Bonnyman, December 17, 1945.
22. Elrod, Col. Roy H. USMC (ret.), interview with the author, October 23, 2015.
23. Price, Harry, letter to Frances Berry Bonnyman, August 30, 1943.
24. Bonnyman letter, March 9, 1943.
25. Griswold letter, July 31, 1952.
26. Bonnyman letter, September 22, 1943.
27. Griswold letter, July 31, 1952.
28. Campbell, Mike. *Amelia Earhart: The Truth at Last*. (Boiling Springs, Pennsylvania: Sunbury Press, 2012).
29. *New York Times*, "Shoup defends Tarawa Tactics 20 Years After Marines' Battle," November 21, 1963.
30. *New York Times*, "Grim Tarawa Defense a Surprise, Eyewitness of Battle Reveals," December 4, 1943.

31. Griswold letter, July 31, 1952.

Twelve

1. Hylton, Wil S., "The Long Road Back," *New York Times Magazine*, November 24, 2013.
2. Noah, Mark, interview with the author, July 18, 2013.
3. Noah interview, March 25, 2013.
4. Owens, Darryl E. "Taps for man's lost WWII cousin brings closure," *Sun Sentinel*, May 27, 2013.
5. Noah, *The Lost Graves of Tarawa*, 60.
6. Alexander, *Utmost Savagery*, 138.
7. Corbett, Kantaake Kerry, interview with the author, April 28, 2013.
8. Belcher interview, September 6, 2015.

Thirteen

1. Stockman, Capt. James R., *The Battle for Tarawa* (Quantico, Virginia: Historical Section, Division of Public Information, Headquarters, USMC, 1947), 29
2. After Action report, Headquarters, Second Marine Division, Fleet Marine Force, In the Field, December 23, 1943.
3. Alexander, Col. Joseph, USMC (ret.), "Across the Reef: The Marine Assault of Tarawa," Marine Corps Historical Center, Washington, D.C., 1993.
4. Salazar, Lt. Col. Chester J., "Report of LTSPCO 2nd Marines," December 22, 1943.
5. Hammel and Lane, *Bloody Tarawa*, 20.
6. Olson, Donald W., "The Tide at Tarawa," *Sky and Telescope*, November 1987.
7. Alexander, *Utmost Savagery*, 76.
8. Ladd, Lt. Col. Dean USMC (ret.), interview with the author, October 8, 2012.
9. Hart, Elwin B, interview with the author, August 28, 2015.
10. Alexander, *Utmost Savagery*, 5.
11. Bale, Ed, interview with the author, July 14, 2013.
12. Salazar report, December 22, 1943.
13. Newcomb, Sgt. Obie Jr., letter to Edna Schneider, March 23, 1944.
14. Newcomb letter, March 23, 1944.
15. Alexander, *Utmost Savagery*, 148.
16. Hammel and Lane, *Bloody Tarawa*, 140.

17. Johnston, *Follow Me!*, 132.
18. Stockman, *The Battle for Tarawa*, 29.
19. Stockman, *The Battle for Tarawa*, 33.
20. Salazar report, December 22, 1943.
21. Medal of Honor citation for Sandy Bonnyman.
22. Alexander, *Utmost Savagery*, 187.
23. Newcomb, letter, March 23, 1944.
24. Stockman, *The Battle for Tarawa*, 34.
25. USMC, "First Lieutenant Alexander Bonnyman," January 16, 1947.
26. Medal of Honor citation for William Deane Hawkins.
27. Dent, J.L. Jr., letter to J.K. Dent, February 6, 1944.
28. Sheppard, Marvin, interview with the author, August 20, 2010.
29. Sherrod, *Tarawa*, 142.
30. Clampitt, Max, interview with the author, June 4, 2011.
31. Stockman, *The Battle for Tarawa*, 41.

Fourteen

1. Elrod interview, October 23, 2015.
2. Hatch, Norman, interview with the author, July 15, 2010.
3. Elrod interview, October 23, 2015.
4. Hammel and Lane, 229.
5. Elrod interview, October 23, 2015.
6. Alexander, *Utmost Savagery*, 188.
7. Alexander, Joseph, interview with the author, May 26, 2014.
8. Hammel and Lane, *Bloody Tarawa*, 233.
9. Szwet, Karl, interview with the author, June 15, 2014.
10. Newcomb, Sgt. Obie Jr., letter to Edna Schneider, May 23, 1944.
11. Elrod interview, October 23, 2015.
12. Elrod interview, October 23, 2015.
13. Sheppard interview, August 18, 2010.
14. Jackson, Col. Gilder D. Jr., letter to Josephine Bonnyman, January 4, 1944.
15. Jacobs, Bruce, "The Island Hoppers, The Story of the Second Marine Division," *Saga: True Adventures for Men*, November 1955.
16. Shaw, Henry I. *Tarawa: A Legend is Born*, (New York: Ballantine, 1968), 115.
17. Manchester, William. *Goodbye Darkness: A Memoir of the Pacific War* (New York, 1979), 283.
18. Alexander, Col. Joseph, interview with the author, May 26, 2014.

19. Crowe, Maj. Henry P., Medal of Honor recommendation for Alexander Bonnyman, Jr., December 27, 1943.
20. Alexander, *Utmost Savagery*, 188.
21. Alexander, *Utmost Savagery*, 190.
22. Hammel and Lee, *Bloody Tarawa*, 233.
23. Hammel, Eric and John E. Lane, "Third Day on Red Beach," *Marine Corps Gazette*, November 1970. 22.
24. Niehoff, Harry, letter to Alix Prejean, October 1994.
25. Niehoff letter, October 1994.
26. Hammel and Lee, *Bloody Tarawa*, 234.
27. Niehoff, Harry, letter to Joseph Alexander, February 27, 1994.
28. Alexander, Joseph, letter to Fran Bonnyman Evans, April 5, 1994.
29. Niehoff letter, October 1994.
30. Sheppard interview, August 20, 2010.
31. Nimitz, Adm. C.W., Silver Star citation for Harry H.W. Niehoff.
32. Hedges, Chris, interview with the author, December 27, 2010.
33. Niehoff, Harry, letter to Alix Prejean, November 1994.
34. Niehoff letter, November 1994.

Fifteen

1. Stockman, *The Battle of Tarawa*, 47.
2. Alexander, "Across the Reef: The Marine Assault of Tarawa."
3. Niven interview, December 11, 2011.
4. *New York Times*, "Scenes of Horror Remain on Betio," November 28, 1943.
5. Noah, *The Lost Graves of Tarawa*. 14.
6. Newcomb, Sgt. Obie Jr., letter to Edna Schneider, May 7, 1944.
7. Newcomb letter, May 7, 1944.
8. Boos letter, April 20, 1944.
9. Sheppard interview, August 18, 2010.
10. The Center for the Study of War and Society, "War Stories: Kyle Campbell Moore: Homegrown Hero," University of Tennessee, Knoxville, Fall 2010. 1–2.
11. Moore, Katherine, interview with the author, June 4, 2011.
12. "Kyle Campbell Moore: Homegrown Hero," 2.
13. Moore interview, June 4, 2011.
14. Moore interview, June 4, 2011.
15. Moore interview, June 4, 2011.
16. DPAA, report on Alexander Bonnyman, Jr., May 2015.

Sixteen

1. Niven interview, December 11, 2012.
2. Emmons, Mark, "Search for World War II hero's remains hinges on South Bay man's research," *San Jose Mercury News*, August 14, 2013.
3. Belcher interview, September 6, 2015.
4. Noah interview, July 18, 2013.
5. Burns, Robert, "MIA work 'acutely dysfunctional,'" Associated Press, July 7, 2013.
6. Burns, "MIA work 'acutely dysfunctional.'"
7. McCloskey, Megan, "The World War II Hero America Abandoned," *ProPublica*, March 21, 2014.
8. US Government Accounting Office, "DOD'S POW/MIA MISSION: Top-Level Leadership Attention Needed to Resolve Longstanding Challenges in Accounting for Missing Persons from Past Conflicts," July 17, 2013.
9. Dedman, Bill, "Pentagon unit held 'phony' ceremonies for MIAs, using planes that can't fly," NBCnews.com, October 10, 2013.
10. Baker, Kristen N., interview with the author, August 16, 2015.
11. Baker interview, August 16, 2015.
12. Baker interview, August 16, 2015.
13. Baker interview, August 16, 2015.
14. *Global Post*, "Kiribati president says climate change is shrinking his country," September 4, 2013
15. Tong, President Anote, interview with the author, November 20, 2013.
16. Hylton, "The Long Road Back."
17. Hewitt, Anthony, email to the author, December 13, 2013.

Seventeen

1. Bonnyman, Alexander, Sr., letter to Fred E. Gore et al, January 26 1944.
2. Clerou, Capt. Joseph, letter to Alexander Bonnyman, Sr., January 15, 1944.
3. Newcomb, Sgt. Obie Jr., letter to Alexander and Frances Bonnyman, May 27, 1944.
4. Spellman, Archbishop Francis, letter to Alexander Bonnyman, January 17, 1944.
5. Russell, James H., letter to Alexander Bonnyman, February 3, 1943 (sic; 1944).
6. Clerou, Capt. Joseph, letter to Alexander Bonnyman, Jr., February 17, 1944.

7. Stanley, Isabel Bonnyman, "I Was a War Baby," unpublished.

8. Bonnyman, Frances Berry, letter to Josephine Russell, August 5, 1946.

9. Bonnyman, Josephine, telegram to Lt. Gen. Thomas Holcomb, January 2, 1944.

10. Stanley, "I Was a War Baby."

11. Russell, Josephine, letter to Frances Bonnyman, March 4, 1944.

12. Russell letter, March 4, 1944.

13. Bell, Blanche Brown, letter to Frances Berry Bonnyman, May 24, 1944.

14. McKeon interview, September 6, 2010.

15. Bonnyman, George Gordon, letter to Isabel Bonnyman, March 20, 1944.

16. Bonnyman, Alexander, Sr., letter to 2nd Lt. M.G. Craig, April 6, 1944.

17. Casualty card for Alexander Bonnyman, Jr.

18. Craig, 2nd Lt. M.G., letter to Alexander Bonnyman, Sr., March 27, 1944.

19. Commanding General FMF Pacific to Commandant of the Marine Corps, memorandum, April 24, 1945.

20. Craig, 2nd Lt. M.G., letter to Josephine Bonnyman, January 5, 1944.

21. Routh, Lt. Col. D., letter to Alexander Bonnyman, Sr., June 6, 1946.

22. Noah, *The Lost Graves of Tarawa*, 11.

23. Allen, Donald K. DVM, "Betio Cemetery—Tarawa's Missing in Action," tarawatheaftermath.com.

24. Bonnyman, Alexander, Sr., letter to Father C.P. Murray, November 6, 1946.

25. McGuire, Bob, letter to the editor, *Life*, July 7, 1947.

26. McGuire, Bob, letter to Clara Hood, November 4, 1947.

27. Bonnyman, George Gordon, letter to AGRS Officer, September 22, 1947.

28. Heil, Lt. Col. John H. Jr., letter to George Gordon Bonnyman, October 30, 1947.

29. Robinson, Lt. H.H., "Dental Officer's Report on Identification Operation on Tarawa," May 31, 1946.

30. "Tarawa Summary, Invasion Casualties," DPAA, March 11, 2015.

31. Eisensmith, 1st Lt. Ira, memorandum to Chief, Memorial Branch, Quartermaster Section, Army Forces, Middle Pacific, July 3, 1946.

32. Shoup, Col. David M., letter to Gen. Julian C. Smith, September 4, 1946

33. Smith, Gen. Julian C., letter to Col. David M. Shoup, August 31, 1946.

34. Marine Quartermaster General's Memorial Branch "Discrepancy Cases—Tarawa 8 June 1950."

35. Proceedings of AGRS Board of Review, February 28, 1949.

36. Marsden, Lt. (jg) W.E., memorandum to Commandant, US Marine Corps, October 4, 1949.

37. Newcomb, Sgt. Obie Jr., letter to Alexander Bonnyman, Sr., July 15, 1945.

38. Bonnyman, George Gordon, letter to Leroy Kain, December 28, 1965.

39. Kain, Leroy, letter to George Gordon Bonnyman, January 14, 1966.

40. Bonnyman, Alexander (son of George Gordon Bonnyman), interviews with the author, passim.

41. Biddle, Attorney General Francis, letter to Alexander Bonnyman, Sr., January 14, 1944.

42. Sherrod, Robert, letter to Alexander Bonnyman, Sr., March 22, 1948.

43. Nierle, President James E., Navy Department Board of Decorations and Medals, email, March 29, 2015.

44. Vandegrift, Lt. Gen. A.A., letter to Josephine Bell Russell, May 10, 1944

45. Bonnyman, Alexander, Sr., letter to John W. Gunn, November 7, 1946.

46. Russell, Josephine, letter to Frances Berry Bonnyman, undated.

47. Vandegrift, Gen. A.A., letter to Josephine Bell Russell, October 23, 1946.

48. Bonnyman, Alexander, Sr., letter to John W. Gunn, November 7, 1946.

Eighteen

1. Hylton, "The Long Road Back," 32.

2. Noah, Mark, interview with the author, February 7, 2015.

3. Noah, Mark, interview with the author, February 7, 2015.

4. Noah interview, February 7, 2015.

5. Frye, John, interview with the author, August 16, 2015.

6. Editorial Board, "Illinois Marines who died 72 years apart are mourned this Memorial Day," *Chicago Tribune*, May 25, 2015.

7. Dedman, Bill, "Pentagon reorganizes effort to ID MIAs after NBC News series," NBCNews.com, March 31, 2014.

8. Baker, Kristen N., interview with the author, August 16, 2015.

9. Baker interview, August 16, 2015.

10. Baker interview, August 16, 2015.

11. Niven, *Tarawa's Gravediggers*, 213.

12. Noah, Mark, interview with the author, June 5, 2015.

13. Baker, Kristen N., interview with the author, May 20, 2015.

14. Baker interview, May 18, 2015.

Nineteen

1. Sherrod, Robert, telegram to Alexander Bonnyman, Sr., November 21, 1948.

2. Bonnyman, George Gordon, Piehl and Bracken interview, 53.

3. McKeon interview, September 6, 2010.
4. Colley, *Safely Rest*, 6.
5. Gomez, Capt. Don, interview with the author, June 16, 2011.
6. Hemingway, Ernest and Hemingway, Sean (editor), *Hemingway on War* (New York: Scribner, 2004).
7. Hathaway, William T., interview with the author, December 9, 2010.
8. Bell, Blanche Brown, letter to Frances Berry Bonnyman, May 24, 1944.
9. Prejean, Alix and Evans, Frances Bonnyman, interviews with the author, passim.
10. Prejean, Alix, interview with the author, August 16, 2015.
11. Russell letter, April 1951.
12. McAllister, Margot, interview with the author, June 19, 2014.
13. *Santa Fe New Mexican*, obituary for James H. Russell, September 3, 2000.
14. Bonnyman, Alexander, Sr., letter to John J. Rowe, November 7, 1946.
15. Bonnyman, George Gordon, Piehler and Bracken interview.
16. Prejean, Alix, interview with the author, August 16, 2015.

Twenty

1. Muster roll for 2nd Marine Division, 2nd Battalion, 18th Regiment, November 30, 1943.
2. Parsons, Hillary, "Biological Profile Report: HF-2015-028," June 19, 2015.
3. Parsons, Hillary, interview with the author, February 23, 2016.
4. Freas, Laurel, "Forensic Anthropology Report: CIL, 2015-125-I-22," DPAA, August 10, 2015.
5. Baker, Kristen N., email to the author, August 27, 2015.
6. Reedy, Capt. Edward A., email to the author, September 18, 2015.
7. Reedy email, September 18, 2015.
8. Alexander interview, May 23, 2014.
9. Clerou George, email to the author, October 21, 2010.
10. Wright, Derrick, *Tarawa, 20–23 November 1943: A Hell of a Way to Die*, (London: Windrow & Greene, 1997), 151–152.
11. McCloskey, "The World War II Hero America Abandoned."

Twenty-One

1. Boylan, Rich, interview with the author, November 30, 2014.
2. Rasdorf, Katherine T., interview with the author, August 13, 2014.
3. Jowdy, Laura S., email to the author, April 7, 2014.

4. Salazar, Lt. Col. Chester, officer fitness report on Alexander Bonnyman, Jr., October 1, 1943.

5. Boylan, Rich, interview with the author, October 7, 2014.

6. Minutes, Horne Board January-September 1946.

7. Hammel, Eric, email to the author, June 26, 2013.

8. Horne board minutes, January 8, 1946.

9. Horne board minutes, January 11, 1946.

10. Horne board minutes, June14, 1946.

11. Nierle email, March 29, 2015.

12. Nierle email, March 29, 2015.

13. Reid, Cmdr. J. Gordon USN, letter to Frances Berry Bonnyman, September 28, 1946.

14. Reid letter, September 28, 1946.

15. US Marine Corps, memorandum to CINCPAC (Commander in Chief, Pacific Command), October 10, 1944.

16. Shoup, Gen. David M. with James A. Donovan, "The New American Militarism," *Atlantic Monthly* (April 1969), 51–56.

17. Shoup, Gen. David M., hand-written note "The New American Militarism," David M. Shoup archives, Hoover Institution, Stanford University, Palo Alto, California.

18. Astore, William, interview with the author, July 6, 2014.

19. Bonnyman, Frances Berry, letter to Col. David M. Shoup, October 3, 1946.

20. Bonnyman letter, October 3, 1946.

21. Bonnyman, Alexander Sr., letter to Col. David M. Shoup, January 24, 1947.

22. Shoup, Col. David M., letter to Frances Berry Bonnyman, March 24, 1947.

23. Shoup letter, March 24, 1947.

Twenty-Two

1. Stone, Rick, letter to the author, October 11, 2012.

2. Senn, David R., "Forensic Odontology Report: HF-2015-028," June 17, 2015.

3. Senn report, June 17, 2015.

4. Linnington, Lt. Gen. Michael S., telephone conversation with the author, June 26, 2015.

5. Walker, Dr. Chet, interview with the author, February 23, 2016.

6. Prejean, Alix, interview with the author, June 4, 2010.

7. Miller, Michael E., "Golden ending: How one man discovered his war hero grandfather's long lost grave," *Washington Post*, July 2, 2015.

8. Headman letter, August 26, 1932.

9. Banks letter, February 29, 1944.

10. Boling, Sgt. Justin M., "Never left behind, forgotten: Honorary Marine recognized for bringing brothers home," US Marine Corps, July 26, 2015.

INDEX